'You've Never Had It So Good!'

Recollections
of Life in the
1950s

'You've Never Had It So Good!'

Recollections of Life in the 1950s

STEPHEN F. KELLY

The
History
Press

942.0855

First published 2012

The History Press
The Mill, Brimscombe Port
Stroud, Gloucestershire, GL5 2QG
www.thehistorypress.co.uk

British Library Cataloguing in Publication Data.
A catalogue record for this book is available from the British Library.

ISBN 978 0 7524 5996 7

Typesetting and origination by The History Press
Printed in Great Britain
Manufacturing managed by Jellyfish Print Solutions Ltd

CONTENTS

ABOUT THE AUTHOR

Stephen F. Kelly is a writer and broadcaster. Born in Birkenhead, he was educated at Ruskin College, Oxford and the London School of Economics and has a PhD in oral history. He was for many years a political journalist working for *Tribune* magazine and Granada Television before becoming an academic at the University of Huddersfield, where he was Director of the Centre for Oral History Research. He has published more than twenty books, many on sport, as well as a number of oral histories. He lives in Manchester.

ACKNOWLEDGEMENTS

There are many people to whom I owe a great debt. First, and principally, all those who gave their time and welcomed me into their homes to talk about the 1950s. These were largely happy recollections, although, for some, memories of being caned or national disasters – such as the Munich air crash – have left emotional scars. Inevitably, many of those I have interviewed were elderly, so their generosity is even more to be appreciated. Sadly, a number of them have died since being interviewed, and, to their families, I would like to place on record my sincere gratitude and hope that the memories of their loved ones in this book will help ease the burden of their grief.

I would also like to thank a number of people who helped to organise interviews and offered their thoughts and advice. These include Chorlton Good Neighbours, who kindly allowed me to invade their regular Thursday morning coffee and craft meetings in pursuit of willing interviewees. I would like to pay tribute to them and all the volunteers who do such magnificent work in the community. Others who have kindly helped me out include Clare Jenkins, Janice Finch, Graham Hobbs of Manchester YMCA, and the Oral History Society. I am also grateful to Nafhesa Ali, for allowing me to use a number of interviews she had carried out for the 'Asian Voices' project, on which we both worked at the University of Huddersfield, and also to Dr Rob Light, for some interviews from the 'Up and Under' project.

My thanks also to all the people who have allowed me to use photographs in their possession or copyright, including Clare Jenkins and Mary Kelly. I would also like to thank John Shepherd for his photographs of the Liverpool docks and in particular the *Empress of Canada*, all of which are from the Captain H.J. Chubb collection; and Steve Hale, for his 1950s photographs of Liverpool. My gratitude also to Reflections of Hastings, who have supplied a number of pictures. While I have endeavoured to trace the copyright on all photographs used in this book, there are some which have proved difficult to identify. If the owners or copyright holders get in touch with the publisher then we shall endeavour to correct this error.

I would also like to thank Neil Kinnock, a friend of almost forty years, for agreeing to write the foreword to the book as well as spending a delightful morning with me in Liverpool reminiscing on his childhood.

For background work on the book I have relied heavily on two highly respected texts – David Kynaston's *Family Britain 1951-1957* and Peter Hennessy's *Having It So Good: Britain in the Fifties*, both of which I would highly recommend to anyone interested in this period. I would also like to thank Peter Hennessy, another friend of many years, for his interview. Needless to say, however, any mistakes in this book are mine and mine alone.

On a technical note, all the interviews were recorded on a digital recorder and these interviews have now been donated to the National Library. I have tried to transcribe them as people spoke, but inevitably I have had to make changes to make their thoughts more clear and comprehensible. Oral historians will understand the difficulties here, but I hope that my interpretations are as accurate as possible. I would also like to thank Matilda Richards and all the staff at The History Press for encouraging this project.

Finally, I would especially like to thank my wife, Judith Jones, for her unstinting support over the years, and to my children, Nicholas and Emma, both of whom have treated me with a neat combination of humour, ridicule and affection while helping to resolve my many computer problems. I am, after all, a child of the fifties myself!

Stephen F. Kelly
Manchester, 2012

FOREWORD
BY NEIL KINNOCK

As the testimonies collected in this very fine personalised portrayal by Stephen Kelly show, the 1950s was a fulcrum decade. In those ten years, British society and economy and politics were levered from an era led by people and conventions that came from the nineteenth century, into a time in which the mass of the population was conscious of a fast changing present and focused, as never before, on the future.

Two world wars and the deep, scarring slumps between them threw shadows over the early years of the decade. But by the time the 1960s came, Britain had moved into the light. The predominant reason for that was that working-class people and communities had their first ever peacetime experience of full employment. That, coupled with the effects of the 1944 Education Act and the Welfare State, established by the post-war Labour government, ensured security, opportunity and care with a breadth and depth previously unknown. It all consequently gave tangible meaning to the liberty for which the British and their allies had fought but few had really hoped to see so quickly or so abundantly. It didn't produce perfection – but it did mean progress on an unprecedented scale.

Such a seismic shift in fortunes and conditions produced radical changes in every facet of life. Dependable work brought continuous pay. For the first time, progressive Pay As You Earn taxation and National Insurance funded greatly expanded universally provided public services, reduced income disparities between classes, and financed pensions and sickness benefits. Monthly salaries replaced weekly wages for public and private sector supervisors and professionals. Trade unions recruited millions more members and framed national standards that were then improved by workplace negotiators.

The mass consumption generated by plentiful jobs fostered new appetites. 'Style' and 'fashion' came within reach of the majority. For many, 'choice' became a reality for the first time.

Advances in science and technology – some spurred by wartime necessity and investment – accelerated the shifts in treatment, taste, development and demand.

In the mid-1950s the vaccines against polio and TB added hugely to the prevention and cure of major killer and disabling diseases. Penicillin derivatives also combated infections, the structure of DNA was discovered, cancer was scientifically linked to smoking, transplant surgery began, most children were born in hospital, contraception came into use, family sizes fell rapidly and made a further contribution to reducing poverty.

Wartime petrol rationing ended in 1950 and, throughout the decade, huge British plants poured out increasingly affordable family cars, bought through 'Hire Purchase' and polished proudly on Sunday morning streets. The first motorways speeded journeys, long distance 'coaches' traversed the land, jet airliners crossed the Atlantic and connected the UK with increasing numbers of capitals in other European countries. The Hovercraft, the transverse engine Mini, and roll-on roll-off vehicle ferries were invented. Britain got its first mainline electric trains. The first business computer, increasing calculation speeds a thousand fold, was introduced (on hire only) by IBM in 1954 and, five years later, Barclay's Bank became the first in Britain to computerise accounts.

With full employment firmly established, something called 'leisure' became familiar, 'pastimes' became 'hobbies', Do-It-Yourself became less of a necessity and more of a diversion. Entertainment was revolutionised, especially with the wildfire spread of television. Over the 1950s Music Hall comedians and novelty acts which had made the transition to radio in the 1940s, gave way to slick and witty duos and spectacular variety shows on the black and white screen in the living room. Live sports coverage flooded into homes and began to turn the cigarette card heroes of football, cricket, horseracing, boxing, motorcar, cycle racing, lawn tennis and (still amateur) track athletics into superstars. Filmed news broadcasts, documentaries and current affairs programmes with mass audiences provided dramatic insights, analysis and opinion. Commercial television arrived halfway through the decade and quickly magnetised millions.

The 1950s, which started with syrupy crooning and bouncy pop songs, was, by 1956, being propelled by the driving beat of rock 'n' roll. 'Teenagers' emerged as an identifiable cohort with particular conventions in taste, consumption and clothes, all – perversely – adopted in defiance of convention. Saturday night queues for black and white pictures dwindled into smaller, more demanding audiences, for Technicolor 'movies'. Ballrooms full of fox-trotters became 'dance halls' packed with boppers and jivers. Coward and Rattigan gave way to John Osborne, Shelagh Delaney and a group of new playwrights who were said to be 'angry'. In reality they were simply radical, brilliantly perceptive commentators on changes that had already arrived without the acknowledgement of the Establishment, and further changes that needed to be made in everything from social class and behaviour codes, to the distribution of incomes, homes and opportunities, to sexuality and the relationships between women and men. Writers may have exercised influence from the stage and paperback books, but from the cinema and TV screens they reached huge audiences and resonated with the changing public attitudes that would help to reshape the character of Britain towards greater irreverence and tolerance.

Women, and the condition of their sex, featured frequently in the work of the new playwrights and authors. That was fitting – the 1950s was an age of female advance in Britain although, in retrospect, it seems to have been osmotic rather than categoric. There was certainly no organised movement carrying women forward. Only the most self-confident and articulate women – supported by parts of the Left in politics and the arts – made the case for changed roles, life chances, status and rights with public force. Apart from pushes from that direction, the major alterations in attitudes toward (and by), and opportunities for, women and girls were pulled by economics. Women in the Second World War – as in the First World War – had again proved their at least equal ability and adaptability in occupations that had previously been monopolised by men. With the return of peace, the demand for women workers greatly receded but – especially in factory and (greatly expanding) clerical and retail work – it was sustained, partly because of what was thought of as 'aptitude', partly – mainly – because their labour was cheaper. In any event, the increase in the female workforce provided independent wages as well as supplementing family incomes. That contribution to increased income brought torrential response from commerce. A massive new 'women's market' rapidly developed in clothing and accessories, and purchases of 'consumer goods' grew exponentially. By the time wartime rationing ended convenience foods were beginning to appear in the shops with vacuum cleaners, electric washing machines, wringers and driers providing 'labour saving' assistance in the home.

At the beginning of the decade, the 1951 Mass Observation Survey (which had started in the 1930s) reported that 'housewives' were working a fifteen-hour day on all or most days of the week. By 1958, the Chief Medical Officer was describing the life of most women as 'dangerously sedate' and voicing concern over 'increasing dependency on tranquilisers'. I clearly remember the *News Chronicle* report of those comments being read out by my father in a semi-jocular tone. The response by my (usually very easy going) mother was anything but light hearted: 'Those people,' she said, with all the authority of a senior – some would say commanding – State Registered District Nurse, 'don't understand a damn thing. Very few women take pills. Those who do aren't sitting down. They have to in order to stay on their feet for skivvying!' 'Tranquilisers?' she spat, 'Those women take them because they haven't got the Chief Medical Officer's housemaids to carry them around!'

There may have been more passion than science in her reaction. But my father and I got the message: You could poke fun at Chief Medical Officers but not at working-class women. It was enjoyable for my Dad, who laughed long and loud, and instructive for me – particularly when the 1960s wasn't far away.

These and countless other evolutions in consumption and commerce brought a new vocabulary to daily life. The Atomic Age came to Britain with nuclear weapons and power stations. Self-service shops spread across the country, though the once universal Co-op adapted too late to prevent eradication from small towns and most cities. Hi-fi radiograms brought stereo sound listening and vinyl record albums provided collections from music performers of every kind. Young women clicked on stiletto heels. Filter tip cigarettes gave sophistication and security – both illusory. Women civil servants got equal pay. Price inflation became the dominant economic challenge and credit squeezes were repeatedly imposed in (vain) attempts to resist it. The new textiles, Terylene and Polyester, made from chemical synthetic fibres covered bodies, beds, windows, floors and furniture of every sort. Jeans became the leisurewear of choice for all young men – and, very gradually, young women – together with slip-on shoes. Drainpipes, drapes and brothel creepers with thick crêpe soles were, however, the preserve of Teddy Boys.

Some things didn't change: While the country got a Queen as ruler, it continued to be a Kingdom, the Queen's sister was not allowed to marry a divorcee, and 'dialect voices' were forbidden for news and continuity readers on the BBC. An industrial proletariat still worked in mass-producing factories, small specialised engineering works, vast steelworks, giant shipyards and increasingly mechanised collieries though, and, by the end of the decade, dozens of pit closures were giving a foretaste of the slaughter to come in the 1960s.

Unchanging, too, was the culture of crime and punishment. Delinquent boys still went to Borstal. Homosexual acts continued to be offences punishable by prison sentences and sensational cases, usually involving aristocrats, clergy, judges or actors were copiously reported in tones of synthetic shock by salacious Sunday newspapers. Despite the repeated attempts at reform in the House of Commons, capital punishment remained for murder. The reports of trials drew avid attention and, for most, the hangings generated frissons of satisfaction that 'justice has been done'. Others, like me, endured anguish as condemned people, some of them later proven to be innocent, were taken on the grimly and graphically reported '8 o'clock walk' to their deaths.

All of these developments provided a backdrop to another major alteration in Britain in the 1950s: From 1954, a country which had received continuous flows of migrants for two thousand years, became the destination for increasing numbers of citizens from the Commonwealth, especially the West Indies and the Indian sub-continent, as full employment enabled British workers to step out of the most menial and lowest paid occupations in the public and health services and from the textile industries of Northern England.

Appreciation of the new supply of essential labour was, to say the least, limited. Landlords either refused rooms or charged exorbitant rents for the crowded accommodation that they were prepared to let. The days when men and women who came from the 'ethnic' backgrounds, became celebrated idols of sports and entertainment, MPs and councillors, leaders in business and medicine and arbiters of taste in food and fashion, were decades of prejudice and disadvantage away. By the autumn of 1958 – when Apartheid in South Africa was seven years old, the Freedom Riders in the Southern States of the USA were beginning to win the support of Federal Courts and Government, and black rule was starting to replace white dominion throughout Africa – right wing hooligans attacking young immigrants ensured that Britain came to know what race riots were.

The bits of former Empire which the Caribbeans, Indians and Pakistanis (Bangladesh did not exist until 1971) were leaving had gained independence. Other former colonies quickly followed through the 1950s and early '60s. Some were awarded nation status grudgingly, some were simply abandoned with little physical or social infrastructure, some stayed in the grip of white rule, some gained nationhood through bloodshed. Malaya, Kenya, Cyprus and Aden 'emergencies' were bitter conflicts that mixed civil war, terrorism and counter insurgency operations that cost countless lives of indigenous peoples and thousands of casualties among British forces who were mainly National Service conscripts. The inevitable finale of Britain's Great Power status came with the 1956 Eden Government's efforts, secretly and illegally contrived with France and Israel, to use force to prevent Egypt nationalising the Suez Canal and gaining regional military significance with Soviet backing. The conspiracy collapsed in warfare and shameful farce as the USA threatened to deny financial support for the pound sterling. The British and French departed and the United Nations assumed interim control of the Canal.

The fact that this final squalid flourish of Empire took place just days after the Soviet Union brutally suppressed heroic demonstrations in Poland and, even more violently, crushed an armed insurrection by freedom fighters in Hungary, added ignominy to shame.

This last adventure, which starkly divided the Tory Party and the country, came as a particular shock to the Britain of the 1950s. The Conservatives, led through most of the decade by Churchill, Eden and Macmillan, were not the supercilious slump-inflicting predators of pre-war Britain. Learning from salutary wartime experience, and influenced by a pragmatic new generation of middle-class centrists, they were mixed economy moderates who gradually accepted the Welfare State, boasted of their ambitious council house building programmes and promised – with continual relaxation of controls on borrowing – to establish 'a property owning democracy'. They regained power from Labour in 1951 and went on to increasing electoral majorities in 1955 and 1959 with a political appeal which was patronising but populist. They kept grouse moor tweed and acres, and Belgravia opulence, but expressed themselves through suburban pleasantries. When Eden shuffled off in a breakdown after Suez, Harold Macmillan – disciple of full employment and high public spending – brilliantly chiseled with the grain of public sentiment. He actively promoted a brand of consensual politics which produced 'Butskellism' – a synthesis of policies between his Chancellor, R.A. Butler, and the Labour Leader, Hugh Gaitskell, and told an impressed electorate 'You've never had it so good!'

Twenty years later, he was to be a relentlessly caustic critic of the Thatcherism which smashed 'the post-war settlement' in which he fervently believed. But then, as the 1950s closed, he was 'Super Mac' – a clever combination of healer and wheeler-dealer, attuned to times of growing affluence and rooted stability and beguiling all but the most diehard detesters of Toryism like my own family.

For me, growing up in the 1950s, life was very good. I was the only child of a blast furnace labourer and a district nurse in a home where hard work was prized and learning cherished. Our prefab in South Wales was 'a little palace' with central heating, a fitted kitchen and a bathroom in which my ritual once weekly immersions had, by the end of the decade, been replaced by daily showers (previously the preserve of men in mining and heavy industry).

My extended family was a strong and generous fortress, full of humour. The surrounding community was socialist in practical deed as well as political thought and vote, and it buzzed with the culture of brass bands and choirs, amateur dramatics and classical performers who came to Celebrity Concerts in a peoples' palace – the Tredegar Workmen's Hall – which was paid for by a universal voluntary levy on all employed men in the area and could, therefore, afford the world's finest. Access to my hyper-creamed, all boys, regimentally uniformed grammar school was won through giddily high marks in the dreaded 11 plus exam. Apart from detentions and canings to punish rebellion, laziness, clowning, and smoking, the following years were a pleasant odyssey through moderate effort (and results), obsessive enthusiasm for sport, and the joy of singing. Adolescence brought the additions of active politics, five chord skiffle (later superseded by pounding rock 'n' roll), and fascination with girls that was eventually (and timidly) requited.

I left the 1950s studying – in the gaps left by fun – for my A level exams, enjoying school for the first time as teachers whom I'd previously hated suddenly became helpful, easygoing adults, and looking forward to going to university. Student grants had made that feeling of certainty feasible for qualified young people from my background for the first time. Even my contemporaries who didn't go on to Higher Education had no doubt that they would get jobs as soon as they looked for them in the locality or in the beckoning world beyond.

Because of realities like that, I'll always think of the ten years between 1950 and 1960 as the Age of New Opportunity. Other periods obviously bring change. The mere passage of years and events always alter possibilities. But in modern history few, if any, periods compare with the 1950s as a time of transformation. Stephen Kelly has chronicled this through the voices of people who are old enough to have known it and still young enough to remember it.

He's performed a service to that and to succeeding generations, as well as telling a story of an era of irreversible advance for the people of our country. I thank him for that. I think his readers will, too.

Neil Kinnock
Westminster
December 2011

INTRODUCTION

In July 1957, Prime Minister Harold Macmillan, speaking at a Conservative Party rally in Bedford, told his audience that in Britain, 'You will see a state of prosperity such as we have never had in my lifetime – nor indeed in the history of this country.'

His audience roared their approval. Macmillan paused briefly, then added a further comment for which he was to be associated for the remainder of his life. 'Indeed, let us be frank about it,' he said, 'most of our people have never had it so good.'

The following morning the newspaper headlines repeated his remarks and Macmillan unerringly discovered that, by chance, he had hit upon a political slogan that would successfully carry him through the next General Election, with the Conservatives recording their highest ever vote. It had been done not by design but from a moment's inspiration by a politician who was blessed with the ability to conjure up a good turn of phrase in a well-delivered speech.

He went on to remind his audience not to forget 'rationing, shortages, inflation, and one crisis after another in our international trade' under a Labour government. 'The pattern of the Commonwealth is changing,' he continued, 'and with it is changing Britain's position as the Mother Country. Our children are growing up'

Judging by the election result two years later, which would give the Tories a third successive term in office, the majority of voters had agreed with his remarks. And so the 1950s became identified with Macmillan and a country that had never had it so good. But just how true was it? Were the 1950s really that good or has the Macmillan slogan tainted our thinking? Is our view of the 1950s simply sentimental nostalgia? Yes, there were friendly doctors who would come rushing to your sickbed, kindly neighbours who would do anything for you, plenty of jobs, and summers when the sun always seemed to shine. And yes, there were fewer cars and fewer dangers on our streets.

But alternatively there were dangerous heavy industries, fatal illnesses, stricter discipline, conscription, and a grammar school system that condemned two-thirds of eleven year olds to a less than decent education.

When the Second World War ended in 1945, the process of reconstruction began immediately. And it was a massive task. Such a task seemed to demand a clean sweep of many of the old ideals. Out went wartime Prime Minister Winston Churchill and the Conservative Party for a start, and in came the diminutive, pipe-smoking Clement Attlee, leader of what was to be the most radical of all Labour governments. Attlee set about his task with considered authority, nationalizing the railways, coalmines, utility companies and so on. He gave his Health Minister, Aneurin Bevan, the task of introducing a National Health Service and encouraged his Foreign Secretary, Ernest Bevin, to forge a closer relationship with the United States in the hope that their economic prosperity might rub off on us.

But the immediate post-war years remained dogged by problems. There were continuing shortages and rationing. There was an unforgiving cold spell in 1947 that saw the country grind to a halt, and getting the armed forces back to work inevitably proved troublesome. But it was not, as Macmillan may have later suggested, all due entirely to Attlee's poor economic planning. These were difficult years for the whole of Europe. Germany was defeated and bankrupt. France, Belgium, Italy, Holland and the Soviet Union were still reeling from occupation or economic and political sterility. Only America prospered and, thanks to the Marshall Plan, some of that prosperity would eventually be shipped across the Atlantic to give a fillip to European recovery. America paved the way and in the 1950s its influence was to be felt in many ways.

It would not be long, however, before Britain was back at war, its armed forces on their way to Korea. While many wondered why we were joining a conflict thousands of miles away, and seeming of little consequence to us, Prime Minister Clement Attlee reminded the nation that it owed a debt of allegiance to the United States. More than 90,000 British soldiers joined forces with neighbouring European countries in support of a UN resolution, many of them ordinary national service conscripts. It was a war that was to drag on for three years, with more than a thousand British soldiers dying and many more casualties. The Americans suffered even more. It has become known as the forgotten war.

Attlee had problems elsewhere as well. His Cabinet had grown weary after the war years and their massive programme of legislation. They had run out of ideas and energy and the electorate recognised it. In 1950, Labour sneaked a poll victory by the narrowest of margins, but in a re-run in 1951 they could not put off the inevitable and Churchill was once more elected Prime Minister.

Although Macmillan is largely associated with the 'never had it so good' remark, in truth his political opposite, Hugh Gaitskell, had already analyzed the situation and come to the same conclusion. As Labour crashed to a second defeat in the 1955 General Election, Gaitskell reflected on the reasons why Labour had been so heavily defeated. It was, he believed, due to the electorate's 'lack of fear of the Tories derived from the maintenance of full employment, the end of rationing and the general feeling that "things were better"':

> I fancy that in the last year or two, more and more people are beginning to turn to their own personal affairs and to concentrate on their own material advancement. No doubt it has been stimulated by the end of post-war austerity, TV, new gadgets like refrigerators and washing machines, the glossy magazines with their special appeal to women, and even the flood of new cars on the home markets. Call it if you like a growing Americanization of outlook. I believe it's there and it's no good moaning about it . . .

Gaitskell was right. The 'growing Americanization of outlook', as he so neatly put it, was changing the face of British homes and British life. New 'white consumer goods' – as the academics liked to call them – flooded onto the market as they had done in America. The washing machine was perhaps the most important item, relieving the weekly drudgery of washing and drying. Then there was the vacuum cleaner (forever to be known as a Hoover), electric iron and, later, the refrigerator, all contributing towards an easier domestic life.

But there was another major change taking place in the towns and cities. Immigration was on the rise and a new ethnic and cultural mix would forevermore alter the face of Britain. Full employment and the call for skilled and unskilled workers had begun to attract interest in the New Commonwealth. With the prospect of employment and wealth, many young men from the Commonwealth began to make the trip to Britain.

According to Home Office figures, in 1953 just 2,000 immigrants from the West Indies arrived in Britain, while there were none from India or Pakistan. By 1954 the numbers of West Indians arriving has risen to 11,000, while again there were none from India or Pakistan. One year later and the number of West Indians coming to Britain had more than doubled to 27,000. More noticeably, however, the influx of immigrants from the Indian subcontinent had just begun, with 6,000 arriving from India and 1,800 from Pakistan. By 1956, 30,000 West Indians had come, with a further 5,500 from India and 2,000 from Pakistan joining them. Throughout the rest of the 1950s the numbers arriving continued to increase, particularly from the Asian sub continent.

In particular they settled in areas such as Manchester, Birmingham, Huddersfield, Bradford and, of course, London. It was in these areas where there was a pressing need for workers and once they had settled their families followed. But of course it wasn't always easy or as rosy as they had anticipated as many testify in the following pages.

There were, of course, people going in the opposite direction. Emigration to Australia, in particular, and also New Zealand, increased as Brits sought a life of sunshine and new opportunities. Almost half a million emigrated to Australia during the period, paying just £10 for their passage. And all of them were white, as Australia imposed a 'whites only' policy. Canada also invited immigrants as its vast frontiers began to open up, offering employment and riches, though not as much sunshine as Australia. Nonetheless, it proved enormously popular.

Neil Kinnock argues that the 1950s saw more changes than in any other previous decade of the twentieth century. And there is much to be said for this assertion. The 1920s and '30s produced steady but minor changes in society. Industry was much the same – coalmining, cotton, steel, shipbuilding, docks – though many of these areas suffered chronic unemployment. But suddenly, in the 1950s, there were massive changes. Manufacturing took off with a host of new industries emerging. The car industry, which had been around for many years, mushroomed as cars became more affordable, even to the working classes. White consumer goods burst onto the market – washing machines, refrigerators, vacuum cleaners, steam irons, even dishwashers – many of them aimed at women, and they had to be made somewhere. For the first time in British history there was full employment, and with it came a new-found wealth among the working classes. They began to buy cars and the white consumer goods that were beginning to pour onto the market.

For many, 1956 was a watershed and a memorable year. In the Middle East, Colonel Gamal Abdel Nasser, the newly appointed President of Egypt, seized control of the Suez Canal, thereby precipitating an invasion by British, French and Israeli troops. The Americans looked on in bewilderment. It was a fiasco. The canal remained in Egyptian hands and, for the first time, there was severe criticism by the public at British military action. Prime Minister Anthony Eden, already dogged by ill health, resigned just three months after the invasion. Also in 1956, the massed forces of the Soviet army brutally invaded Hungary in an attempt to quell a revolution. Communist Parties throughout the world were split, with many British members of the Communist Party resigning and never returning. For any communist, 1956 was a soul-searching moment.

And always there was the threat of nuclear war. As the decade progressed, so the size and power of nuclear weapons increased. New missiles to launch the warheads were being constructed, each one able to be travel further afield than the previous. And with it came greater fears of a nuclear holocaust.

The Cold War was at its height. The Soviet Union, our strongest ally during the Second World War, was now our sworn enemy. There were spies, hydrogen bombs, nuclear shelters, early warning stations, and atomic bomb tests.

A pressure group – the Campaign for Nuclear Disarmament (CND) – emerged with its annual Easter march to Aldermaston, where the weapons were constructed. CND would soon enter the common currency and its famed symbol would survive to the present day, perhaps the most iconic emblem of the period.

In his splendid study of the early years of the 1950s (*Family Britain*), David Kynaston lays particular emphasis on the family being central to the era. And indeed it was. For a start families were smaller. The days of five or more children were gone. By the 1950s far more people were beginning to use family planning methods. Many of them were primitive but they were not wholly unsuccessful. As a result, family sizes fell. Improvements in health also meant that there was far less infant mortality, relieving many women from years of pregnancy. With fewer children, families were able to plan their own economic destiny.

But the question remains as to whether all these changes could ever have developed as they did without the underpinning of economic stability. For the first time in its history, Britain enjoyed full employment. A mere 150,000 were unemployed at any time and this figure took account of people changing jobs, those too ill to work, students and so forth. Hardly anyone could be described as long-term unemployed. Jobs were aplenty. A scan through the job pages of any newspaper showed hundreds of jobs advertised. Employment was also far more localized than it is today. Jobs were close by and didn't necessitate moving house or long commutes. And that, in turn, helped foster the strength of the nuclear family.

Trade union pressure was also stimulating wage growth. It might not have been the most militant of eras in terms of strikes, but there is no doubt that there was a growing confidence among trade unionists to take action in support of higher wage demands if necessary. Similarly, employers were happy to pay up as the economy thrived. As a result, salaries increased steadily over the decade and there was also the added bonus of overtime and improved holiday entitlement.

Indeed, holidays became an essential part of family life. Prior to the war, few working class people would have gone on holiday and certainly not on a regular basis. They may have had honeymoons but not an annual week at the seaside. The 1950s marked the heyday of the seaside resort, when the family went to the coast, played on the beach, and saw a show in the evening. But none of this could ever have been achieved without economic stability and wage growth.

The boom in housing meant that many newly married couples, for the first time, were able to buy their own home. The two-bedroom terrace or three-bedroom semi-detached became the norm. With smaller families, there was less demand for larger houses and more bedrooms. But, importantly, full employment also meant that they could pay off their mortgage and begin to afford the small luxuries that were coming onto the market.

And of course there was television, a revolution in itself. In just five or six years we were transformed from a radio-listening nation into a television-viewing nation. Life became centred around the home as the family huddled around the set in the corner of the room, enjoying *Sunday Night at the London Palladium* or *Hancock's Half Hour*. And it is true to say that television itself was far more family-oriented than it is today. Almost all programmes could be viewed by the entire family. Grandparents and grandchildren alike could all laugh to Hancock. It was as Peter Hennessy says 'a shared culture'.

Both Prime Minister Harold Macmillan and opposition leader High Gaitskell were astute in their observation that we had never had it so good. It was true, although that is not to say that everything was rosy. Attitudes were far from liberal. Homosexuality remained outlawed, women played a subservient role in the workplace and home, backstreet abortions continued and there was capital and corporal punishment.

The distinguished historian Peter Hennessy, in an interview for this book, recalls the 1950s as 'a success story nation'. It was, he says, an era of optimism but also a forgotten decade, falling between the heroic fighting 1940s and the dazzling 1960s. And of course there was the Queen, with her Coronation in 1953 playing a role in this success story. He also rightly points to the technological advances that were being forged in civil nuclear engineering, space travel, and aviation. Science was the new frontier and interviewees in this book, like Mike Prior, were keen to become scientists, even though their politics were on the Left.

So while David Kynaston is right to call the 1950s a 'family era', it is perhaps even more important to acknowledge that none of this could have been achieved without economic stability and growth. Of course, the obvious question is *why* was there was such economic stability and demand-led growth? This is a far more complex question, and possibly not one for detailed consideration here. Nonetheless, the Marshall Plan, European growth, the foundations of a more equitable economy established by the Attlee government with its nationalisation programme and health service, plus a booming American market, are factors to be considered.

This collection of interviews is far from comprehensive. Indeed, it never can be. But I have attempted to balance it regionally and to give as wide a circle of interviews as possible. As people grow older, it is more difficult to capture memories of those who were in their forties or older during the 1950s. Anyone who had a childhood in the 1950s is likely to be over the age off sixty today. In fact, a number of those I have interviewed have sadly since died.

What is undoubtedly true is that most of the interviewees here still have fond memories of the 1950s, particularly those who had been children at the time. They all valued family life and, apart from the cane at school, the eleven plus exam and living in the shadow of the bomb, a 1950s' childhood was not far off being ideal.

CHAPTER ONE

THE WAY WE WERE

What was Britain like in 1950? As the New Year broke, Labour was still in government, though only for a further year or so. Prime Minister Attlee and his leading Ministers, Nye Bevan, Ernie Bevin and Herbert Morrison, had all gown old and weary, worn down by the war years and a punishing period of frenetic activity in office after the war. Industries had been nationalised, a health service established and a new education system introduced. All that, plus a massive rebuilding of the nation after the Second World War, had left Labour exhausted. A General Election a few weeks later, in February 1950, would see Labour's massive majority begin to crumble, slashed from an overall majority of 145 to just five seats. Labour was a tired party and the country knew it. The writing was on the wall and before 1951 was out a Conservative government, under wartime Prime Minister Winston Churchill, had been voted back into power with an overall majority of sixteen seats. The Conservatives would remain in office throughout the 1950s, steadily increasing their vote, and turning the 1950s into the Conservative years.

Yet despite six years of Labour government and a raft of radical changes, Britain was still much the same as it had been prior to the war. The old divisions remained: rich/poor, rural/urban, North/South. Indeed, it would not be until the 1960s that attitudes and divisions began to be seriously challenged. But for the main part, 1950 was much as it had always been.

The Church of England dominated religious life, homosexuality was outlawed, lesbianism simply did not exist (or so we were told), abortions were illegal, the police were respected and obeyed, we smoked like chimneys, industrial life was dirty and hard, sex was not to be enjoyed, and women did not work once they were married.

But one area of major change was the National Health Service. Introduced by Health Secretary Aneurin Bevan in 1948, it was to radicalise healthcare in Britain. The previous system of private healthcare had led to anomalies, with poorer members of society unable to afford even the most basic of medial treatment. But the new system promised free healthcare for everyone. The impact would be far-reaching and, along with such innovations as immunisation against fatal diseases, would lead to the eradication of certain deadly illnesses that had prevailed prior to the war. Infant mortality fell sharply and, correspondingly, life expectancy rose dramatically. In 1951, life expectancy for a man was just sixty-six years of age and seventy for a woman. By the end of the decade, however, the average man was living until sixty-eight and the average woman until seventy-three.

In the 1950s it seemed that fewer people died of cancer. Far more dangerous was tuberculosis, or TB as it was more commonly known. Anyone contacting TB was liable to die and the only cure was a long stay in hospital or an extended period of convalescence in a healthier climate, such as Switzerland, where the air was free of smoke and smog. TB sufferers were frequently shunned by those who knew of their illness, as anyone coming into contact with them only enhanced the possibility of contracting the deadly disease. Bronchial illnesses generally were a common problem, particularly in cold, damp, and industrial areas such as the North of England. Polio also began to emerge as a serious problem. It was not at all uncommon to see young people wearing callipers or limping. Many also died from the disease.

The 1950s were notorious for their fogs, often caused by pollution rather than meteorological events. In London, and many other major industrial cities, the smog would descend for days. Traffic would come to a halt, people would walk around with scarves over their mouths, or wearing facemasks, football matches would be cancelled, traffic would be slow and in London policemen often walked in front of buses in order to guide them along the road.

And there was conscription or national service, as it was more generally known. After the war the call-up continued, with all young men, apart from those in Northern Ireland, enlisted to serve for two years in the armed forces. The majority served in the army, some finding it a challenging and life-changing duty, while others hated every moment. For most it was the first time they had ever been away from home and there were always indelible memories, even if it was only of square-bashing or the sergeant's bellowing voice. In 1950 the Korean War had broken out, with many conscripted soldiers making the long voyage to Korea to fight alongside the Americans. Many died. And in 1956 conscripted soldiers were called once more to fight, this time in Egypt at Suez, in a conflict that was to prove as controversial as any that the British had been involved in up to that time. The Second World War may have ended, but war was never far away. Conscription thankfully came to an end with the last intake in 1960, and a generation of young men gave a deep sigh of relief.

Many of Britain's city centres remained dominated by back-to-back terraced housing, much of it built before the war. Amidst the city centre streets German bombs had left a landscape of craters and wasteland.

Labour had set into motion a massive rebuilding programme that would continue under the Tories and well into the 1950s. But as they were rebuilt, the tendency was not to replace bombed terraced houses with more city centre housing but instead to begin a process of shifting the population to the suburbs. And where they did keep the population in cities, the new architectural fashion was for high-rise flats. At the time they seemed like luxury, a new beginning for working people. But in time they would prove to be otherwise and would soon become a blot on the social landscape of our cities. The camaraderie, which had been so prominent during the war, was quickly disappearing. People complained about the lack of good neighbourliness and increasing social alienation. Nobody seemed to care for their neighbours and friends as much as they did before the war.

In 1951, Britain celebrated the forthcoming age with a Festival of Britain. The war had ended and there was a new optimism for the future. Houses, offices, workshops, factories were being rebuilt and beginning to thrive. Britain was on a new course. Events took place throughout the country but the main event was on the south bank of the Thames, just across from Westminster Bridge. A whole site was constructed, including a Festival Hall, which was later converted into a concert hall. A giant sculpture, known as Skylon, was also erected. The Festival was a vivid memory for many people in the 1950s and attracted more than ten million visitors. It was about art, architecture, medicine, science and the new world ahead. And further down the river, at Battersea Park, a massive funfair park was built purely for enjoyment. There were even sporting events around the country, with English football teams welcoming European teams as a gesture of friendship. The Festival was deemed a massive success and even today, sixty years on, its legacy remains in the Festival Hall as well as indelible in the memory. Not everyone was in favour, however, the chief critic being opposition leader Winston Churchill, who promptly had everything, apart from the Royal Festival Hall, torn down when he became Prime Minister.

The hit parade in 1950 was dominated by American artistes such as the Inkspots, Billy Eckstine, Doris Day, Mel Tormé and Frank Sinatra. It was the era of the crooner and the Broadway musical. By the end of the decade, however, music would have changed dramatically as Elvis Presley and Bill Haley burst onto the scene with their loud, rhythmic music.

In sport Tottenham Hotspur had just won the football league title, while their north London rivals, Arsenal, had beaten Liverpool in the FA Cup final at Wembley. Over the next few years Manchester United would emerge as a major force in English football, alongside Wolves, while Everton and Liverpool would slip into the second division.

In cricket Lancashire and Surrey shared the title, with Surrey going on to become the dominant force in English cricket for much of the 1950s. The West Indian team arrived in England in 1950 as well and thrilled crowds up and down the country with their swashbuckling style that saw them defeat England 3-1 in their four test series. The three W's – Worrall, Weekes and Walcott – would forever live in the memory as elegant batsmen, while spinners Sonny Ramadhin and Alf Valentine tore the English batsmen apart.

Our cities may have been changing but you could still walk down a high streets in any village or suburb and buy whatever you liked. There was never any need for a trip into the city or town centre to buy a suit, shoes, record or washing machine. You could buy it around the corner. There were no charity shops or fast food restaurants, and, of course, there were no supermarkets. People shopped each day at the local butcher, greengrocer or grocery shop. Produce was fresh and local, whilst buying anything out of season was unusual. Figs, pineapples, grapes and even bananas were a rarity, and, if available, they would be for only a brief period.

Meanwhile, back in rural England, life continued much the same as it always had. The village was the centre of activity with a church, pub, post office and a variety of shops to cater for every need. Much of village life revolved around the church, with the four seasons appropriately celebrated, while in the evening the pub was the hive of local activity, though not for women.

Life for women remained constrained and restricted. Only a third of women worked and, once married, they tended to leave work altogether and concentrate on home life. In some professions, such as teaching, women were forced to resign as soon as they became pregnant. Certainly once women had children they left the workplace. And for those who did work there was no such thing as equal pay and work was often menial, uninteresting and tiresome. Women rarely went to the pub or attended sporting events, which remained the preserve of men. A woman's life was not ideal; chained to the kitchen sink and pregnant was the way some described it.

Whether you lived in the town or country, however, you always felt safe. Crime was almost at an all-time low. In many areas, particularly in the country, doors were never locked and burglaries were unheard of. Muggings and street crimes were also rare. Murders were few and capital punishment still existed, at least until 1964, though Ruth Ellis, the last woman to be hanged in Britain, was sent to the gallows in 1955 amidst massive protests. The prisons seemed empty by today's standards. In the mid-1950s there were a mere 20,000 prisoners in Britain's gaols. Today there are over 85,000.

On the streets children would play free of traffic and wander off to parks or into the countryside without any parental control. Indeed, parents usually had little or no idea where their children were most of the day during the summer holidays. Nobody felt threatened.

They may have been much to commend life in 1950s Britain but there was also much to denounce. Attitudes were very different from those of today. In the 1950s we feared authority, the Soviet Union, the local priest, teachers, Teddy Boys, and even television. We were far more subservient. Divorce was still rare and abortions were illegal. Nonetheless they took place, sometimes helped by the local 'expert', as well as self-inflicted on many occasions. Contraception was poor, buying condoms a furtive and embarrassing experience. Single women had unwanted pregnancies and did not wish to marry, though many did. The alternative was a backstreet abortion. Many married women simply could not face the prospect of a further addition to an already overstretched household and, consequently, paid the necessary going rate for an abortion.

Throughout the 1950s, homosexuality was outlawed with a threat of imprisonment. As a result it was swept underground. Nobody was openly gay, but there were clubs and pubs frequented by homosexuals and it was not difficult to discover where they were. The police often turned a blind eye to these establishments, although they were more likely to take action if gay men were to be found soliciting in public toilets. Any concept of lesbianism was just unimaginable.

For Michael McCutcheon, living on the border of Northern and Southern Ireland, life was considerably more primitive than on mainland Britain. There was no electricity, gas, newspapers, radio or television, and money was so tight that life on a farm had to be self-sufficient. You grew your own vegetables, reared your own animal stock and cut your own peat. It was the same in remote parts of Scotland.

For those coming to Britain in 1950 from America, life was a considerable cultural shock. There was no central heating, nor any of the white consumer goods such as refrigerators, vacuum cleaners or steam irons that were commonplace in the United States. England seemed stark and primitive compared to the gloss, optimism and friendliness of America.

ESTHER SHERMAN

I came to England in 1959. I was American and my husband was English and, after he got his PhD, we came to Liverpool, where he had just got a job. One of his professors at home in America said, 'Esther, you're going to get chilblains.'

We came on the Furness Withy line and when we arrived and I saw the land, I just burst into tears. I don't know why – I love travelling but I burst into tears. We were met by my father-in-law, who took us to the Childwall Abbey Hotel, which was the most grotesque building I had ever seen. Living in the light and warmth and luxury of America had been so different. In this hotel we had this huge room, with this electric light hanging down from the ceiling with no shade on it. It was horrific. I remember about a month later, I began to rub my toes and, yes, I had chilblains.

I was very intolerant of the lack of refrigerators, central heating, washing machines and so on. There was no warmth in the house, we just had electric bars to keep us warm and an open fire, but I never got the hang of that. All in all I was quite miserable. It was cold in Boston but we had central heating, fur-lined boots and fur-lined coats. It was cold outside but warm inside. We never had vests until I came to England.

The cultural contrast was stark. We had friends in America and they would introduce us to one another. At the university in Liverpool nobody talked to us because my husband had a lowly post. People were just not friendly at first. I eventually got a job as a part-time librarian in the science department at Liverpool University. I remember the professor of the geology department. He came into the library to collect a book put aside and I asked him what his name was. Professors were on a higher plane and he was shocked that I did not know his name. In America we always called everyone by their first names, but not in England. Everyone was so much more aloof. I was aware of the poverty because we lived in a poor street in Liverpool. I remember the poor children, poorly dressed, running noses, always having colds. I was very aware of the poverty.

MARY JAMES

There was a very blonde-haired girl with plats at Daisy Hill School. She was German. We were pretty awful to this girl – I still feel ashamed. I think she may well have been a refugee. It would not have come from my family as my father had respect for Germans. He had gone to Germany after the war as an officer in the R.A.F. He had great sympathy, even though he had fought against them. He brought over a lot of Germans to work for him. I think that was because things were so bad in Germany after the war.

There was also a school nearby where I thought all the children were very beautiful – blonde-haired and blue-eyed. I didn't realise this was because they were albinos. Why they had a separate school I don't know.

MAX EASTERMAN

We had so many bombsites in England, particularly in Bradford and Leeds. In Germany there were no bombsites. In the village we went to in Germany they were building their own houses, all under the Marshall Plan. It was astonishing that after so much bombing, places like Koblenz were totally rebuilt.

STEVE HALE

As a family we lived in a council house, which was pre-war built and had an outside toilet; it wasn't really very good. Five of us were living in it – me, my mum and dad, my nan and my Uncle Peter, my nan's son, who was more like a big brother to me. When he left home to get married my nan, who was the head of the household, decided we should move. 'It's time to get out of here, let's go to one of the new estates that are being built.' So we moved out to a place called Gillmoss. It was a lovely house. I remember running around it when we got there. I had never seen a bathroom like it; separate bathroom, toilet upstairs. It was a brand new house, really light and bright because the back faced south. We were really lucky as we had all this sunshine coming in all the time. The other house had been quite a dark house with small windows. I was brought up by my mum and my nan. They were very important to me right up until I left home.

CLARE JENKINS

I was born in Rutland, which, in the 1950s, was still a rather feudal county. My father worked for the Lord Lieutenant of Rutland and his wife and so we lived in a tied cottage on the estate. My mother's still got a photo of the Lord Lieutenant and his wife, in the clothes they wore when they went to the Coronation – he was in uniform and she was wearing evening dress. They had three daughters and, as we were growing up, my sister and I sometimes got their hand-me-downs, and some of those were evening dresses as well, which we used to dress up in. The daughters were debutantes. It was very much that kind of era, although we were at the other end of the scale.

When we'd moved from Rutland to Leicester, the Queen came to Abbey Park, where we were living – my dad was the park gardener – and we were all out there with our little flags. There was great excitement. I don't suppose she would have been Queen for very long then, maybe six or seven years.

There was a huge upstairs/downstairs existence in those days. I've talked to other people whose parents were in a similar situation – butlers, housekeepers, gardeners and maids – and it was very much that. You lived in a tied cottage and your whole livelihood depended on these people. Actually, the ones my parents worked for were very good but not everybody was. As I say, Rutland, at that time, was very feudal so there were lots of people around who were in service.

My parents lived in this little row of cottages and all the people living in these cottages worked for the Lord Lieutenant. He worked in London, in the City, and he was also a director of the railways, and the train used to stop specially for him – this was before Beeching and there were more rural lines. [In 1963, a government report headed by Dr Beeching recommended major changes to the railway infrastructure, with thousands of miles of rural railway lines being closed.] The train would specially halt at the next village, stop for him to get on to go to London and then drop him off in the evening. My mum still has the letters from him and his wife congratulating her on the birth of my sister Ruth and then me.

NEIL KINNOCK

I was born in 1942 and would have been eight years old when the 1950s started. I was living in Tredegar where I was born, which is a mining town to the north of the South Wales coalfield, now called the Heads of the Valleys road. It was a thriving community, rich in all of the cultural outlets, mainly undertaken in the Workman's Hall, which was a beautiful, massive cinema and leisure complex with snooker rooms and chess rooms and a wonderful library, which Aneurin Bevan called his university. It really was an extraordinary standard of library. The life of the town revolved around the hall and was used by the male and female choirs – world renowned – the Tredegar town band national championship winners and the Tredegar thespians, who used to win every competition they went to, and the operatic society. Throughout the winter, on the last Sunday of the month, there would be celebrity concerts and the finest players and voices of the generation – Beniamino Gigli, Jussi Bjorling, John Braine and others – everybody played or sang there. And the reason was that this very sophisticated hall paid Covent Garden rates for the world's best performers. There was a collective voluntary contribution of a penny a week, and by 1952 two pennies a week, by every worker in the district. And the result was that the collective subscription enabled them to get access to the very finest quality in the world. And they fully exploited it.

If you hadn't got a ticket for the celebrity concert in this 1,200-seat theatre-come-cinema a month before, you weren't going to get in. If there was a particular popular demand they would put up tannoys outside. They used to do that for Aneurin Bevan meetings as well. Twice a year he would come to the Workman's Hall – he never conducted an MPs surgery or anything like that in his life – he would come here frequently because his family still lived here and he would come and do the great meeting in the hall. I was privileged to go there with my father one Sunday night. The meetings used to start at half past seven, immediately after chapel, and they were wonderful occasions.

Without romanticising at all, I can safely say that I was born and brought up in a small industrial town where poverty was a very recent memory – deep, deep poverty – and tragedy was very familiar because we had mining and steel-working and it was a thriving community because of collective support for individual taste and brilliance. And out of it came world champion snooker players, sportspeople, performers, actors, singers – because they got the chance. That is the Tredegar I remember very clearly, when I was eight years of age.

MICHAEL MCCUTCHEON

In 1950 I would have been seven years old. In those times we lived in a house with an outside toilet and two and a half bedrooms. There were seven of us living in the house, so basically I was farmed out. I was sent to my uncles and my grandparents, who had a farm about thirty miles away, but it was over the border in Donegal, in Southern Ireland. I would have been about six years old when I went to live on the farm with my grandmother, grandad and uncles, away from my parents. At the time I never thought anything about it. I enjoyed the farm, I liked animals. You only think about it when you're older. I had to go to school there. The Irish was taught but my uncle had a word with the school and I didn't have to learn it, which I should have done. A little bit always helps. I probably came back from there when I was about twelve and a half and I then finished my last year and half in a local school, in Northern Ireland, until I was fourteen, when I left to find work.

The farm was self-sufficient. It was poor land but you survived. We had cattle and we had to grow everything – potatoes, animal feed, the lot.

The only thing we bought was sugar. We made our own bread and butter and we had our own corn. We would get it grounded, take it to the miller, then get it sacked for the winter. It was the same with potatoes, turnips, swedes, carrots. We made pits, put straw down and all the potatoes were stacked up, straw over and then soil, it grew like a mound, free from the frost. Then, when you needed potatoes in the winter, you went down and took some from the mound. It was the same with apples. You had to keep everything like that because you had to be self-sufficient for the winter. We had pigs as well and we'd kill one every so often, chickens as well, we'd have one once a month – that was a luxury. But generally we survived on bread, porridge, flour.

It was a hard life at that age. I would be up at six in the morning in winter to feed the cattle, bring the hay out; I'd then go off to school. Saturday was my only free day. In the spring we would be in the bog cutting the turf – that's peat – for the winter, stack it for the whole winter. If the weather was bad you might not have enough turf. Good years you had plenty, bad years not a lot.

I lived on the farm with my two uncles, my grandmother and my grandfather; though he died the first year I was there. Funnily enough, I had my own room, the uncles shared the large bedroom and I had a small room, grandmother was downstairs. At home I would have been sharing. I didn't go home very often. Mam came down every weekend, she had a bicycle – there were no buses – she would cycle about thirty miles; that was the only way. We were Catholics and I always went to church on a Sunday on a bike, it was about four miles.

Steve Hale

I was always excited to go down to the pier head on the tram or the bus. The first thing I always looked for were the trains on the overhead railway. If I was on the tram or the bus and we were downstairs, I would ask if I could go upstairs and stand at the front, because you could get a good, clear view. I must have gone a few times in the winter time because I remember the lights in the dusk, they fascinated me more than seeing them in the bright sunlight of day. The next thing you see is the River Mersey. I was always thrilled to go down to the pier head and see the railway. I can only remember going on it once, and that was down towards Seaforth, Bootle. What I remember most is the noise, the banging and the rattling, the sheer noise.

There were lots of horses and carts, lots and lots of people; the train, trams and buses. All these people milling about and I'd be clutching my nan's hand.

MAX EASTERMAN

Nobody thought twice about me going down on the underground on the northern line from Colindale to Tottenham Court Road at ten years of age and walking up Oxford Street. It wasn't considered dangerous. When I went to stay with my grandmother in Harrogate I was about six years old. I had been ill. They said go to Harrogate and stay there, it's much fresher. So I was put on a bus and told to get off at Harrogate. All the way from Hartlepool. Six years old!

CHRIS PRIOR

My father was a policeman in the City of London Police. He joined in 1938 and worked as a normal, above-ground policeman until 1943, right through the blitz in the middle of London, which was all very traumatic. All the young policemen were then put in the army, but he was demobbed early on and came back into the police force as a detective constable. By the time I was nine or ten we had moved down to Essex and therefore I wasn't very likely to see him at work. Just occasionally, if he worked on a Saturday, I might go up and see him in his offices in London.

Being a policeman was something he could never stop thinking about – and that carried on for the rest of his life. He believed in police ideals. He had a certain legal status and would have to sign official documents and papers. We moved away from London in 1954, down to Essex, where they bought a little bungalow that was newly built in Hockley, on a mortgage. I knew they were really pushed for money, what with travelling to London, bringing up myself, and so on.

NEIL KINNOCK

There were more changes in the 1950s than in any previous era. Little changed between the 1920s and '30s. Life was still pretty much the same – poverty, unemployment – and in the 1930s it didn't change much again either. It was the same kind of jobs, or lack of them – the same kind of housing, poverty, illnesses and so on. And in the 1940s any progress was hampered by war. Then, in the late 1940s, it was all about rebuilding after the war. But the 1950s were different. For the first time things really changed. You could physically see the changes. There was more housing and buildings, there was the National Health Service, education until you were fifteen and, of course, there was work. They may have largely been the same industries but at least most people, if not all people, had jobs.

So much changed, all those consumer goods coming onto the market as well as changes in popular culture. And there were cars, not many, but a whole lot more than there had been in the 1930s and '40s. In fact, I think you could say that things changed in the 1950s more than in any era certainly before or even since. No, I can't think of an era when so much changed.

JOAN FINCH

I was born in December 1931. In 1950 I was living at home with my parents. I had met Bill and he had to go in the army – that was in 1951. So we got married in two days, two days notice. He was going to Egypt for two years. He wanted me to save up for the deposit for a house while he was away, so I lived with my mother so that I could save. It wasn't much, but at least I was saving.

I was nineteen and Bill was twenty-one. We met when I was fifteen and he was seventeen. We met dancing at the Barracks on Cross Lane. As I say, he had to go into the army. Lots of people got married young then, some had to, but I was a good girl. I had a little job at weekends as an usherette at the Theatre Royal in Manchester, selling ice-cream, taking the tickets and so on. It passed the time while Bill was away. Sometimes I would go and look after his parent's off-licence when they were away. We got married on April 5th and he went away on the 21st of April, we had just two weeks together. We went to the Fairhaven Hotel at Lytham for a few days, just before he left. I didn't see him then until December the following year, when he came home. He was a painter and decorator. He got a job and I was working as well. We managed. It was very hard, but my husband was always a saver. All his army pay went straight into the bank. We saved £100 for a house deposit; that was a lot in those days. The house was £250, a little terraced house. Employers had to take you back if you had been off in the army. He didn't like the firm he worked for so he only stayed for six months, then went into decorating on his own.

NEIL KINNOCK

Tredegar was a very safe community. There was a sergeant of police and two constables in the Tredegar police station and that was the total police strength for a town of then over twelve thousand people. The greatest discipline was of course the discipline of the community. I was brought up substantially in my grandparent's house in South Tredegar, an area called the Tip; it appears on maps as the Tip and had been that since the exploitation of coal in that area from the 1820s on. My grandfather – my grandmother was dead – lived in a classic terrace alongside the River Sirhowy, facing on to Ty Trist colliery, and at the back was the Tredegar gasworks and the main railway line running down the middle of the street. Hence with the pit in front and the gas works and the steam-driven railways behind, my mother would come out at about half past four and shout, 'Neil, Neil! Come in your tea is getting dirty.'

PETER HENNESSY

I don't look at the 1950s through rose-tinted spectacles because to appreciate its specialness you don't have to. In terms of the rise in living standards, along with the transformation of consumer goods came a growing awareness, certainly from the mid-1950s, of items such as fridges, washing machines and televisions. By the end of the 1950s, labour-saving devices, entertainment facilities in your own home, and all the rest of it, absolutely transformed society.

And there was the first flush of affluence in terms of being able to go out to a Berni Inn and eat a proper steak for the first time. Until then, steak was stuff you got stewed from tins. But that first flush of affluence plus the optimism of the post-war reconstruction period, which had set in motion reforms in terms of health, education and welfare, would, for generation upon generation, produce benefits. It was by no means a pessimistic era.

Of course the great paradox was fear of the hydrogen bomb and the possibility that everything would end in the space of one afternoon in a huge ball of flames and heat radiation. We were the first generation to grow up in the shadow of the bomb. The bomb was very, very real and menacing, yet at the same time, in terms of our everyday living patterns, we were the most privileged generation our country had ever seen. And that's how I remember the 1950s. It didn't produce the dramatic changes in lifestyle that the 1960s did, or the personal liberation and charismatic pop music of the 1970s, but it really was a time of optimism. That was true in sporting terms too. Even though the decade had ended before Jimmy Hill got rid of the maximum wage, the Manchester United phenomenon from the moment of the crash onwards was extraordinary. But I remember the glow of the Wolves, collecting cigarette cards, and the great cricket summer of 1953. I remember that Roger Bannister, when I met him many years later while making a film on the post-war era, lived up in every particular to what one wanted a sporting hero to be – unassuming, properly amateur and all that.

Stella Christina

I think things were marginally better in the 1950s than the '30s, but people were less concerned about each other in the 1950s than they had been. Some people had more money than they had in the '30s, but there was still a big gap between the rich and poor and if you smoked that was it; all your money went on ciggies. I smoked until I was in my seventies and I never had any money.

Joan Finch

Because I was nineteen and we wanted to get married, my fiancée wrote me a letter to say he was coming home and to make plans to get married. His mother came up on the Sunday morning to see my mum and dad and my dad said, 'She's got my permission; she couldn't have a better man.' We got married by special licence at St Clement's Church. Then he went away in the army and I didn't see him again for ages. My mum and dad thought the world of him. We didn't have two ha'pennies to rub together.

Chris Prior

I can vividly remember the smog. Now, it must have been 1952 when that huge smog descended on London and everything was blacked out for days on end. I used to live on Hermitage Road in Harringay and I had to walk to school, about a mile down the road. My mum made me a smog mask, which was layers of muslin and cotton wool, and you tied it over your ears and you'd walk to school. As soon as you got to school they took you inside and closed the doors quickly, and when you took the mask off it was all brown inside, like marmite. You'd have a fresh one to come home with. There was no traffic on the roads except a police car, which had a policeman walking in front of it because the fog was so thick you could not see beyond the bonnet. And it went on day after day.

The effect on my dad was not good. He got a bad chest and had severe bronchitis and he was ill for weeks on end. I remember they brought the bed downstairs so that he could be ill with the family around him. When the fog lifted he recovered, but he still had trouble with his chest. In the end they allowed him to leave the City of London Police and move to Essex. They normally did not allow you to live more than ten miles from where you worked. He got special dispensation from the Chief Constable because the doctor said that if he stayed in London he would get bronchitis every winter with the fog and would finish up off work again. So we moved to Essex.

JOAN MATTHEWS

I was in the last great smog. I went up to work that day and by two o'clock in the afternoon you couldn't see across the corridor. It was thick, yellow, and somebody knocked on the door of my office and said, 'Go home, we're closing.' There weren't many trains after four o'clock so we all departed and went home. I'll never forget it because the smog was so thick you really felt like you were walking into a war. Extraordinary. That was an experience we were all pleased to put behind us. I walked to Waterloo and, of course, they were all steam trains, so that didn't help.

JOHN STILE

There was a pub in Liverpool called the Magic Clock, which was frequented by homosexuals during the 1950s. It was close to the Playhouse theatre but has now been pulled down. Everybody knew it was a gay pub, maybe actors went there, I don't know. Any rate, me and my mates went there one night. We were teenagers and going for a bit of laugh, you know, go in, wink at the fellas in there, see what they were like, and so on. Then we'd come out and fall about laughing. It was very naughty and certainly not the kind of thing you'd do today. But in those days gays had a hard time. It was appalling the way they were treated. Thankfully, attitudes have changed and things are so much better now.

LES GORMAN

Attitudes in the 1950s weren't good. It all began to change in the 1960s, but in the 1950s it was still pretty hard-going for most minority groups. Homosexuals in particular had a difficult time, ethnic minorities as well. Homosexuality was illegal and you could be imprisoned. But of course that didn't stop it. It was just driven underground. There were clubs and pubs where gays would hang out and could meet other gays without too much fear of police action. Generally, I think, the police were quite happy to leave them in peace if they weren't causing any trouble. But if they stepped out of those bounds, for instance, and started cottaging in toilets, then the police would arrest them. The Labour MP Tom Driberg was arrested on a number of occasions; although once the police got him down to the station and discovered who he was they generally released him. There's a story that on one occasion he asked the arresting policeman if he was a Labour voter. When the policeman said 'Yes', Driberg told him who he was and reminded him that if this all became public, Labour's slim majority would disappear and there'd be a Tory government. This must have been some time between 1950 and 1951, when Labour had a majority of about one. The policeman let him go. Gays would be discriminated against in the most appalling way. To some extent, you were probably better off if you were part of the establishment class, as there seemed to be more of an acceptance there. The further down the social ladder you were, the more likely you were to get beaten up.

Attitudes to black immigrants were also bad. They couldn't get housing, jobs or whatever. And of course they would be called all sorts of names. There weren't too many immigrants in the 1950s, but there were many more coming from the West Indies, Pakistan and India in the '60s, that was when things got progressively worse for them.

Women also had a hard time. They were expected to stay at home and look after the family. Indeed many women, once they had married, stayed at home. And certainly once they had started a family they would stop work. And even if they did work, opportunities for progression were few and far between. Women either became teachers if they were bright, secretaries if they were reasonably bright, or production line workers if they weren't that bright. In those days they never rose to become company managers, directors or whatever. You would never see a woman in a high-powered, highly-paid job.

JENNIFER WORTH

In the 1950s, illegal abortions went on all around us. In 1957 I met a fourteen-year-old Irish prostitute, who was fleeing a brothel where a girl had died after a backstreet abortion. Her body vanished. We, as midwives, were never directly involved, but we often had to clear up the mess after a bungled abortion, especially on gynaecology wards. Doctors, midwives and hospitals were required to report to the police if they suspected an abortion, but I never heard of this happening. We all knew what the woman had suffered; prosecution would have been too cruel. But by shielding the woman, we were also shielding the abortionist, whom most of us would have wished to see behind bars. It was a dilemma.

I have heard stifled screams as I entered the tenements many times, and seen dubious-looking women, who were not local, leaving the balconies or stairways. It wasn't difficult to spot them. A woman who avoided eye contact, or hid her face if she saw one of the midwives approaching, was in stark contrast to the cheerful housewives who greeted every midwife like a long-lost friend. I have heard two matriarchs conferring about a teenage daughter, who looked visibly pregnant, and muttering about 'getting it done' – a conversation that stopped abruptly as I approached. We could never find out exactly what went on, but we knew it was pretty grim.

The film *Vera Drake* tries to imply that the heroine was acting on principle, and never took payment, but I very much doubt that this was ever the case. From everything we heard, abortionists were in it for the money (the going rate was between one and two guineas). I never heard of one who was conducting a philanthropic practice. Ignorance, incompetence and avarice seem to be the folklore memory of abortionists. But I wonder if this is fair. When medical treatment was illegal, they were in demand. They performed a service that was widely used. It was not their fault they were medically untrained; the legislation was to blame.

Fatalities among women undergoing an abortion were high, but they was far higher among women who tried to do it themselves, unaided. Knitting needles, crochet hooks, scissors, paper knives, pickle forks and other implements have all been pushed into the uterus by desperate women who preferred anything to the continued pregnancy. How a woman can push any instrument through a tightly closed cervix is more than I can imagine. But it has been done and I have heard so many stories in such diverse circumstances, and they are all so dismally similar, that the evidence cannot be doubted.

Chronic ill-health frequently followed a backstreet abortion – infections, anaemia, scar tissue or adhesions, continuous pain, cystitis or nephritis, incontinence, a torn cervix or perforated colon. I remember a girl of nineteen who developed renal failure due to damage to the bladder. Her kidneys packed up, but, amazingly, she survived. In 1967 the Abortion Act was passed, and abortion was no longer illegal. When I was a gynaecology ward sister at the Elizabeth Garrett Anderson Hospital in London, I was sometimes asked whether or not I approved of it. My reply was that I did not regard it as a moral issue, but as a medical issue. A minority of women will always want an abortion. Therefore, it must be done properly.

(From an article written by Jennifer Worth for the *Guardian* in January 2005)

STELLA CHRISTINA

If girls got in trouble they would usually get married or have an abortion. Abortions were illegal then. I don't think women always knew where to go, but they would ask around. I remember a girl coming and asking for help at the church. We took her to Didsbury (a suburb of South Manchester) and bought her a meal. She said to me, 'How many abortions have you had?' I said, 'None.' She was shocked. She'd had about a dozen. It seemed horrendous to me.

JOAN MATTHEWS

Illegitimacy was frowned upon. When I went to live on the Isle of Wight, a girl who got pregnant and was not married was whisked away. She'd be taken off to a home somewhere else in the country, that's all we'd know. She'd come back with a baby. I had very strict non-conformist parents and that kind of thing was not mentioned in my house. Whether or not the babies were adopted often depended on class more than anything else. I had a hairdresser and she was the daughter of a woman she thought was her elder sister, but who was in fact her mother. You still get situations like that. There was a home for unmarried mothers on the island when I first went there in the 1950s. People pitied them. They were mainly Catholic homes, I think. These women would go to these homes, have their babies and live with them, away from society. There's a lot of things now being revealed about the dirty tricks that the Catholic Church got up. People were told their babies were dead when they'd been whisked away for adoption. Abortion was illegal but obviously it happened. My parents were so straight-laced and so severe that even with two sisters we never mentioned the word sex. I was engaged for three years before I got married and I was a virgin when I did get married. A girl at college did get married in a hurry and we all helped with money. I was very ignorant about what went on. I was brought up in a purist bubble.

PETER HENNESSY

Looking back, people's attitudes were appalling, inherently appalling. But we were not shocked by it because that was the norm and it was beginning to ease. I became an abolitionist on capital punishment when Ruth Ellis was hanged in 1955. I was eight. I never believed in corporal punishment at school and things like that because of my upbringing. And I wasn't in a household that reacted in an unpleasant way to the arrival of immigrants. Of course, I didn't know what that meant until the 1960s. You were warned about men of a certain type – that was all. But one did go to school on one's own. When I was eight, nine, ten, I'd walk about one and a half miles to my primary school, sometimes with friends. It was an age of innocence really.

PHILIP LLOYD

The trams stopped, I think, about 1953. They sent around an illuminated one in 1953 for the Coronation, and then there was one for the last tram. They followed a similar route as the buses do today. They were double-decker trams, although the number 46 was a single-decker as it had to go under a bridge. We even had our own railway station, until Dr Beeching came along. It was the London line, via Derby, although the London train didn't actually stop in Chorlton – it was just a local stopping station.

STEPHEN KELLY

We went to see some new flats that had been built in the dock area of Birkenhead. They were very smart, or so we thought at the time, and the top flat had been opened to the public. I went with my mum and some friends. Everyone thought they were wonderful and as we stood at the top someone was saying how you could feel them sway when it was windy. I don't know if that was true though. Anyhow, the thing is that everyone was envious and fancied having one of these flats. Twenty years later they were pulled down, harbingers of all kinds of social problems.

JOAN FINCH

You could go out and leave your door open. I wouldn't open my door to anyone, being on my own these days. It was better in those days. There was trouble just the same but not as bad as it is today. There were Teddy Boys then, as well.

STELLA CHRISTINA

I got married in 1957. We had a small wedding. The wedding was in the church and the reception was in the Co-op. My husband's father worked there and he wanted us to have it there. My husband was a teacher at St Aloysius School. I met him at the tennis club. My leisure time was spent mostly at the tennis club. I played tennis in the summer and table tennis in the winter. We'd have get-togethers even in the winter. We used to go hiking at weekends, bring our own sandwiches. We'd go up the Cat and Fiddle. We used to go on a picnic once a year to Ainsdale and have a meal.

ESTHER SHERMAN

People were anti-American. My in-laws accepted me, they were fine. But we Americans were very chauvinistic. We thought America had won the Second World War. We were told that on the radio and television back in America. The English didn't take too kindly to the arrogant ways of Americans.

STELLA CHRISTINA

Only the wealthy had cars. I remember someone in the tennis club getting a car and everyone was extra nice to him so that they could get lifts.

JOAN MATTHEWS

I remember that first wave of immigration. I worked in Bethnal Green, which was very interesting. Hackney was Jewish, Stepney was quite considerably Jewish, with some Chinese because it was a dock area, but Bethnal Green was strictly fascist. I used to get the *Blackshirt* magazine pushed through my door every week. Extraordinary, isn't it! I remember people buying and selling silver in the street and having little scales, and the tailoring trade was all over the place. People didn't make a suit in one place; they just did a little bit of it and then you'd see little boy runners taking bits to another place up the road where collars were made or turn-ups were done or buttons put on. It was like a whole ants' nest, all moving around all the time.

I distinctly remember walking down Mare Street in Hackney one day, on my way back to the office after lunch, and seeing black people sitting on the doorstep. They were as happy as Larry but we just stared because we hadn't seen anything like it before. But I was more aware of it than some people because my father-in-law was a crew member of the *Windrush* that brought the first load of immigrants over from the West Indies. He was one of the most amazing people I have ever met. He was the son of a Welsh miner, illiterate, emigrated at fourteen to the United States, went on the stage – he could play any instrument – went across to the west coast of America and worked as a lumberjack, then on a turkey farm, came back to this country before the First World War and got a job on a ship. The he bought some papers from a drunk engineer in Istanbul to prove that he was an engineer, met my mother-in-law in Odessa – she was Russian – married her, came back to this country and got work as a deep sea diver with a salvage company, and when I knew him he was still diving. He was an absolute rogue, a terrible rogue. He could never keep a penny in his pocket. During the war he was earning £40 a day diving, but he never had any money left by the end of the day. This had an interesting effect on his children because my husband and his brother would never bet a penny. You could not sell a raffle ticket to my husband even if you held a gun to his head, because he had seen what misery his father's life had brought to his mother.

OLGA ATKINS

I came over in 1959 from Grenada. I was nearly eighteen. I travelled by boat. The journey took about ten days. I paid $365 Caribbean dollars – about £50 – for my ticket. At the time it was a lot of money. Travelling on the ship was a very big experience because we met people from all races and we had to make friends with everybody and get to know them. I always remember my mother said to me, 'You don't know where you will fall, so be good to everybody.' I used to do the washing and ironing on the ship for all the boys that couldn't do their own ironing. So the journey was very interesting and pleasant.

The first place was the station and we travelled from Victoria to Huddersfield. I was somewhat disappointed because the buildings and the surroundings weren't what I expected. I expected to see beautiful painted houses. Back in the Caribbean, no matter how old the building was, it was beautifully painted and very pleasant to look at. When I saw the blackness of the buildings I was very much surprised and, looking at the smoke from the chimneys, I thought, 'My God, the houses are on fire!'

When I arrived, my brother-in-law fetched me from London, and when I got to where they were living, again I was taken back quite a lot because I had to share a room with my sister and her husband. That was very hard to handle, that I didn't have my own room, my own bedroom, my own space.

Grenada is a very small country and there wasn't a lot of work. I like to stress this, though some people don't like to hear it; we came over at an invitation; there was plenty of work in England, work which the British didn't like doing. So we decided to come to England.

In the house itself it was all West Indians, so that was alright. We got on very well because my sister knew most of the people, some of them I met when I was a little girl but couldn't remember, and then I got to know them again. We got on very well but the problem we had was the reception we got from the native white people.

It was not very pleasant. I can remember looking for rooms, you'd see vacancies on the window and would knock on the door asking for a room to rent. Some shut the door in your face, some would just say, 'Sorry, no vacancies'. I found that very hard to handle.

Some people might say it was a racial issue, but I would say it was an ignorance issue. I've had things done to me personally that was discrimination. I've had people spit in my face; I've had people call me black monkey and people say, 'Get back to the jungle'. It's just pure ignorance.

We were brought up in the West Indies to be polite. When you walk in the street you say 'Good morning'. We would say 'Good morning' even if we didn't know the person, but saying 'Good morning' to people here was like speaking to a stone, nobody replied. They'd look at us as though we didn't know what life was all about.

When I came, there was the shop which sold West Indian stuff. As I said, I came to my sister's, so they were here before me, so for me it wasn't difficult finding things. The way was paved for me by those who came before. By the time I got here, in 1959, there were a lot of people who had come in the early '50s, so things were already beginning to improve for West Indians.

At the time, the early days, the English didn't really take to the West Indians; we were isolated in certain ways. It didn't happen to me, but I know people that went to church and nobody would speak to them and there were people who wouldn't even sit near them. We found it very hard; we just weren't welcomed.

We had to try and push our way in because we realised we were strangers in a different land and we had to integrate and get to know people. I said, 'Just give us a chance and get to know us.' Never mind we might have different skin, we carry the same red blood and we're human just the same. We had to really struggle to integrate and interact with people.

Mike Prior

I remember that our lodger was pleased when we gave him the room. He said we were the only people who would take a black man. This was the era when there were signs up saying 'No Blacks, No Coloureds'. He was from a very well-connected family and was respectable and was studying law. He was a tribal chief and could easily pay his rent. But black men didn't find it easy to find lodgings. He was, in fact, the first coloured resident in our street. His name was Kofi and I thought he was wonderful. I used to play with him and he would wrestle with me and carry me on his shoulders. He used to have parties and quite a number of what would later become nationalist leaders would come, including Nkrumah. The parties didn't get out of hand, they would just play music and there would be white girls, but no one complained. My parents were communists and were simply not racist and it was because of their beliefs that he was able to live here. He came back and visited us in the 1990s.

Joan Matthews

I really enjoyed my time at the LCC (London County Council) and I was there at the time of the Rachman business. [Peter Rachman was a notorious London landlord who used extreme methods to evict sitting tenants in his properties and replace them with new tenants paying considerably higher rents under new terms. The word Rachmanism became common currency for this type of activity.] In 1952 the Rent Restrictions Act was either amended or cancelled, I don't remember which, because, during the war, there had been rent restrictions and private landlords couldn't put rents up, and also properties were requisitioned. When people were bombed out of their homes, the local councils just found other empty homes and put them in, but then, at the end of the war, the previous owners wanted them back and it caused lots of problems. When the Rent Restrictions Act was amended, suddenly landlords wanted tenants out so that they could raise the rents or sell the properties and it really was a racket. There were people coming to our office crying their eyes out; the landlords had been around with large dogs and changed the locks and there was a great deal of unhappiness. The name Rachman only crept into the news gradually, but it was a wicked time and I have a feeling it's being repeated now because there is such a shortage of housing today.

MARY JAMES

We had relatives in places like Australia. We had people from all over the world at the YMCA. I think that is why I was so much more open to other cultures. I can remember my mother being horrified when she called the doctor into the YMCA to see one of the Africans who was unwell, and the doctor, who was an Austrian Jew, making some racist comment about them always pretending to be ill and you couldn't tell if they were ill because they were black! My mother was horrified. We later had many from Northern Ireland coming in order to give them a break from the troubles and again there was never any trouble. We had lots of students from Liverpool University, Birkenhead Technical College, seamen, unemployed. It was male-only, although eventually the hostel was mixed – my father would have been horrified. One boy from Ireland brought his clothes in a record case. That was all he had – such poverty. All sorts of groups came to stay. We got lots of gifts from people coming from other countries. Mainly they came from Commonwealth countries to stay, study, work, whatever.

STELLA CHRISTINA

I went regularly to the library, daily sometimes, but usually once or twice a week. I spent most of my time reading, anything. There were books all round – you had to push it through a wire netting so that it was pushing out at the back, and the librarian on the other side would collect it and call it out.

PHILIP LLOYD

I did my national service in the RAF. The King had died in the February and I was sworn in to Queen Elizabeth II just a few months after she had acceded to the throne. I wasn't looking forward to doing my national service. It wasn't my scene. I've never liked regimentation and square bashing. Once I was in the RAF, however, I was alright, getting around different places. I met a variety of people, most of them okay, not many I didn't get along with. Anyhow, I signed on for three years, even though I only had to do two. If you signed up for three years you got more money and a choice of jobs. So I chose to go into the signals section. After a month of square bashing I was sent to Bridgnorth in Shropshire, then to Wiltshire to train up in signals. I was there two months, then to Suffolk for on-the-job training. Then they asked very nicely where would I like to go? I said Manchester or Cornwall, so they sent me to Northern Ireland! When I was in County Down I lined the route when the Queen came, standing there with my rifle. She hadn't been long crowned Queen. Of course, this was before all the Troubles started. I thought the RAF would not be so regimented and I think that was probably true. I spent most of my time in a little van in the middle of an airfield with an aerial on the roof. Then I went to Germany – north Germany – the nearest big town was Bremen. I tried to learn a bit of German and toured around a bit. It wasn't long after the war, only eight years or so. The places round there hadn't been hit by the war as it wasn't an industrial area. There were quaint little towns and villages, like something out of Hans Christian Andersen. At Christmas-time in the town there were lots of lights and decorations. Really nice. For the last few months I was at a gliding centre. It was up in the hills. They had all the equipment there for skiing. There was thick snow, so I did a lot of skiing. That was very nice for the last two months. Then back to England, near Gloucester, to get demobilised.

WILF McGUINNESS

There was national service. I missed it through ill health. Nobody wanted to go in the army. There wasn't a war on and it just seemed to interfere with your training. David Pegg and I didn't make it. Bobby Charlton, Eddie Colman, Duncan Edwards, Tommy and Gordon Clayton all went in. They got £1 a week wages from the club, it was ridiculous. You couldn't possibly manage on it. I trained here and I got in the first team before Bobby Charlton, Eddie Colman, even though they were older than me.

JOHN PALMER

We knew we had to go into the army before we got the letter. When I got the letter, I was eighteen; I was told where I had to report to. I met one of my friends on the bus going to Romford and I asked him where he was going and he said Palestine and I said, 'Ah, so am I'. We had about six weeks of basic training, came home for a few days' leave, and then we were off to Palestine. I was there until we all came out. I went to some wonderful places in Palestine. I went to Petra – I'll never forget that. We piled into these lorries and started off alright. Then we were climbing these hills and all these hairpin bends, we drove as close as we could to the edge and then we all had to get out and the lorry had to back up a bit, then go forward again in order to get round the bend. We'd all jump back on and off we'd go again.

I spent a lot of time hiding from the provost sergeant. He's the guy who looks after the prisoners and he says, 'You, you, come and do this'. I had some lovely friends. I made good friends with the Arabs. I was in Gaza, I was in Hebron, Be'er Sheva. I used to drive the lorry down to the border with Egypt. I had some wonderful experiences. I got on this boat, it was sailing to Port Said and Benghazi, and all we had was a corporal, me and another guy, only nineteen. Going along I used to spend a lot of time lying on the deck in the sun. Eventually we pulled into this dock at Benghazi. There was a little army camp there so we went to this camp, very small, a few tents, and there was a square tent with an officer. We were allotted a tent, had something to eat, went back to our tents, got up in the morning, dressed smart, ready for parade. We looked around and there are all these guys, some with no shirts, some wearing shorts, no hats. They said, 'Why are you dressed? You don't come like that.' These guys did nothing all day apart from cook and eat, and their officer was always drunk. He used to sit in his tent with his gun, shooting holes through the tent.

ANTHONY HANBURY

I had a letter telling me to go to Aldershot. And to be honest I was quite keen to go. It seemed very exciting. But I had not been in very long when I realised what it was all about. I think I was at Aldershot for about eight weeks. I met a very interesting bunch of lads from completely different backgrounds, from a lad who was in a gang to these very bright lads, extremely well educated, who had degrees and God knows what. For one reason or another they'd been on the War Office Selection Board, which is what you go on to become an officer, and these fellows were considered potentially good officers because they had been well educated and so on.

But for one reason or another, they found it difficult to become an officer. I believe one did make it, eventually.

If you went to a good school you would become an officer. You might be the thickest nut head, but if you'd been to the right school you became an officer. After Aldershot, when I'd finished my training, I went to Bicester. I was based there for the rest of the two years.

I was on the reserve list at the time of the Suez Crisis in 1956. Because I was in the Territorial Army, I think they had us on the Z reserve, and if you were on the Z reserve I think you were on it for about twelve months, and if anything happened like Suez then you'd get called up and you would have to go off at a minute's notice, but I didn't have to because I was in the Territorial Army. I had to do three and a half years in the TA, which was no great bind really. I had to do the odd weekend – going for training – and in the summer they would have a camp. You would have to go on these camps – I think it was a fortnight you were away. After conscription it was back to Civvy Street to find a job.

CHRIS PRIOR

I remember thinking about conscription and calculating whether I'd be called up. My uncle had been in the merchant navy during the war. My dad had been in the army and they'd talk about the war. You knew there was Korea happening, and then Suez as well, I remember that. But then they stopped conscription and I breathed a sigh of relief.

ROGER TOMES

In 1950 I was in the army. I had just joined the Intelligence Corps and had done a course near Loughborough, and then I was transferred at the beginning of 1950 to GCHQ at Eastcote, in London. [GCHQ is the Government Communication Headquarters, now based at Cheltenham, and otherwise known as the government's listening-in station.] I had been conscripted. I think I approached it with resignation. Most of my chums had done their conscription before they went to university. I was one of the ten per cent who went to university first. I had already been to Oxford. I finished my degree at Oxford and then went into the army. I joined up at a place called Bordon in Hampshire, which was a depot of the Light Infantry Brigade. It soon became clear that I was not officer material, so in view of my degree they thought the Intelligence Corps was the right place for me, so I went on a course in what was originally a farm near Loughborough and learnt how to interpret wireless signals. I then transferred to GCHQ, which was at Eastcote near London in those days. I logged intercepts of radio signals, so I suppose in a way I was a spy. I worked on intercepts, particularly from Israel, which was a new nation at the time. I had done a little bit of Hebrew before I went into the army. It was a sort of modified army service as I was working in a civilian office with mainly civilians, who were very envious when we got Wednesday afternoons off for sport. I did quite a bit of cross-country running at the time and I would end up in a café where they sold brandy snaps. Towards the end of my time at Eastcote (which was extended because the Korean War had started, I was originally in for eighteen months but it became two years), I met a very interesting young woman who I later married. But we only had a month to get to know each other before I was demobbed. My future wife was in the Russian section. I was quite interested in the job but she wasn't, she couldn't get out quick enough.

I wasn't called up to serve in the Korean War but my services were offered to the Americans as an intelligence officer when war broke out, but they said, 'No thank you.' I enjoyed my time at GCHQ because of the relative freedom we had. I made good friends, took part in the life of the local church and so on. But it was a very much modified national service. I didn't have too much drilling. They once announced that there would be parades on Saturday mornings. They said it would be in full uniform and we got our kit out of mothballs. And then they announced that it was cancelled, as they had no Blanco. Blanco was the material you cleaned your uniform with.

CLARE JENKINS

Just outside the park gates there was a playground and we would go there and play on our own because it was so close. I was out there one morning with John, on the swings, and this strange man came along and he was chatting to us and asked, 'How much do you weigh, little girl?' and I said, 'I don't know,' and he said, 'Well, let me pick you up and see how much you weigh.' Then he picked me up and put me down. John and I must have thought there was something wrong because we ran straight home. Mum was absolutely furious and she came running out with a broom, but of course he had left by then. But you've always had that 'stranger danger'. There were always people like that. They weren't called paedophiles, they were just called strange men.

Mum told us never to take sweets off strangers. The next time I was offered sweets, it was from one of dad's colleagues. He was from the Ukraine – there were a lot of Ukrainian people who had moved here after or during the war. Anyway, I threw the sweets down the drain and was very proud of myself and ran home and told mum and she said, 'Don't be silly, he's not a stranger.' And I thought, well, you never told me what a stranger was.

TREVOR CREASER

When I was in the choir at Leeds parish church we went on a yearly camp to Hovingham Hall, Sir William Worsley's place near York. Sir William's lawn was used as the cricket pitch. We organised a match and I had to go in as the last man. I was a bowler, really, but I had to go in as the tail-ender. Anyhow, I received this ball and smashed it straight through a window at Hovingham Hall. Sir William was sat on the grass in all his regalia, with his family and all this food around him. His daughter Katharine Worsley, who later became the Duchess of Kent, was there as well. We used to play with her. Anyhow, this ball had gone through the wire mesh on the window and had smashed the glass. Sir William stood up; he was a big fellow with white hair and a ruddy face. He came striding down towards me and I thought, 'Hells bells!' He grabbed hold of my hand. 'Well done, sir, come and have tea with me tomorrow.' I thought, 'Oh my God!' So the next day I got dressed up and went for tea and he showed me around the place – the stables and so on. He had about six beautiful old cars. I had to be on my best behaviour. There was a massive class divide in those days, but the Worsleys were a smashing, real down-to-earth Yorkshire family. Mind you, Katharine was a bit of a bugger.

STEPHEN KELLY

When I was about ten I got a verruca on my foot and could hardly walk, so I was taken to the doctor's and then had to start a course of radium treatment at the Liverpool radium hospital, opposite the Philharmonic Hall in Liverpool. I went once a week for about six or seven weeks. My mum would buy me a comic to read while I was waiting around. They laid me on this bed – on my stomach – and put this thing on the verruca – it was like the end of a vacuum cleaner. I would lie there for about half an hour and, presumably, they shot radium at it, or something. Whatever it was, it worked. Years later, when my son had a verruca, you either just put cream on it or, as in his case, have it cut away. It took about five minutes.

CLARE JENKINS

There were certain things you heard about polio, and you were fearful of it – the idea that you could pick it up in swimming baths. In fact, somebody

I knew did contract polio, though I'm not sure if that was to do with swimming baths. You had your polio jabs — we all had to line-up for that — and we had the nit nurse as well, and that awful black tar shampoo to use. It was little wonder children didn't like having their hair washed. It was foul-smelling. But we knew it was important to have those jabs. Children got whooping cough at school, and chickenpox. But I got neither. It's probably a pity because if you get that later in life, it can be shingles. Measles; we all got measles.

We had regular check-ups at the dentist. My mum had had all her teeth out before she was twenty-one because the diet was poor and they hadn't got much money. So she had false teeth before she was twenty-one. Dad had his last teeth out when I was a child — he would have been in his late thirties, early forties. It was much more common then for people to have their teeth out as it was a nuisance — and an expense — looking after them.

JOAN MATTHEWS

A girl in my class at school died of TB and we were very carefully examined for it when we had school medicals. We had them regularly, and dental medicals. I was a healthy youngster. My first encounter with the NHS was when my daughter Josephine was born and I stayed in hospital for a fortnight. They were so concerned to have a healthy generation of babies. My husband was not present at the birth, that didn't happen until my fourth child. It was not encouraged at all. I remember polio. I have a friend who got polio as a child and has been in a wheelchair ever since. There were regular scares about polio. Our local pool closed, it was a devastating illness. Polio and TB were still very common in the 1950s.

VERONICA PALMER

I remember polio; we had friends who caught it. I knew a little girl who had a withered arm. People didn't talk about things like that then. They would whisper it; they wouldn't talk about it. As it was highly contagious, people would be afraid to come near you if you had TB.

STEPHEN KELLY

Illnesses like TB and diphtheria were widespread. If you'd had TB, you didn't tell anyone. A friend's mum had had it and it was all kept very hush-hush because there was always a worry that you might catch it by being in contact. But the biggest scare at that time was polio. We had a lad in our school who'd had polio and he had a calliper on his leg. Everyone was terrified of getting it. Lots of kids wouldn't go swimming because it was said that this was where you might pick it up. And then there was the iron lung. This is what they had to put you in. It was a terrifying prospect. Then came vaccination. I remember a footballer – Jeff Hall – who played for Birmingham City. He was an international, a fullback, a really good player, and he was stricken down with polio and put in an iron lung. Eventually he died and it was headline news. People thought, well, if a fit man like him can get polio, so can anyone. It was at the time that the polio vaccine was being introduced, so people went out and started to have the vaccine. So, in a way, his death was not in vain as it probably spurred many on to get vaccinated and that, in the long run, saved many more lives and led to the eradication of polio.

John Hectorball

I had a breakdown when I was seventeen or eighteen. I was in hospital for seven months, in Prestwich. I think it was the thought of national service that brought it on. I was afraid of being killed, bullied, being out of my depth. I was called up but got out on medical grounds. I had been off my head, talking nonsense, I didn't understand what was being said to me. I just flipped; it was over a couple of weeks. I just didn't want to go in the army. Prestwich hospital hadn't changed much; it was primitive, quite old. They had electric shock treatment and they used to give it without any anaesthetic, shoot a current through your head. That was supposed to make you see reality better. I had electric shock treatment about twelve times. You lie on a stretcher and they wheeled you into a room and put, like, headphones on you. There's no injection, they just flick a switch and the next thing you wake up in a room. It's like being kicked by a horse; you come round in another room with a terrible headache.

The electric shock treatment helped but it mustn't have helped enough because they then put me on insulin treatment for a while. An injection in the arm and you go to sleep for the morning and then they bring you round. It put you into a coma. I had fifty comas. I was with two men; one was Polish and one Ukrainian. They had the tattoos; they had been in the concentration camps. There were six of us taken every morning for the insulin treatment. It was one a day. I had it ninety-six times. They had to be careful you didn't have sugar because it upset the balance; they did a test each morning. It was quite expensive treatment. I don't feel bitter about my treatment, it did me good, gave me a second chance.

It was an old Victorian hospital with rows of beds and about twelve patients in each ward. You couldn't go outside. I was confined to the hospital. I was

in the same ward; it wasn't mixed, just men. I mucked in, got used to it. I had
visitors. My father came to see me, and my mother, though on separate days.
I was allowed other visitors as well. In the ward there were games, billiards.
We just sat around; about twenty of us in a day-room. I went to bed at half
past eight. I had a radio but there was no television. I made a few friends. I
chatted to the ones who had been in the concentration camps. They had been
in German camps; I think it was Auschwitz, not sure. There was occupational
therapy as well, making baskets, needlework. I got out of hospital after seven
months. They sent me to live with my father; they thought it would be more
suitable than living with my mother.

John Palmer

I had TB. I was working in the Fire Brigade and they said I could go to either
Sevenoaks for treatment – which would take two years – or to Switzerland,
which would be much shorter. A friend came to see me and he said he'd
been to Switzerland and it was wonderful, they don't mess about and you'll
be operated on. He said if you want a cure go to Switzerland, they have
everything. So I went, for nine months. It was a bit terrifying going to
Switzerland on my own. A lady met me at Euston, carried my bag for me,
then put me on the train, and when I got off at the other end, I was met
as well. I had a bunkbed and a sleeper on the train but I never slept. In the
morning I went for breakfast. I got off at Aigle and there was a pretty young
nurse waiting for me, she was Swedish. From there she took me to the
vernacular railway and we went up this mountain to a little village, where
the hospital was. They took me off all the drugs I was on and prepared me
for an operation known as AP, they inject in your lungs – reduce your lung
size down to a fist. They only work on one lung at a time – if you cure one
lung, the other will cure on its own. Any rate, they did the operation and
I could barely breathe but after a few weeks I found I could breathe more.
Every week they were reducing the size. After nine months I came home
and they continued the treatment here. They kept that lung down for two
years all told.

I didn't get homesick, I just wanted to get cured and get home! But yes, I
did miss my wife.

Veronica Palmer

Our honeymoon was just three or four days. John was in the Fire Brigade
and he couldn't get a full week off. We went to a hotel at Richmond, in
London, and we got the first signs there that John was not well. He didn't

eat much and it wasn't until six weeks later that they diagnosed him with tuberculosis. He started coughing up blood on duty so they sent him home. It all happened so quick. They sent him to hospital for checks. When I got the letter, I thought he was going to die. It was devastating. In those days it was like being told you had cancer. You usually didn't survive it. They soon packed him off to Switzerland. The Fire Brigade said our benevolent fund can send him to Switzerland or to Sevenoaks in Kent. I said I don't want him to go to Switzerland 'cos I'll never see him. They said if he goes to Sevenoaks he'll be there for two years. They said if he goes to Switzerland he'll be cured in less than a year. I'm not sure how true that was. My mother-in-law said let him go to Switzerland.

The Fire Brigade were very good at the beginning; they paid all his wages and said that when it was all sorted he could come back to an office job. They gave him a pound spends, as well as paying my wages. After two years, however, there was no job. But they were good at the start. It cost the Fire Brigade £1,000 for the cure – the benevolent fund paid that. That was a huge amount of money. It was remarkable. John was so ill, he looked so thin, and by the time he came home he was a different person. I wrote to him every single day and he wrote to me.

After two months in Switzerland he wrote to me and said, would I come and see him. Well, I had never travelled any further than where I used to live, or gone anywhere on my own. All the family said I had to go. In the end the Fire Brigade said they would meet me at the station and put me on a train. It's all very vague. I got on the train to Gare du Nord station in France, in Paris. What I didn't know was that the first half of the train was carrying on, while the back half didn't – it stayed in Paris. Well, I didn't know. I was sitting there and there was a knock on the window telling me to get off. This inspector was talking away to me in French and I didn't understand. They got an interpreter to tell me and I said, 'I can't stop here I'm going to Switzerland,' and they said the train's gone; you got in the wrong half. I sat on my case and cried and cried. Well, as luck would have it someone came out of the office who could speak English and he said, 'We'll put you into a taxi and drive you to the next station, where the train will stop'. So they put me in a taxi and it was hair-raising. The driver was on the horn all the time, the traffic was crazy. Anyhow, he got me there and got me on the train. I don't know how I did it that day. I was only twenty.

MIKE PRIOR

In my second year at senior school I got tuberculosis. It was unusual because TB had almost been wiped out. Most people got it from drinking milk from infected cows. In the 1920s they invented a test – you put a patch on the cow and you could tell if it had TB. Up until then you had no way of knowing. It was often fatal and was called the white death. It was common in working-class communities and was associated with overcrowding, spitting, but mostly it came from drinking infected milk. Many farmers didn't want to have to do these tests because it was expensive. Manchester City Council had a brainwave. Milk was only sold in dairies at that time as they maintained strict standards of cleanliness. They realised that under their by-laws they could put a label on a milk bottle saying whether or not it had been tested. So there would be labels saying it had been tested and labels on other bottles saying it had not been tested. So, of course, people simply bought the milk that had the tested label on. Eventually farmers realised and soon changed their attitude about testing.

I got a form of TB in the stomach. They opened me up and found that I had TB, so I was sent to a sanatorium. This would be in 1955 because it was in my second year at school, so I would have been twelve or thirteen. It was a hospital out in the country, near Alton in Hampshire. It was a long way away and I was given complete bed rest. This is what you did if you had TB, you had complete bed rest; you just stayed in bed, which I loathed. You didn't get out of bed even to go to the toilet or wash. Because I was an only-child with a room of my own, I couldn't stand being in a ward with other kids, although not all had TB. I was there for six months, the first four months was bed rest. I eventually ended up in a room of my own. I just was not used to being with other kids.

I had a new drug, which was experimental, called streptomycin. I had ninety doses injected – two a day. Nowadays you just take it orally and don't even need to go to hospital, but it was then the new wonder drug. The injections left a lot of bruises. By the end of it they were finding it hard to find a place that wasn't bruised. I remember they told me how much it cost; it was £80,000 at 1950 prices. It was an enormous amount of money, mainly because it was still experimental. But of course it was the NHS. We were five years into the NHS, the drug was there and I got it. No question – in it went.

One parent would come to visit on a Saturday, the other on a Sunday, there was only two-hour visiting. They could not come in the week because they were working. But I would write to them. I found a letter some years back that I had written to my mum and it was all tearstained and even when I think about it now it brings tears to me eyes. It was awful. The thought of my mother getting this letter with me saying, 'It's so horrible here . . . I hate it,' and my tears staining the letter. They would take a bus to Victoria station and then come down on the train to Alton, and finally a bus to the hospital. It was something like a three-hour trip. They brought me books because what I did all the time was read. There was a visiting tutor who gave me a bit of education but, basically, I just read, and by the end of my time there they had persuaded the library to give us extra tickets and they had their own tickets too. I was reading twenty books a week. I would read them and then they would go back. I used to read everything, all kinds of things, fiction, non-fiction. They weren't school textbooks either.

I remember one day they had a fête, an open fête with stalls and people came down, and those of us on bed-rest had our beds pushed out onto the hard standing area just outside the ward and we just watched from our beds.

Even now I can't bear the sound of someone playing a recorder because they had music classes and I can still remember lying in bed in my little cubicle listening to people playing recorders. Whenever I hear a recorder I remember being there and being so miserable.

I came out in November, so I spent basically the whole summer in that hospital, six months. For the last two months I could get up a bit. When I came out I was very fat. My muscles had disappeared. I had eaten a lot of biscuits and things people had brought like cakes. I weighed fourteen stone and I was only twelve years old. I was so fat they couldn't find a school blazer to fit me. I went back to school after a couple of months at home and I had a bad time. I was bullied because I was a fat little kid with no uniform. I wasn't allowed to do gym because I had no muscles, they had all gone. I could barely walk, I literally could hardly walk.

WIN HINDLE

We had a crowd from school. A few of us would go out together, watch the football, go to the cinema together. When I went out with George he was a loner. At that time he was quiet but later everyone knew him. He went in the forces when he was eighteen, he was called-up, he was an officer's batman. I went to Folkestone to see George and my mother gave me a lecture about what I could and could not do. Now things are so different.

He was in the army for just eighteen months. It should have been two years but he came out early. When he came out he wanted to get married. My mum asked, 'Where will you live? Have you got any money?' Well, no.

My mother-in-law, who I had never met because George's parents were divorced, suddenly turned up. My mother said, 'George is outside in a car with a red-haired lady.' She didn't believe it was his mother. There was a house near the station. His mam said, 'If I get this house, will you let them get married?' And my mother said, 'Oh, I don't know. Let's see how it goes.' Well, the house was seven shillings and sixpence a week, it was a one-up one-down.

His mother got us a settee, a bed, an old chair and a sideboard. About twelve months after we were married we got this lovely bed and table. I got a China display cabinet at half a crown a week – mother had to be the guarantor, it was lovely. I used to leave the front door open so people could see it. I pegged a rug as well; it was a half-moon rug and had coconut matting at the back. But it was nice, our own little place.

I had to ask mum's permission to get married; she thought I was too young at eighteen. But once we got the house, it was okay. George got a job at a pet shop in Rusholme. My mother had to get papers to prove that she had said I could get married because I was under twenty-one. George was twenty-one but I wasn't quite. George's parents had got divorced when he was just a little boy, before he was evacuated; it was unusual in those times.

HUGH CAIRNS

The English were not very popular with the Scots. My grandmother was from Sunderland, so we had to be a little bit careful. The Tories were hated with a passion; Churchill was detested with a passion. I once asked my grandmother why he was so unpopular and she said it was because of what he did to the miners. She said that at the General Election he came up to campaign and got such a bad reception that he never came back. Labour was popular, certainly in Shettleston, which was a solid Labour constituency. Politics was very much Labour. The Communist Party tried to get a foothold but didn't get very far, and not with the Catholic population. And certainly after the Hungarian uprising they were detested. The Royal Family was greatly respected, but some folks weren't bothered. I went out with my dad and played football on Coronation day. We didn't have a television and the family wasn't interested. My mum may have listened on the radio. It was a class thing. Most people in the East End of Glasgow were downtrodden. They didn't have much money. Their only get-out was to go and get drunk, though my father never did.

MARGARET WILLIAMS

I went to Paris in about 1953. I went with a friend I had been in college with. We enrolled in a French-speaking course at the Sorbonne. It was only three weeks or something. It was very different from what I had experienced before. The course wasn't very good though and after a couple of weeks we gave it up and just went around Paris. It was a bit of a culture shock from Nelson! I found it all very interesting, the food was very different; it made me think about different cooking. My mother's cooking was very good but it was also very traditional. Most of the time we were eating in the canteen at the Sorbonne. I was fascinated to hear children speaking French in the streets. I've had an interest in French ever since and now we have a French daughter-in-law.

I don't think I went abroad again until 1957, when I went on the World Youth Convention in Moscow. Everyone said we'd never get home after being behind the Iron Curtain. We flew to Prague and then got a train to Moscow. We were told the train would stop frequently and lots of people would come out to see the train and us, which they did. In Moscow the food was horrendous – awful. But we saw a lot of the things you'd expect to see – Lenin and so on. It was very exciting because it was so different. My husband, Frank, was very interested, being so left wing. Being an architect, he was interested in the buildings and seeing all the reconstruction after the war. Frank was in the Communist Party. That visit to Moscow was a big excitement after being married a year.

We moved to the North Riding in 1958 because Frank was doing an MA, so we both got jobs up there. We lived on a farm near to the Catterick army camp. All the local accommodation was taken over by officers, so we couldn't find much.

We had a 1936 Alvis car – it was a great big thing, ridiculous. It was a very thirsty car and we had to drive from the farm to Northallerton every day. I don't think we were there for a year even. We felt isolated on this farm, so we came back to Manchester. Frank went back to the Town Hall. We had a flat belonging to the council on Altrincham Road. From there we bought our first house. I think it cost something like £1,800, which was a lot of money in those days. We only had one salary, as I was pregnant. I think we put down a ten per cent deposit.

BRIAN HULME

I left home when I was seventeen – my dad threw me out. I lived with my maternal grandmother for the last year at school. I only went back to see my dad when I'd got to university. He pretended he didn't know where I had been, but he must have known, someone must have told him. My mother and father didn't communicate very much. There was a cultural divide – he was an ex-Methodist. He would come home after work and just sit there gazing into space, doing nothing. Eventually he started working in the wines and spirits department of the brewery and he became a bit of a local expert on wines. In those days a straw-covered bottle of Chianti was the height of sophistication, followed by Liebfraumilch. He even visited vineyards in

France on several occasions, ordering for Robinson's brewery. And he would give talks about wines. People would have wine and cheese evenings.

MARGARET WILLIAMS

In many ways things were better then. People's expectations were lower, satisfied with much less than they have now. We didn't have the easy things like freezers and so on. It was a very different life, but people helped each other a lot. People's attitudes to everything were different. You expected life to be like that. It was a happy life. We had lovely holidays on the beach, went to see our parents; it was very different. Living in Manchester was fantastic – libraries, theatres, and so on.

IAN RALSTON

I was born in Oxford Street in Liverpool and I spent all of my childhood in Hunts Cross – that was a lower middle class area, semis built in the inter-war years. And that's where I went to primary school as well.

I remember the trams and the noise they made. Some of them must have been ancient and survived the Second World War. They had flat roofs whereas the newer ones had sloping roofs. Some were open at the front. There was a terminal up at Garston, a huge tram station, and one in Old Swan. But it was the noise, sitting on leather seats with the occasional stained-glass window, seeing the driver get out with his pole to turn the tram around.

One of the great losses to Liverpool was the overhead railway. I recall going on that from the pier head all the way up to Bootle with my mum after it was announced that they were going to pull it down. One of my hobbies was ship spotting and going down to the old floating landing stage, which was a whole city itself. You'd have to walk under the old overhead railway, seeing the steam-powered trucks on the dock road move material around the docks, going under the overhead – the Docker's Umbrella it was called. I remember looking out of the window of the overhead railway and seeing all these docks full of ships. I'll never forget that. A great loss to the city.

BRIAN HULME

I was always surrounded by women, except for my grandparents. All the men were in the army, at war, and I remember being three when my father came back from the war and that was the first time that I had consciously met him. I remember standing on the sofa in our front room and seeing this tall, sunburnt guy in a khaki uniform coming down the road with a kitbag over his shoulder – it was my dad. Lots of people in my generation had the same experience and to some extent they were estranged from their fathers, who came back from the war expecting everything to be tickety-boo – which of course it wasn't – and the resentment they felt towards their children affected a whole generation. My mother used to say, 'One day I'll write a book entitled "The Casualties of War". It won't be about the troops, it'll be about those who were left behind.'

Ian Ralston

I can still remember large areas that had not been repaired after the war. Gaps between houses – 'bombies' we called them. The Liver Building was black with all the pollution. Liverpool was a dark city in the 1950s. There was a lot of poverty and the buildings were dark. Some of the new building on Dale Street stood out but the municipal buildings – St George's Hall, the Liver Building – were all dark. When they cleaned them up it came as a great shock to see their real colour.

I broke my arm and was taken to the children's hospital and, as we were driving up to the hospital, the entire street was blocked by a huge brawl. There were Black Maria's [the nickname for secure police vans with separate locked cubicles] there – that was the first time I had heard that phrase – there were police, people fighting. And even though I was in pain, I was fascinated by all this. People go on about violence in the streets today but there was always violence – this was a mass brawl.

Pat Tempest

In 1950 I was thirteen years old and still living in Wolverhampton, where I had won a scholarship to the high school.

My father was something of a chancer and he had made a lot of money during the war. He had a company that re-stamped industrial files and because they used a lot of industrial files during the war he made a small fortune. He took us on holidays to the Isle of Man because he loved the big bands. We stayed in a posh hotel. He loved the beach. He loved the fact that there was no rationing; there was beef to eat, eggs, milk, all of which you didn't have on the mainland.

The Isle of Man had been used as an internment camp during the war and many Jews and foreign nationals were all caged up on the island. They were all people considered suspicious, some were fascists, some had connections to the Royal Family and were right wing.

Father was worried that my brothers would not pass the scholarship and would go to a secondary modern school. The family had been rich at some point but had lost it when he was young. So he came back from a visit in February 1950 and said that he had found a house, so we were all loaded into a van and went to live in the Isle of Man. It meant the break up of friendships and so on. The house was called Seaview; it was crumbling but had barns, an orchard, a tennis court, a wood, and a huge field at the front. There was no water, no electricity and no gas. Never had. He decided we'd live there and he would be a sort of boss of the village. We had to walk a mile over fields to the bus stop to get to school. We'd get on the bus in filthy clothes after this walk. He thought that by going to these private schools we'd learn to talk proper, but we didn't. He didn't fit into the village, he was a terrible drinker. He was very embarrassing as a father.

He used to take us around in his Bentley. My father would bring strange vehicles back from the Midlands with the idea of making his fortune with some invention or other. My parents used to go out all the time, usually drinking, leaving us with the other children. Father smoked a hundred cigarettes a day, my mother about fifty. They were very neglectful. There were some very nice, ordinary working class people who were our friends and a millionaire who had married a local girl. It was basically a tourist economic. Our house was about three miles outside of Douglas so that if you missed the last bus, which was at about 8 p.m., you had to walk home. In a way it was quite bohemian. We had a billiard table as well.

BRIAN HULME

My dad worked in Gartside's brewery at Guide Bridge, in the offices. He was a very introverted person, not outgoing. I think the war had turned him in a way. He came back rather bitter and he didn't have a lot to do with me, really. I can remember my grandad taking me to cricket matches and it used to bore me out of my skull. It was always in hot weather and he'd take this little case with bottles of stout and these smelly sandwiches with Gorgonzola cheese and I'd sit there just waiting for it to be over.

PAT TEMPEST

We used to go and see all the stars when they came to the Isle of Man. The big names – Ted Heath, Joe Loss, Two-Ton Tessie O'Shea – stayed at the same hotel that we did. And there was Norman Evans – Over the Garden Wall – and The Ivy Benson band as well. There was something called 'Soldiers in

Skirts', which must have been something gay. Of course we never realised that there was something called gayness.

OLGA HALON

I used to do a lot of charity work; I used to help the old people in a hospital-type home, taking the trolley around to them with sweets and chocolates and things they needed and then I used to go to the prison and serve tea. I belonged to the League of Jewish Women and this was one of the things we'd do. They'd take us into this big room, down at Strangeways gaol it was, and you'd go in this room and there was just tables, like a canteen. The visitors would sit on one side and the prisoners on the other. We'd stand at the back and provide tea and coffee; the prisoners weren't allowed to come up to us, it had to be the visitors who came up and paid for the tea or coffee. Then we would clear the tables. You had to be careful. We never really saw inside the prison, just this room. We never knew what they were in for.

MAX EASTERMAN

All around us was the aftermath of the war. This was particularly evident when we got to grammar school. The school had a very progressive attitude because there were people who believed that there should never be another war, so they taught us never to want war. I remember wearing my CND (Campaign for Nuclear Disarmament) badge at school and one particularly unpleasant member of staff got angry at me for wearing it to school. Afterwards, quite by chance, I heard another member of staff arguing with him that it was his duty to encourage this kind of thing. 'Do you really want another war like that?' he was asking. They had seen the horrors of war. Some had fought with Monty in the Western Desert. You saw it all around you, with the bombsites, war books, war movies – *Dam Busters*, *Reach for the Sky* and *Prize of Gold*, which was set in Berlin just before the workers revolt in Berlin in 1953. I remember seeing the Hungarian revolt in 1956 on television and my father was so angry at the Russians. I think we were quite rightly terrified. Teenagers today have no clue; we were growing up in a divided Europe.

OVERHEAD
RAILWAY

A ROUND TRIP 13 MILES
GIVES
UNRIVALLED VIEWS
of **DOCKLAND**
& **SHIPPING**

CHAPTER TWO

FAMILY LIFE

Mention food in the 1950s and the first memory that springs to mind is rationing. After the war, rationing continued long into the 1950s, though, as Pat Tempest recalls, it did not exist in the Isle of Man. It seems the Isle of Man was self-sufficient. Nevertheless, it was to dominate the lives of so many housewives on mainland Britain, who had to take their ration books to the grocers, sweet shop or butchers every day. As many testify, you didn't choose your food, it was determined for you by what was available and what you were allowed. During the 1950 General Election, the Conservative opposition had campaigned on ending rationing as quickly as possible. Although the Tories were not elected, the victorious Labour government did go on to end petrol rationing in May 1950. But once the Conservatives had been elected to office in 1951, rationing began to disappear. Sweet rationing ended in February 1953, followed by sugar in September. Most other food rationing ended in September 1953, with meat the last to go in July 1954.

Although restaurants were exempt from rationing limitations, few working-class people went out for a family meal, apart from holiday time, when your hotel would serve evening dinner. Restaurants were generally expensive and beyond the means of ordinary working-class people. Workers might go to a café for a quick breakfast or lunch, but it would be very basic and an evening meal at a restaurant was out of the question. It was simply too expensive and, anyhow, was not really part of the culture. Chinese and Indian restaurants were not to be seen on the High Street until the 1960s. Meals were eaten at home and were often very ordinary. It was usually meat and two veg, perhaps fish on a Friday and a roast on a Sunday. Other favourites were shepherd's pie, stew, streak and kidney pie, chops, sausages and mash. Salads were rare, very run of the mill, and only eaten in the height of summer, when lettuce and tomatoes were freely available. There were also cuts and types of meat that have since lost popularity, such as corned beef, spam, tripe and pig's trotters. Vegetables also tended to be basic and seasonal; sweet potatoes, asparagus and artichokes were rarely, if ever, seen at the greengrocers. It was the same with fruit, which was always seasonal, fresh and generally British-grown.

Puddings like apple pie, rhubarb or gooseberry crumble with custard, jelly, blancmange, rice pudding and trifles were always popular, and might appear on a Sunday if you were lucky. And of course there were always cakes.

It was part of the housewife's ritual to bake at least one cake a week, as well as cupcakes and jam tarts.

Most shopping was done locally and certainly all food shopping. The local High Street was a glut of food shops – butcher, baker, greengrocer, fishmonger, and, of course, the Co-op. You could even buy most of your clothes locally – shoes, dresses, knitting wool, men's outfitters, and there were usually newsagents, cycle shops, toyshops, a post office, a hardware shop and a sweet shop. A visit into the centre of a town or city for more substantial items was barely necessary. There were no freezer aisles or frozen meals in those days. Most people would never have tasted fresh figs. And of course there were no fast food outlets apart from the fish and chip shop, which was a favourite with everyone. It was cheap, nourishing and quick. But there was no McDonald's, no Starbucks, no Indian or Chinese takeaways. Yet, as Ian Ralston points out, home deliveries of groceries are nothing new. Indeed, it was quite common in the 1950s to have your food and vegetables delivered to the door. You simply dropped your list off at the Co-op, or wherever, and, later that day or the following day, at your convenience, a box of food arrived.

All food was cooked in the home and daughters learnt the rudiments of cooking from their mothers. Men rarely cooked or did much in the way of housework. The kitchen was the domain of the woman.

Clothes were also rationed in the early 1950s. Generally this didn't cause too many problems, but if there was a major event that necessitated new clothes, such as a wedding, then families would pool their coupons so that the bride and her bridesmaids could be fitted out. The making of the wedding dress and those of the bridesmaids would generally be done by a relative, friend or neighbour, perhaps in lieu of a wedding present.

Many women made their own clothes. It was far cheaper. Buying clothes from a shop (they were never called boutiques in those days) was expensive and most women had learnt needle and sewing craft from their mothers. Once children had grown out of their clothes they would simply be passed on to a younger member or another family with young children. There were no charity shops because nothing was wasted or thrown away; even pullovers would be unwound so that the wool could be used again.

Above all, women dressed smartly and femininely, taking great care with their appearance. Dresses were often brightly coloured with floral prints. Skirts would be pleated and always well below the knee. Waists were tight and slim fitting, often with a belt. Few women wore trousers and certainly not jeans. The fashion was for pencil skirts, tailored suits – pinched in at the waist – and high-heeled shoes. Cardigans and blouses were also close-fitting. At weddings and other grand occasions women wore hats and gloves. They carried handbags rather than shoulder bags, and often wore headscarves.

Fur was also popular, particularly shoulder wraps. Older women aged with dignity, often wearing widow's black or darker clothes. Lingerie was practical rather than sensual, with full-length body corsets to hold you in and, of course, suspenders to hold up your nylons. Petticoats were also popular and were often hooped for dancing, so that they swirled outwards as you jived around. It was smart femininity

Men would often dress quite formally if they were going out for the evening. After all, they might have been in boiler suits for most of the week so that even a visit to the pub or local club warranted a change of clothing. On a Saturday night though, a suit, sometimes a three-piece, was obligatory, with well-polished shoes and a smart tie. Grey flannel trousers and a tweed jacket were another favourite. And hats. Most men wore a cloth cap to work and a trilby when they went out. Look at any photograph of a football crowd in the 1950s and almost all the men will be wearing cloth caps. City gents wore bowler hats and trilbies were a casual favourite. Most men also smoked and many women too; some men also smoked pipes, taking great trouble with stoking them up and cleaning them, as well as having different pipes for different occasions. Cigars might also be smoked, though more commonly at Christmas.

The 1950s also saw the advent of the family annual holiday. By the 1930s, those who had money – mainly the middle classes and even more wealthy – were regularly holidaying. But holidays for the working class tended to be restricted to either a honeymoon or a one-day trip to the seaside. But once full employment had begun and wages were on the increase, along with paid annual leave, then families began to go off for a week's break, maybe two weeks if they had a bit more money. The favourite spots, as ever, were at the seaside. In particular Blackpool, but also resorts like Scarborough, Ilfracombe, Bournemouth, Torquay, Skegness, Redcar and the Isle of Man. Wales too was popular too, with Rhyl, Anglesey, Llandudno and Conway being favoured venues. Scotland, on the other hand, was better known for its spectacular scenery, rather than sunny seaside spots. Scotland wasn't always the ideal place to holiday with young children.

And once you were at the seaside it was usually beach activities; sunbathing, paddling, kite flying, swimming and sandcastles. The sun, of course, always shone! But when it didn't shine there was always the fairground, the zoo, and plenty of good shows to go to. Every summer the nation's leading comedians and singers could be found at some resort or other, and you always booked to see at least one show. Mainly you stayed in a bed and breakfast. They were far cheaper than hotels. Some offered just a bed with breakfast but others offered an evening meal as well. Some even had full board that included lunch. But if you couldn't afford a week in Blackpool then a caravan holiday was becoming popular by the end of the decade. The other alternative was Butlin's.

Founded by Sir Billy Butlin in 1936, they came into their own during the 1950s. Each camp, usually by the seaside, offered a chalet and laid on entertainment. They all had swimming pools, bars, dancing and other entertainment, while all meals were taken together in a large canteen. Everything was organised and overseen by an army of famous Redcoats. But the regimented style of Butlin's was not to everyone's taste, with many considering it a tad 'common'.

During the war much of Britain's housing stock had been destroyed by German bombers, making the reconstruction of our cities the number one priority in the immediate post-war years. In most cities and towns evidence of the war could still be seen, even in the 1950s, with bombed sites and rows of houses or buildings coming to an abrupt end. By the beginning of the 1950s, houses were being built once more. But it would take time. There were still rows upon rows of terraced houses, ginnels, back entries and passageways, as well as outside toilets with torn-up newspaper for toilet paper. Children often shared a room well into their teens, with a pot under the bed for emergencies. Gardens were few and many grew their own vegetables, a hangover from the wartime campaign to grow your own.

As a result of the lack of new housing stock, many newlyweds were forced to begin their married lives in their parents' home, saving as much as they could and waiting for houses to become available. At the beginning of the 1950s, a brand new two-bedroom terraced house could be purchased for as little as £200. High-rise flats were also beginning to appear by the end of the decade and although they initially seemed like the answer to a housing crisis, in time their shortfalls would become apparent to everyone, but especially to those living in them.

The 1950s was remembered by many women for the gadgets that suddenly flooded onto the market. The vacuum cleaner, manufactured by the American firm Hoover, was a godsend, making cleaning so much easier, while the washing machine revolutionised the weekly wash. In the past much of it would have been done outside, in a tub filled with hot water, with a dolly tub used to turn the clothes, or even just scrubbed on a flat surface. They would then have been rinsed and put through a mangle. It was a painstaking, laborious and time consuming task, leaving your hands red and sore. Many women would also go down to the local laundry, where there were facilities to allow to do your own wash, particularly when it came to washing larger items such as towels and sheets. The new washing machines, however, could do everything. And once the clothes were dried, new electric and steam irons turned ironing into a far more pleasurable occupation. Also, into the kitchen, came electric kettles, toasters and pressure cookers. They became known as white consumer goods, mainly flooding in from America, but they were to make the job of the 'housewife' much easier.

Joan Finch

When Janice was born I took her in the pram to Chapel Street and the food office there. It was bitterly cold. We walked all the way and I left her outside in the pram – you wouldn't be able to do that today – while I went in and got a ration book for her. I think it was that year or the year after that they did away with them.

I always did my own cooking. When I first got married I bought a new gas cooker. I paid for it – only £37 – and I always did my own cooking, and baked as well. We always had roast dinner on a Sunday. If I didn't cook, we'd go to my mother's on a Saturday. She idolised the girls. I've had a good life, touch wood! You've got to work together, but we had fall-outs same as everybody else.

Joan Wood

My daughter, Janet, was born in 1953 and she had a ration book for the first year of her life. Clothes rationing had finished in 1949, just in time for me to get enough material for my wedding dress, in April 1949. I did all my own dressmaking, made all my own clothes, everything for the children as well. That was fairly common, though not everybody made their own clothes. You always saw babies in nice knitted things, knitted by mums and grannies.

Esther Sherman

You couldn't get things like carrots in the wintertime. In America you could get them whenever you wanted. It was just such a cultural shock. Those white consumer goods that we had in the States just did not exist in England for so much longer. I remember getting swindled in a shop. It was two shilling for whatever I was buying and I gave the man half a crown and he accepted it and I had to demand my change.

Mary James

My mother used to order peppers. She had to get them in especially. She was before her time in a way. You couldn't get things like that from the shops then. We ran the YMCA so she tried to give the foreign residents something of their own food culture. She also used to mend our shoes. With rationing, she would cut down her old clothes to make clothes for me. She also made rag rugs. We would normally eat what was on offer in the YMCA canteen. By the time it came up to us it was lukewarm.

Stella Christina

You didn't go and choose your meat, you got what you were given – it could be quite fraught. We used to have an Irish captain who would come and sleep on our sofa. He'd bring us bacon and we'd give him tea and sugar.

I made our own clothes. You used to do things like unpick an old jumper and then knit it again. I remember when I was a little girl getting a dress that wasn't a pass-down. It was new, the only one I had. We used to send our old clothes to Ireland and we used to think they must be badly off over there having to have our old clothes.

Towards the end of the 1950s I got a washing machine, it was a twin tub washing machine. I thought it was wonderful. I used to do all my washing by hand before that – put it all in buckets to soak. My mother had a big dolly tub, it was a big tin drum, and then there was a plunger that went up and down and you had to do it all manually. We had a mangle to wring all the water out. It was hard work. We used to have one of those push cleaners – a Eubank – that was before we had a Hoover. I was never house-proud.

Joan Matthews

We got very good at making things out of nothing. I remember my father coming home once with a bundle of old parachute silk. You were really lucky if you got hold of that. Mostly it was nylon and it was a great spur to the manufacturing of nylon. We used to cut them up, make petticoats and things like that. Clothes were very hard to get hold of and to afford. When I met my husband, he brought me things from America such as nylons, shoes. He brought me a dress which was quite nice. You were lucky if you had a source of supply like that, very lucky. In Southampton they used to say that you only had nylons if your husband was a sea captain or you were a prostitute. That was the only way to get nylons. I made a lot of clothes for the children. When Jo was born we got an allowance of, I think, twelve coupons for baby clothes and we were allowed twelve nappies. People helped and there was a great market in second-hand baby clothes. I can remember unravelling jumpers to make new ones from them. Things were rationed for a long time, but everybody was in the same situation. When I got married, in 1951, six of my college friends got together and bought me a complete dinner service. It was Denby ware and it was green and it was the first coloured crockery we had seen since before the war. That was quite an event. When I got married, my father's tailor moved heaven and earth to get me some fabric for a wedding dress.

IAN RALSTON

Some think home deliveries are a new idea. It's not. I distinctly remember a van that went round delivering tea, with a giant tea-kettle on top. It was exciting to see it. You could also hand your grocery list in at the shop and they would deliver from a real grocers shop or a real vegetable shop. I remember harassing my mum for a lemonade delivery. They would come round every week with their screw-top bottles, but we never got one. We had a man from the Pru – Mr Flynn – who used to come round for the insurance money. He always dressed in a long overcoat and trilby hat. We had a coalbunker and coal would be delivered. It would be my dad's chore to fire up the fire. We had a gas poker to do this. I would sit for hours looking at the gas poker. We didn't have central heating until well into the 1960s. We had a back boiler when we had a coal fire and you could hear the water rumbling and think the whole house was about to explode. If we hadn't had the chimneysweep around, my dad would set fire to the chimney with burning newspaper to try and clear it and one day he nearly set fire to the house. There was smoke everywhere, coming from underneath the tiles. We were on the point of calling the Fire Brigade.

You forget those smogs, which would stay for days, they were not good; and they always had the smell of a coal fire. I loved to just sit and look at the coal fire, to see faces and all sorts in the burning embers.

MAX EASTERMAN

I can remember sugar coming off the ration when I was about five and I was given a shilling to go down to the shops to indulge myself with a big bag of sweets.

NEIL KINNOCK

We were very well fed. Poverty was gone for the first time in history, completely gone from those working-class communities. Nobody was opulent, but by the mid-1950s people were buying family cars – very few of them – but it was becoming increasingly evident. The earlier evidence of the gradual effect of the first ever period of full employment in the history of the South Wales valleys and communities, like mine, was that rush matting and stone floors were replaced by wall-to-wall linoleum and then, very, very quickly afterwards, by wall-to-wall carpet. And that really was the point of lift-off – the building of indoor toilets, or at least lean-to's against the back of houses rather than at the very back of the garden, and then the gradual conversion from gas light to electric.

Aberdare was a coalmining town, where my grandfather and uncles worked in the pits – one right through to retirement in the 1970s. In Aberdare they always had electric light because they had started burning garbage in the 1890s to generate power, from which they ran a tram system and put electric lights in every house and on every street. But that was a particularly revolutionary enlightenment. They were the only community I came across when I was politically active in the late 1950s and early '60s where I still found people who regretted the fact that there was now a national electricity grid, because they paid virtually nothing at all for the locally-generated electricity, whereas now they were having to pay the same price as everybody else for their national grid electricity.

Michael McCutcheon

The house on the farm in Ireland had a big open fireplace and you just hung the pots around it, the kettle was always on the boil, bread was made on the pots. It was peat (turf) that kept us going all winter. From mid October to March you needed a lot of peat. Sheds were built especially to keep the peat dry. We had an old tin bath, like in Victorian times. We had a bath once a week but there were rivers where you could go and have a dip in summer, but no heating apart from fire. All the rooms were freezing in winter time, but everyone seemed to live longer.

Joan Wood

We'd always cook; we didn't go out to eat like they do these days. It'd always be fresh, we didn't have such a thing as a freezer, didn't have a fridge even until I went back to do some teaching. I had forty-nine four- and five-year-olds in my class, on my own, plus my own son. I didn't know anything about teaching infants. I had done science with senior kids but the headmistress – a nun – was very persuasive and wouldn't take no for an answer. I said, 'I know nothing about teaching infants,' and she said, 'Of course you do, you've got two of your own. Bring your little one in with you.' I couldn't say no.

Chris Prior

My mum had worked for Boots the Chemist in the City of London, which was where she met my dad. When I was born I don't think she worked for a few years, but when we moved down to Essex she took on work at some local shops because she needed the money. We never had very much money.

We didn't, for instance, have a car and we didn't get a fridge until at least the late 1950s. We got a TV in late 1950s as well, but didn't get a car until 1963/64. My mum was never into clothes-making. I never understood that, as my grandmother had been a domestic servant when she was younger. But she did knit, she'd knit jumpers, swimsuits, socks, anything that could be knitted. I don't remember anything being done on the sewing machine, even though she did have one. I never felt denied clothes, but then we never had an obsession about clothes in our house. The only person who was concerned was my dad, who had to have smart suits for work and was always going to tailors to be fitted for suits. They never complained about money.

STELLA CHRISTINA

Chorlton was lovely. You could get anything you wanted in Chorlton. There were clothes shops, shoe shops, furniture shops, china shops, hardware shops. Now all you have are bars and eating places. Helen Fletcher's was my favourite shop, a lady's outfitters. They used to do very nice two-piece skirt and jacket suits. We used to go on the Whit Week march and we had to have something special for that. It was a lovely shop.

I used to have an order delivered from the grocers, especially after I'd had a couple more children. I used to go out every morning before that, then I started ordering. He'd send someone with the order, drop it off.

MARY JAMES

I remember Bradford very well. I used to go with my grandmother to Busbys, a large shop, like House of Fraser. I remember we used to go in the winter because my grandmother used to put her fur coat into storage for the summer; you used to take you fur coat to Busbys, where it went in for cold store. We used to go there and we'd have tea. I remember the centre of town where my father worked and I remember, I think it was 1953, the centre of Bradford went up in flames and the whole of the centre was destroyed. And because my father was in the YMCA, and it had a hostel there, he had to find accommodation for all the people who had been made homeless by the fire. And also his assistant and wife lived in the building. They came temporarily to live with us in this little semi and stayed for a year, or certainly for a while. I can remember going round the day after and being quite shocked. Everything was black, floors were missing, everything black. I think it started in a building nearby dealing with the fat from the wool which they used.

CLARE JENKINS

When you went to a school party for Christmas you were supposed to bring your own dish and spoon. Food at home was traditional – pork chops, meat and two veg, roast dinner on a Sunday, dandelion and burdock or 'Tizer the appetizer' – that's what it said on the advert – to drink. And mum always did us good cooked breakfasts. For sweets we had Spangles, Lovehearts, Opal Fruits – I can still sing the Opal Fruits advert song – Jubblies, Cadbury's Five Boys, fruit pastels, pear drops, flying saucers, sherbet fountains, liquorices, aniseed balls, jelly babies and dolly mixtures. Which is probably why I have so many fillings!

BALWANT SINGH SANDHU

When I came here in 1956 there were approximately twenty Pakistanis and twenty Indians living in Huddersfield – all in six or seven houses. The ones that came then, even Pakistanis, were from India, Punjab. We were all from the same area. When people came from India you would ask them to bring some spices or you could get them from Bradford. There were no shops in Huddersfield where you could buy spices. In Bradford there were only two shops – both Asian shops – where you could get spices and lentils and you'd go there every month.

JOAN MATTHEWS

We moved to the Isle of Wight when Josephine was about seven, and I became a housewife, so that was a big change for me. We were very prudent and careful. We lived next door to a manager of Woolworths, and they always had the latest of everything. We bought a second-hand gas cooker, one of those old mottled blue ones, and we paid £5 for it. And my neighbour came in and said rather disdainfully, 'I remember my mother having one of those in 1925.' It didn't bother us because it was an excellent cooker and didn't show the dirt. We were careful with our money until we got the offer to move to the Island. My husband was head of the techniques group and he was asked if he wanted to go. He took four people with him and they worked on a special project.

I had a washing machine early on because my father, before the war, had an electrical shop. He sold radios, washing machines and the first televisions. So we got a washing machine early. My mother had a washing machine in 1935.

ESTHER SHERMAN

I couldn't cook at first. I eventually got a fridge and I was the only person who had a fridge. I insisted that we had a modern block with central heating and that was in Sefton Park. We also had to share a house at one point, a semi, and we had one room upstairs. We had to share the kitchen with another woman. We also stayed in a temperance hotel for about four or five days. I asked for some grapefruit segments for breakfast and was told we only had them on a Tuesday. For Thanksgiving we had lamb chops; chicken and turkey was a luxury.

CLARE JENKINS

Mum always turned us out beautifully. I've got photographs of us at a wedding as children and we looked so spruce in our dresses, white socks, shoes with a strap across the front, and hats – we had these little white hats on. It was very important for mum, who also looked smart, that we should look smart, even though we didn't have much money. I think we had little bags to go with the dresses as well. So we did have some nice clothes, just not lots of them. It's such a different world from what it is today. You know, I've spent Christmas with people where it's taken two hours to open all the presents. As children we had a stocking and one main present, and in that stocking would be a tangerine, sixpence, a pack of chocolate pennies and you might have something wrapped up like some pencils. That was it – one present, a stocking and a selection box. When we lived in Leicester we had these little dresses, seersucker dresses. Sometimes they would have elasticated sleeves, puffed sleeves. You'd look around at the other girls who were seventeen, eighteen, and they were starting to wear those pencil skirts and heels. So one game we used to play was borrowing mum's heels and you'd tie your dress behind, so it would feel like a tight skirt, because this was what these sophisticated older girls were wearing.

ROGER TOMES

This was a time when members of my congregation bought their first car. We didn't buy our first fridge until 1963, but we had a very cool cellar. I did notice that people were prospering a bit even though I didn't have a lavish lifestyle. I got £1 day. We got our first washing machine from Rolls Razor. We had a lot of trouble with them. If it broke down it was difficult to get them to accept any responsibility. But the attraction was that it was a twin tub.

Trevor Creaser

In 1950 I would have been in Meanwood, in Leeds. I grew up there with my two sisters, Jenny and Wendy, and my mother. My father got killed in the war when I was very young. He was a machine-gunner or something, so my mother, two sisters and me lived together until I got married at twenty-four. It was very difficult for my mother bringing us up. She worked for various doctors as a domestic help, cleaning. It was hard, very hard. I remember once, when I was very young, and we had snow. Me and my sisters tunnelled under Highbury Street to check on a woman over the road. My mother couldn't get out to work and we were desperate for food. As kids it didn't affect us as long as we got fed. We had nail soup. I don't know if my mother invented this term but she would send us three kids to find things, a potato, a turnip, and she would put this nail in a pan of water with whatever she could find, bits of Christmas cake, cheese, or whatever. But it was sustenance. She even had me going through pig swill. There were some allotments at the end of the street and I had to go and root through all the stuff that people had put out for pigswill and see if I could find anything that we could eat.

My mother, when she went to work, always left us kids with a list of jobs to do. Mine was always to chop and chips, that's cutting up the wood for the fire. We'd go down to the market every Saturday night when things were cheaper and being thrown out and get an empty orange box or two to bring home, and then I'd have to chop them up for the fire. My other job was to sort through the ashes in the morning to save the cinders. I'd throw all the ash out but kept the cinders so that they could be used for the fire again.

We had a tin bath; my mother used to fill it and then put a clothes-horse over it with a sheet or blanket over to give us a bit of privacy. I used to have get in after my sisters had used it. I didn't like that. We only had one room at that time. It was a one-up one-down, with an outside toilet. We had a guzzunder, which was a pot under the bed. We had a man who came to pump out the midden (the toilet). There was one for our two houses and one for next door. Later, when we'd moved, we had three bedrooms and a proper iron bath in a bathroom. I later went to live with this girl, who I finished up marrying. I used to stay at her house and they had an outside toilet over the other side of road, down three steps which were stone flags, then down another four, which was under the house. One night I had to go to the toilet. I had some moccasins on and they had no grip. It was a beautiful clear night, about two o'clock in the morning, and the steps were iced over and I slipped in these moccasins and I went straight down on my back. I was stark naked as well. I hadn't been able to find my coat.

I had school meals, which I loathed. We had semolina; I hate milk puddings to this day, and there was lumpy custard. That thick stew – I'm sure they used to chop it with scissors – but it tasted beautiful. Mum always cooked basic stuff, potatoes but very little meat. She told the neighbours that we always had meat but, in truth, it was brisket, the cheapest cut of meat.

Right from the age of eleven I smoked. They sold tiny little pipes with people's heads on them, and you could put your cigarette ends in them. I used to smoke Woodbines. You got four in a paper pack. Then there were joysticks, which were long and you only got one. I later smoked Piccadilly, Park Drive, Robin and there was Capstan Full Strength as well. Phew they were strong.

WIN HINDLE

We were only allowed two ounces of tea and two ounces of butter. Now and again you might get a little bit more under the counter. If you got a tin of corned beef you couldn't get any meat, you had to have one or the other. Things were getting a little bit better when we got married. Anyone getting married would buy coupons off people so that they could get things – for a wedding dress you needed the material.

We cooked anything that was going – pork chops, we did quite a bit of stew. If you got the meat you could also make potato hash with it the next day. Get some bones, make some soup, put some bits of bacon in. I never made my own bread, I tried it once and it looked nice but it wasn't good, even the birds weren't interested. It was the same with puddings, it was never successful, but I made plenty of cakes. My favourite was rice pudding, but I hated sago.

We had spam, but used to dip it in batter, chips and corned beef but never tripe through. We'd put cow heel in potatoes to strengthen them.

My mother could make a meal out of nothing 'cos she had to. It was all done by hand, no mixers, she'd make fruitcake, apple pies, cheese and onion, bubble and squeak, Madeira cake; it would do for the whole week. We never went out to eat then, at least not until after we were married. The one thing we did do was to go to the Lyons corner house on Market Street, that was great. At Christmas we used to go to Henry's – a big store on Market Street – for Christmas dinner.

TREVOR CREASER

I had rabbits from the age of seven until I was fourteen or fifteen. They kept disappearing and my mum would come up with these reasons about where they had gone – it had died or escaped – so I would then get a new one every year.

Then I finally discovered that we had been eating them, my mother must have been killing them and cooking them after I had fattened them up. But she never told me. It never crossed my mind that we had been eating them. I was fifteen or so when I found out. Of course food was short.

WIN HINDLE

The mother-in-law bought us a little sweeper. We had squares from the carpet shop, very colourful and warm. I said, 'I'd love to have a fridge,' so George bought this unit and we had a small fridge. But we didn't get a washing machine until 1966. I used to have a mangle. They were brilliant. They really squeezed out every bit of water. You didn't need to iron sheets after that. You had to be careful with shirts though because of the buttons, as they would break. I used to go to the old washhouse. If you were lucky you'd get into the big boilers, but at the cheaper end it wasn't so good; you'd scrub with your scrubbing board. On the wall were heating racks and you put your washing on it to dry. All the women went; you had to book early otherwise you wouldn't get in. I think it was half a crown.

HUGH CAIRNS

Initially we lived in the Parkhead area of Glasgow, very close to Celtic Park. My first recollection is living with my mother and father in what is known in Glasgow as a single end, a one-roomed apartment, in Shettleston Road in Shettleston. Shettleston was not a prosperous area in those days. Today it is one of the poorest areas in the country with possibly one of the shortest life expectancy in the country. But in the 1950s it was reasonably respectable area.

This single end had a kitchen as well and we lived in this one room until my brother was born, shortly after my sixth birthday, in 1953. We then moved to a new house, known in Scotland as a housing scheme but elsewhere as a housing estate, and we moved to a three-bedroomed house in Barlanark. I lived there until I moved to Manchester in 1959.

The flat was one room, just one room with a little kitchen. There was no inside toilet in the tenement. The tenement had five or six closes and it is still standing. You walked in and there was a house with one bedroom on the left and one with two rooms on the right. My grandmother, my aunts, uncles and grandfather all lived in the tenement. The stairs took you up to our room. There was a loo and everyone had a key to the toilet.

In the one room my parents had a double bed; there was also my bed and a settee. I don't remember it terribly well as we moved on shortly after my sixth birthday. But it was very cosy and we were very happy there. Many of the extended family lived very close.

MARGARET WILLIAMS

I moved to Manchester in 1956 to take up a new job at Aspinal School in Gorton. I lived in Denton and I cycled or went on the trolleybus to work. It was an infant and junior school.

We hadn't any money. Frank had been at university for five years and he was working in the Town Hall in the architecture department, and what money I had managed to save went on furniture. We had a ground-floor rented flat. It was a house split into two. There were smallish shops nearby – no supermarkets – and a police station right next to our house. It was easy to get into the city centre and it was also easy to get a bus out to places like Lyme Park. We had a washing machine that you filled from the tap and then emptied into the sink. It had rollers that folded into the machine and had to be hand-turned. We had a gas cooker and we bought a fridge. We had a coal fire in the sitting room and we used to roll the paper up and tie it in a knot in the morning so we could light the fire when we got home. We had quite a big yard with an outside toilet and a coal place out there, I think. We didn't have any heat in the bedrooms, I remember. We had two lounge chairs which had belonged to Frank's grandfather and I made some covers for them. I didn't knit much but I did make clothes. When I went to college we still had ration books.

In Manchester we continued to do our rambling but not as much cycling. We went into the city for the theatre and to the Free Trade Hall. I remember Artur Rubinstein at the Free Trade Hall; he was fabulous. I was quite keen on swing, Glenn Miller-type stuff, but I don't think we went dancing.

We would go back to visit our families regularly on the X43 bus from town. We started a family in 1959. Our oldest son was born then and the younger one in 1961. I gave up work in 1959, that was the norm, and I was at home until the youngest one was three and a half – six years altogether. I then got a job at Chorlton Park School.

BRIAN HULME

Until I was eleven, sweets were rationed. One point, torn out of the ration book, entitled the customer to buy a quarter of sweets (four ounces), meagrely meted out from a large glass jar onto the scales. Shopkeepers often argued the legality of supplying two ounces for half a point, but I found it a useful way of widening my selection. The tiny corner shop near my primary school – Joan's Sweetshop – attracted a noisy crowd of children with non-rationed sweet substitutes, such as fizzy sherbet, liquorice roots, coltsfoot rock and – my favourite – Spanish. These were small, concentrated sticks of liquorice stamped 'Sicilia'. I discovered they had a baleful effect if consumed in quantity, but I was not deterred. Philip Marsland once stuck one up his nose and had to go to the school clinic to have it removed, an early beneficiary of the NHS.

Veronica Palmer

I started courting at sixteen. I used to go to a youth club when I was fourteen and we'd have table tennis and dancing. Doris Day was a favourite. I learnt the quickstep there but I wasn't very good. I could never dance very well. I was married at twenty in 1953. My mum saved – things were still on ration – not a lot, but you still couldn't get everything. I had become engaged at eighteen and for two years my mum saved, not money but food, tins of food, as much as she could save. My aunties made the bridesmaid dresses and I bought my wedding dress secondhand and we had the reception in the Labour Hall. My mum did all the catering and we employed someone to do all the cooking. It was a beautiful day 'cos I didn't have to worry about anything. It had all been taken care of. It chucked it down all morning, then the sun came out at midday. It was done on the cheap, all our friends and family came and my cousin had a band and he played for us. Didn't cost much at all that wedding.

Brian Hulme

I was at a Catholic primary school in Openshaw, at the back of St Anne's Church. It was an ordinary sort of school, but I was seen as posh because it was put about that I was the only boy who wore underpants. Mum made some of my clothes, she'd knit, and I remember lots of corduroy that lasted for years and years. I can't remember much about clothes until fashion dawned on me in the mid-1950s. There was a school trip to Rome. It was £27 to go to Rome, so I saved up. I worked in the summer weeding on the market gardens on Ashton Moss, 6p an hour, just weeding lettuce beds and watering tomatoes. I noticed that people's clothes in Rome looked different from those in Manchester, so we all came back wanting that style. I took an old jacket of my dad's and put an extra button on. I found an old jumper, which my dad had brought back from Italy after the war, and wore it until someone told me it was from Mussolini's old Blackshirts. And it was; it was one of his war trophies, so I stopped wearing it then. The other thing about fashion was that when I was cycling my hair got blown back, so I got a hairdryer and blew my hair back Italian-style. We didn't have a lot of money for buying posh clothes.

VERONICA PALMER

I did knitting and had a sewing machine but I didn't make lots of clothes. But we didn't buy loads of clothes either; we weren't fashion conscious like today. People weren't looking at you wondering why you were wearing the same clothes as you wore yesterday. We had grown up through the war years. My mum thought I was frivolous anyrate.

John taught me to cook, he was a good cook. We made soups, pies, cakes, we never thought of going out to buy a pie or cake, wouldn't dream of that. We're vegetarian now but we weren't then. Nobody was vegetarian then.

I got a washing machine, which was absolutely wonderful. The first one was a Hotpoint and it had its own wringer. We didn't have a twin tub so you had to rinse the clothes in the sink after they had washed and then put them through the wringer. When I got the washing machine I washed everything, it took me all day! I thought it was wonderful. Before that I did it in the sink. We had a washboard, which became a skiffle board later on. My mother had a dolly tub. And we had a mangle as well. It was terrible in the winter because your clothes were drying for days. When we first got married we were living with John's mum. You'd put clothes anywhere you could, there were no radiators. And when we had children there were nappies to be washed. They would be all over the place. Not disposable ones like you have today.

I got a Hoover when they started to appear. It was a cylinder machine. It was very smart. If we could afford it we would get it. We had an electric iron and John made the ironing board. In fact he made them for everyone in the family. In fact, you couldn't buy them, so he went and got a load of wood and made them all.

OLGA HALON

I was born in 1921. In 1950 I was living in Manchester, in West Didsbury, close to Chorlton. I was married in 1944 and had a daughter in 1948. I used to look after her myself, so I didn't go out to work. But we'd go out most days – we'd walk to my sister's in Didsbury. She had children and my daughter would play with them. I used to go on my bike to do all the shopping. Usually in Burton Road – butchers, greengrocers or whatever –

I'd give them my order and they would deliver and I would pay them the following week, when I gave them my next order. They were all shops in Burton Road – no cafés or restaurants – they were all shop, hardware shops, food shops. In fact the hardware shop is still there. I didn't go down town much unless I wanted clothes. There was a shoe shop in Didsbury village called Kellys, and a fish shop as well. I never made my own clothes as I can't sew, but I did knit and I knitted quite a lot of clothes. I got my first fridge in 1948, when my daughter was born. But we didn't have a washing machine until later – we sent sheets, pillowcases and so on to the laundry.

MIKE PRIOR

In 1950 I would be coming up to eight years old, so just old enough to remember a bit about the end of the war. I'm a war baby. In 1950 I lived in a house in Stroud Green, now called Crouch End, which was up on a hill rising up from Finsbury Park. It was a large house which at one time had been owned by relatively wealthy families – there were bell pulls and speaking tubes so that you could communicate with servants. It was, however, an area that had come down in the world largely because of the war. One thing that had happened during the war was that a lot of well-to-do people simply left and there were large areas of empty housing – it's one of these undisclosed secrets of the war. A lot of the better-off people departed London – reasonable enough, I suppose, as there was fear of bombing – and there was a lot of empty property and a lot of property that was sub-divided. My parents had bought a house using as a deposit a gratuity my father had received on being demobbed. There was a scheme that if you weren't taken back on at your old job you received a year's salary. My father hadn't been taken back because he was a shop steward, a communist shop steward. He received this money and put it down on the house. So in 1950 we had just moved into this house. It was, and indeed still is, a large terraced house with a large garden, but was shared by two families. The top floor had sitting tenants. They lived in the top three rooms and we lived in the remaining four rooms. This was common at the time as houses hadn't been physically sub-divided into flats, as happened later. There was just one bathroom in the house and we shared it with the Ardents. One evening a week they used the bathroom for baths. There were fixed times for using it. Then, in 1950, we let one of our rooms to a lodger – a student from what was then the Gold Coast. It was an odd arrangements – these families living separate lives, we didn't socialise at all. I was an only child and had my own bedroom.

STEPHEN KELLY

There were lots of prefab houses – prefabricated houses, a sort of bungalow – that were thrown up after the war. They were cheap to build, easy to erect and they provided important housing for many people. Of course they didn't last, although there are some still standing near the railway line close to Stalybridge. When you think of those flats being torn down after twenty years it makes you wonder if prefabs weren't a bad idea.

DENNIS GILLIGAN

I went on holiday to Jersey, and to the Isle of Man when I was courting, that's where I saw Joe Loss. We used to stay in a bed and breakfast and I went to Blackpool a lot. My daughter was suffering with her eyes so they told us to go to Blackpool – lovely air, they said. I never thought of emigrating, I always wanted to live here in Salford.

JOHN PALMER

We bought a motorbike and we'd go out on it. We couldn't afford a top motorbike so we had this 350cc BSA. The sidecar came later on, when I met Veronica. We also had a 250cc BSA. I later had a 600cc Norton and sidecar. Once we had children we had to give up the motorbike.

HUGH CAIRNS

Holidays were mainly taken in Scotland – Ayr, Saltcoats, Troon; those were the traditional places you went during the Glasgow Fair weeks, the equivalent of Wakes Week. This goes back to the travelling fairs that came to a city at the same time every year and the city would shut down. When the fair came to Glasgow Green, Glasgow shut down for two weeks in July. There was known as Fair Monday. You had the same fair at different places. Paisley fair was before the Glasgow fair, and everywhere in Paisley would be shut on Fair Monday. I came to Manchester in 1969 and in 1970 or '71 I phoned home to my parents in Scotland and I hadn't realised it was Fair Monday and my mother said, 'Well, you won't be working today?' and I said, 'Of course I'm working, I always work on a Monday.' She couldn't conceive that people outside Glasgow did not have a day off because it was Fair Monday. Lots of people going to those coastal resorts would bump into people they knew because it would be full of Glasgow people.

One year we went to Blackpool. Now that was really something because you needed money to go South. There would be two or three queues, 100 yards long, two or three deep, waiting at Glasgow Central station for trains for Blackpool for their holidays. You'd stay in a boarding house. I can remember going to Blackpool on holiday and on the Sunday going to church and you couldn't get in because it was absolutely packed.

We'd go to a show on the pier in the evening, or the cinema. We had little chance of going to the cinema in the evening back home in Glasgow as we couldn't afford it. We had donkey rides on the beach and so on. Some people would really push the boat out and maybe go to Bournemouth. Blackpool was the bees' knees. Lytham St Anne's was really posh as well and people would wonder how you could manage to afford to go there. My mum always wanted to be a bit better than everyone else, but there was no chance of my father getting a better job because of glass ceilings and the education system. Holidays were wonderful, but I do have some horrible memories because sometimes the weather was so bad.

Roger Tomes

My parents were still living in Cardiff and when we had children every year we spent a fortnight with them in August. They lived reasonably near the sea so the children were very happy. We also tried to have a week around about Whit somewhere else. The only one I can remember was at Sandsend, near Whitby. It was the only fine week in that spring and early summer. There was a cold northeast wind blowing most of the time and as Gummersall was on a hill, the east winds were felt.

Before I was married I had my first overseas holiday. I went with a party to Germany and it was very interesting visiting cities like Cologne, which was rebuilding after the war. We also visited Munich and Nuremburg and they were further advanced with their rebuilding. They had maybe not been attacked in the same way as Cologne. Making first contact with churches in Germany was very good for me. I don't recall any particular anti-German feeling but what I did notice among the German Christians was a feeling of guilt.

Steve Hale

I got picked out at school to be one of six lads to go over to Lourdes. Me and the lads got escorted over by two teachers, one male and one female, who took us from Liverpool Lime Street all the way down to Folkestone on the train, got the ferry over. and then all the way through France to the Pyrenees and Lourdes. That was quite an experience. We were there for two weeks.

We were just helping out at the hospital there. At various times the people in the hospital wanted to go up to the shrine and we had to take them up on these old antique stretchers and wheelchairs with beautiful ironwork and basketry. They were magnificent pieces of furniture. That was my first taste of what I'd call a proper holiday. Prior to that holidays were a day out to New Brighton. One day we broke the bank and took the boat from Liverpool to Llandudno in North Wales for the day, it's a trip of about three hours. I remember the ship had gone out into the Irish Sea and the colour of the water changed from the brown muddy colour of the Mersey to aquamarine blue, and I remember being surprised and excited and saying to my dad, 'Look how blue it is!'

BRIAN HULME

We had some family holidays, to friends at Llanfairfechan in North Wales. There'd be lads of my age and we'd do exciting things – catching eels in mountain streams and messing about on the beach. Three or four times we went to Norfolk. The guy next door had made a caravan and towed it to this caravan site near Yarmouth and we'd go there. Me and my brother Stephen used to wander off, exploring. There was an airfield next to the caravan site and we'd spend all day there, watching the planes. There were also RAF planes on flights round there – Meteors – and later planes that could break the sound barrier – you couldn't miss the sonic boom.

JOAN FINCH

We went away every year. We'd go to places like Torquay or Newquay. We'd stay in a B&B or hotel. We always had a decent holiday. We had to save up throughout the year for our holiday. Bill was a good saver; he was a good man, a good husband. I miss him terribly.

CHRIS PRIOR

From the age of four onwards I would spend four or five weeks in the summer in Essex with my grandparents, while my mother and father stayed in London working. Grandfather was quite an old man, but he was a countryman. He had been a tram driver in London but brought up in Essex. It would be the middle of summer and he'd be up at half past four and we would go out into the fields looking for the horse mushrooms that had grown overnight. He'd find these massive mushrooms and we'd bring them back and by then grandmother would be up and we'd cook these mushrooms with bacon and fried bread and we'd have them for breakfast – mushrooms that were growing just a few hours before. We would also go out picking blackberries and grandfather would show me grass snakes, adders, whatever. He knew where they were; he'd just pick up a stone and there would be some insect or something beneath it. He knew all the birds as well. He always had a whittling knife and he would cut a length of branch and would cut the bark off, then cut the ends off and make a whistle from it. Sometimes my two cousins would come down from London as well. They were four or five years older than me. My grandparents would take us to the seaside. We'd take the bus into Southend and then the bus that would take us to Shoeburyness, which was at the edge of where you could get before the army military range. They'd take buckets and spades, not the small ones for the beach but proper large zinc ones. And at Shoeburyness, which cut out into the Thames estuary, was the old sea barrier for submarines. The tide at Southend goes out a mile and a half. We'd walk out on the estuary and catch eels in these big pools of seawater and we'd put them in the bucket and then walk back, picking cockles. We'd have a picnic on the beach with grandmother and then go back home and pickle all of the cockles and have jellied eels – which I never liked that much – but it would keep us going for days.

We used to go to Southend and the pier a lot. It's a very long pier because the tide goes out a mile a half. We'd get the little train that went up and down the pier. We'd walk one way and then, as a treat, get the train back. After we'd been in Hockley for a few years (I was nine or ten by then), rather than join the Scouts I joined the St John Ambulance, which was quite active in the area. They taught you lots of first aid. My duty as a ten year old was to man the post on Southend pier. I did it every Saturday throughout the summer. There would be properly trained men there and I would run around helping them. Fishing hooks used to scratch people on the pier, particularly in the face, as the fishermen cast their lines into the sea. One week the men never came and I was there all day by myself, hoping to hell that nobody would need any medical treatment.

Olga Halon

We used to go on family holidays to Cornwall and also to Tenby in Wales. We would stay in a hotel. The very first holiday we had was in northern France, Brittany. That was the fist time we had been abroad. My husband wouldn't take a lot of holiday because he was always busy with the shop. We went in the car on most holidays but when we went to France we flew, that was the first time we had ever flown. You could only take so much money out as well; I think it was £50.

PHILIP LLOYD

We used to go to our mother's parents in Cornwall every year for our holidays, usually about Easter time. I also went youth hostelling sometimes with my sister. I remember going to the Welsh borders, Cornwall was another venue, and Scotland and in Ireland. I went with my sister to Southern Ireland and then into Northern Ireland. We were quite adventurous.

CHRIS PRIOR

We didn't have any big holidays until the end of the 1950s. We'd have a week in the Isle of Wight or a week in Bournemouth and always went on the train. All travel was done on the train or bus. We stayed in guesthouses, which were one up from a B&B because we had an evening meal there as well. I was an only child but we did have other relatives living close by – my grandmother was living nearby and my mother's sister. They essentially lived down the bottom of our garden. They had two daughters who were older than me by about three or four years.

My parents were good at taking me to the beach when we were on holiday. My mother in particular was good at that. But I've never known my father go into the water apart from paddling; never known him put a swimsuit on. Mum would go into the water and we'd play on the beach, walk a bit, have an ice-cream, and so on. In retrospect it seems an incredibly dull holiday but that's what we did, we didn't know any different. The guesthouses were always friendly and the sun always shone.

IAN RALSTON

When we went on holiday it was always to a caravan in Devon or Cornwall, which was owned by Coast Lines. This was one of the perks of benevolent employers. We'd go to places like Newquay. I have very distinct memories. We always went by train and we'd get a pass from the company as well as reduced fares. I remember standing on Crewe station at one in the morning waiting for a connection to Liverpool. Those were the days when it was sunny all the time on holiday. We'd go for two weeks – mum and dad would prepare a trunk packed with all the clothes and it would be picked up by the green British Rail van a few days before and it would arrive at the caravan site before us. The first thing we always did on arrival was to check that the trunk had arrived, otherwise we'd be up the creek if there were no clothes. We'd also meet up with other people employed by Coast Lines, particularly from Belfast. We'd make a lot of friends from Belfast and would go over on holidays in later years to see them.

We never went to anywhere like Butlin's. Butlin's was too organised and regimented for us. I never went to a holiday camp until ten years ago, and it was a riot. We went everywhere by public transport or pedal bike. We didn't have a car then. When we did get a car, my dad had won £250 on the football pools and he went out and bought a blue and cream Hillman Minx with bench seats and a column gear change. One of our neighbours, who had been a First World War veteran, taught him to drive.

VERONICA PALMER

Before the children and after we were married – we had our first baby within two years of getting married – we didn't go on holidays. We had a motorbike and sidecar and then got a little car when the children were a bit older and went on holidays to Margate, Clackton – to a caravan site. On holiday the men all went to the clubhouse and the women had no holiday 'cos they still had to look after the children and do all the cooking in even more cramped conditions. But I was lucky because John did all the cooking. He said, 'You see to the kids and I'll cook'. So we both got a holiday. My women friends used to ask if they could borrow him. There weren't many men like him. We did things together. The holidays were pretty good. We had one lovely holiday when John had won £25. The children were a bit older and we went to Butlin's for a week. We didn't have the children all day long because at Butlin's they entertain the children all the time. It was safe so that was good.

STEPHEN KELLY

We never went to Butlin's. It was considered a bit down market and while the regimentation of Redcoats and hi-de-hi meals might appeal to some it certainly never appealed to my dad, so we never went. Although my dad didn't earn very much money he always insisted that we should have a holiday each year. We always went to places like Blackpool, Ilfracombe, Torquay, London, the Isle of Man. I think we may have gone to Scarborough as well but I can't remember. We'd stay in a B&B, sometimes full board, sometimes half board, and do all the usual seaside things, going to the beach, ice-cream, fish and chips, maybe a trip somewhere, going to see a show, especially at Blackpool. Unfortunately the sun didn't always shine.

MAX EASTERMAN

Our first family holiday was to the Lake District, to Stonethewaite. We were in a farmhouse with walls that bulged and floors at an angle. We had an old

Singer car that wouldn't engage with first gear. We never went over the Honister Pass because dad thought the car would not make it.

My father had been with the occupation forces after the war – he had been a senior customs officer at Aachen – and he had some tales to tell about that. We had German neighbours and the husband worked for a German firm that manufactured sweet-wrapping machinery. Father had talked to him about going by car on holiday to Germany, and this man knew someone who ran a small guesthouse and said he'd write to them. So he did and off we went. I'd been learning French at grammar school and we had to drive through France. My father was very suspicious of French and Italian people, but we had to ask directions and because I spoke French I was made to wind the window down and ask. What I remember most was the thrill of going on the car ferry, it was a completely different world. My father didn't believe in planning because booking in advance was difficult. It had to be done by letter or a phone call, so we just got off the ferry at four o'clock and set off, hoping to find somewhere to stay. There were border checks at all the borders. You needed lots of car documentation, as well as passports and so on. The border guards would salute you and then you'd go through no man's land and come though the other border.

We found this place in Ghent but they didn't serve dinner, so we had to go out and find dinner. My father only spoke German and in those days – it was not easy in France or Belgium to use German – memories still lingered. My father asked for coffee in German and the waitress asked if he was German or English. He said English, and she said, well don't ever speak German here, never. It would have been occupied during the war and there was a big Jewish community there; memories were still very raw. But it was all a real experience. The food was not so different because we always ate a lot of Jewish food at home and it was very central European, we'd have black bread and so forth. I loved the food.

The family we stayed with had a son who was bit younger than me. We were going down to Luxemburg for the day and he asked if he could come. He didn't have a passport and my father said, 'Don't worry, we'll sort it out'. He'd discovered that the people on the border were people he'd worked with in the customs service after the war. And indeed we got down to the Luxemburg border and he said, 'I've got someone without a passport,' and it was all okay.

JOAN FINCH

My brother emigrated to Vancouver. He was a draughtsman; he had quite a good job. He went to see a cousin who had emigrated to Canada and he liked it, so he sold up and he went. We went to see him – we've been five or six times. He used to say to my husband, 'Bill, why don't you come over?' He thought about it but I was not enthusiastic at all. 'No, this is the finest place in the world,' he said.

CHAPTER THREE

A 1950s CHILDHOOD

The 1944 Education Act promised a fairer education for all. It was revolutionary. The idea of the Act, devised by the then Conservative Education Minister R.A. Butler, was to open up education for all, especially for girls and those from working-class backgrounds. Secondary education would be free to everyone, with the introduction of grammar schools, secondary modern schools and secondary technical schools. Children would remain at school until they were fifteen (this was later changed to sixteen). An examination at the age of eleven was also introduced to determine the best kind of school to suit the child's ability. It became known as the eleven plus and was to have a profound effect on the lives of almost all schoolchildren during the 1950s, and in many cases, far beyond.

The exam meant that the top third would go to a grammar school, where they would learn more rigorous subjects such as foreign languages, chemistry, biology and Latin. They would remain at school until they were sixteen, when they would take the General Certificate of Education in a range of subjects. Their success in this examination would then determine whether they left school and sought work or whether they would remain at school, taking an advanced certificate of education and leading to a possible university place. Less than 8 per cent of students would end up going on to university. Meanwhile, secondary modern schoolchildren did less rigorous subjects such as woodwork, art, cookery, domestic science, plus a few other traditional core subjects to equip them for an immediate entry into the workplace, often via an apprenticeship. And, of course, there was far less of the dreaded homework.

Given this discriminatory system, it is little wonder that the eleven plus examination hung like a giant shadow over the lives of so many young people. In effect it was an exam which generally determined the academic outcome of their lives and, with it, their employability. It was a life-determining examination and that it should come so early in everyone's life was to lead to it becoming a controversial issue until it was repealed towards the end of the 1960s. Astonishingly, in some areas of the country it still exists even today. Talking to so many people, the evidence of its detrimental effect is clear, condemning many to run-of-the-mill jobs whilst for others it paved a way to higher education and professional high-earning careers.

Of course there is an alternate view. The grammar schools bred success and for many working-class children it opened the door to a pathway that hitherto had never existed for them. Young boys like Chris Prior, whose father was a policeman, were able to take advantage of the system and go on to Cambridge and a successful career as a university academic. And Clare Jenkins, whose father served as gardener to the Duke of Rutland, went on to become an outstanding broadcaster and journalist whilst her brother went on to Cambridge and is now a British Ambassador. Many of these children of the 1950s would be the first in their families to ever go to university. But, generally, the universities remained elitist institutions. Less than 8 per cent of the school population would find their way to university (compared with 46 per cent in 2011). Degree courses were also traditional – English, French, history, medicine – though they would gradually change as a batch of new universities were created in the 1960s.

But having said all that, many others found themselves condemned to low earnings and poor prospects by virtue of having failed their eleven plus. The looming presence of the examination was always there for many ten year olds. One interviewee ended up in a convalescent home, overcome by anxiety and nervousness said to emanate from the pressures the school was putting on students about to take the exam.

Schools were very different then. No computers, whiteboards, modules or variety of subjects. It was almost, but not quite, rote learning and a core set of subjects. Discipline was far more rigid than it is today. The cane, slipper, or, on more than one occasion, the gym rope were acceptable forms of corporal punishment. Even girls had their knuckles rapped in many schools. And usually you got caned for not very much – talking in class, poor homework, cheating. I myself saw teenage boys with blue bruises on their backsides from the gym slipper or, as happened to me, a lump on the head when hit with the school bell by a rather pompous teacher known as 'nogger' Morris. It was normal in my school for the gym master to force boys to lie across the vaulting horse while he slippered them or even used the end of the thick gym ropes that we climbed up to belt them. Today it would be tantamount to assault.

The grammar schools were elitist institutions whose teachers saw themselves as a cut above the rest. The majority of them were university educated, whereas secondary school teachers often had a vocational background. The one thing that was exceptional was sport. Yet even here there was elitism; the grammar schools played rugby while the secondary schools played football. These were winter sports; in summer there was cricket and athletics. There would also be regular cross-country running and at least two PE lessons a week, with the whole of Wednesday, or some afternoon, often given over to sport.

A regular visitor to all schools was the nit nurse who would inspect each child, running her fingers through your hair to see if you had nits. Nurses regularly inspected children to make sure they were developing as would be expected. Prior to the 1950s the major health scare had been tuberculosis, but by the mid-1950s it had largely disappeared among young people, though, as Mike Prior testifies, it could have devastating consequences if you did catch it as a child. During the 1950s the major health scare was polio, a disease that could kill or maim young people. It seemed to be seasonal and every summer, as the weather improved, outbreaks would occur. Swimming baths were said to spread the disease and any localised outbreak would lead to an immediate closure of all local pools. Many schools had children in leg irons, a sign that they had at some point contracted the disease.

The disease came to particular prominence in March 1959, when the 29-year-old Birmingham City and England fullback, Jeff Hall, was struck down. Hall remained seriously ill for some days before dying. Birmingham's Easter fixtures were called off and anyone who had come into contact with Hall was checked out by doctors. The Football League also advised all football clubs to have their players immediately vaccinated. That someone so young and talented should be struck down hit the headlines and may well have helped persuade families of the need for wholesale vaccination. The vaccination programme that followed almost certainly led to a fall in the number of cases and the eventual eradication of the disease. Other diseases, such as tuberculosis and diphtheria, also began to disappear as the 1950s wore on.

Games dominated the lives of young people. The streets were generally free of traffic and street games abounded, from hide and seek to hopscotch, and other games. Children could play in the streets, racing from one side to the other without fear of accidents or their games being disrupted by passing cars. Public parks were also a haven and some parks offered football pitches, cricket pitches or enough foliage for cowboys and Indians or other such war games. Many in this volume testify how games were about make-believe or even playing on your own. As ever, swings, slides and an assortment of bars offered exercise galore, many of which would today be considered dangerous.

One of the great delights of childhood was the cinema and in particular the Saturday morning cinema club that was a regular in most towns and cities. Every Saturday morning kids would flock to the cinema; prices were cheap and there was a diet of kids' films, usually cartoons, a western, Batman and anything else that might appeal. It was often a riotous affair, screaming noisy kids, ice-cream, sweets, sometimes a birthday club and a photo, but always great fun and memorable.

Every week many children would buy a comic. The most popular were the *The Beano* and *The Dandy* at 2 pence each, cheaper than most other comics and featuring characters such as Dennis the Menace, Gnasher and the Bash Street Kids, Korky the Cat and Desperate Dan. Also hugely popular was *The Eagle*, which cost 3 pence and was said to be a favourite of the young Prince Charles. Its comic strip characters included Pilot of the Future Dan Dare and his sidekick Digby, Captain Pugwash, PC 49, Harris Tweed and adventures from the French Foreign Legion. There were also illustrated biographies of famous historical characters and in the centre spread of the colour comic was always a cutaway of a warship, aircraft, racing car or other mechanical vehicle. Much of *The Eagle*, which began in 1950, was drawn by a man called Frank Hampson, whose unique style of draughtsmanship would not be fully recognised until some years after his death. It was the nearest thing to cinema. There was also *The Tiger* with the world's most famous footballer, Roy of the Rovers, or, to be more precise, Roy Race of Melchester Rovers. Girls had their equivalent to *The Eagle* with *Girl* and characters such as Susan of St Bride's and Wendy and Jinx, though most of those interviewed seem to have been fans of *Bunty*, which began in 1958. The highlight was the Four Mary's of St Elmo's boarding school. And if that was a touch elitist there was also Penny's Place, which centred around a family café. For younger readers there was *Robin* and *Swift*.

There were also plenty of American western comics around, which were readily available, such as the *Batman* and *Superman* comics. Some were even in colour. Kit Carson, Gabby Hayes, Wyatt Earp, Wild Bill Hickok and Roy Rogers, with his famous horse Trigger and wife Dale Evans, all had their own comics as well. Many of these were replicated on television, especially the Lone Ranger and the Cisco Kid. The British also had their comics, with one inspiring series reproducing the classic novels. *Great Expectations*, *Sherlock Holmes*, *Dr Jekyll and Mr Hyde*, *Treasure Island*, *The Hunchback of Notre Dame*, *A Tale of Two Cities* and *David Copperfield* all featured. Indeed, a whole generation of youngster swore they had read these classics when, in fact, all they had ever read were the comic strip versions. Still, it was probably better than nothing.

But for young people there was no time quite like Christmas. Although there is a tendency to remember Christmas in the 1950s as a time of receiving only meagre gifts, this was not altogether true. Top of Santa's list for most kids was a train set, Meccano or Bayko. Meccano was enormously popular with boys and there were varying sets, each with more equipment and the ability to build more complex structures, from cranes to cars and bridges. Bayko was a plastic construction set with which you built detached and semi-detached houses, perhaps encouraging a whole generation into property ownership. But the best present of all was an electric train set, preferably a Hornby Dublo, and one of the great steam engine locomotives of the period, such as the *Duchess of Montrose* or the *Sir Nigel Gresley*. But of course they weren't cheap. But if you had the basic track layout and a transfomer you could at least build on it and buy new locomotives, wagons and carriages, as well as signals, points, stations and scenery for birthdays and subsequent Christmases. Scalextric racing cars, which raced around a slot in a track, came later in the 1950s and is still produced to this day.

Footballs – a leather casey – or, towards the end of the 1950s, the newly developed plastic ball, were always popular with boys, along with football boots, though at the time they were always leather and with a steel toecap. Cricket bats, balls and stumps were popular, along with boxing gloves. Bicycles came high up on the list of favourites and if you had one with gears then it would be rather special, as well as expensive. Girls also enjoyed Bayko sets, dolls' houses and even toy Hoovers.

And there were a myriad of board games including Scrabble, Monopoly, Scoop, Totopoly, the Amazing Robot, Wembley, Test Match and Snakes and Ladders. All were guaranteed to keep children amused for hours on end. There were annuals too, usually based on the weekly comics – *The Eagle*, *The Beano*, *The Dandy* and so on. Plus there were the more serious Commonwealth annuals, which told of life abroad. But, contrary to popular belief, it didn't always snow at Christmas and summers were not always hot!

But perhaps more than anything, the startling difference between childhood in the 1950s and childhood today is that children roamed free. They would go, of their own accord, to the local park, playground or fields. Even children as young as seven or eight would wander off to the park without any grown-up supervision. Parents rarely knew precisely where their children were, but they knew that they would always return once they got hungry. Children would play in the street as well. Old bombed sites were another ideal playground, and even in the 1950s there were still many such sites in our towns and cities. It was, in many ways, an ideal time to be a child. They were few threats, few pressures – apart from the eleven plus – and some surplus cash.

Mary James

I followed my elder brother David to school. This was an infants' school on Howarth Road. I remember there were lots of air-raid shelters and we weren't allowed to go in any of them. I remember Mrs Bartlett who had a magic knee so that if you fell over you would sit on her knee and everything would be alright. But of course that wouldn't be allowed today.

Stella Christina

I was teaching at St Wilfrid's School in Hulme. I was in the boys' school teaching junior one. You taught everything then, you didn't specialise. The boys' school started at seven or eight to fifteen years of age. It was a Catholic school, very different then to what it is now. We had a mass register and you had to check that the boys had been to church. And there was a strap which you used if they had done anything wrong, like stealing lead from roofs. Sometimes I dished out the punishment, sometimes it was the head, depending on how bad they had been. It was a leather strap. I hit them over the hand. I didn't enjoy doing it but it was just accepted that you did it. It wasn't enjoyable. I've since seen some of the boys and they were ever so nice, they didn't resent anything that had happened to them.

There were two other ladies teaching there and about seven men. The priests would come in and they would all start working quietly and then when they had gone there would be laughter. After that I went down to infants at Bishop Bilsborrow School. We used to have some religion but not as much as you might have thought. Albert Scanlon[1] was there. I taught him – but not a lot. But he was alright at playing football. I wasn't that interested in football so don't remember much about the Munich disaster.

Mary James

May Day was special and we always had a May Queen. One year my brother David had to crown the Queen. In the year when it came to me, I remember that the May Queen was chosen and it wasn't me, and then her attendants were chosen, and again it wasn't me, and I thought, how can I tell my parents that I have not been chosen after my brother had played one of the main roles, I was only an extra. It was so important to me that it stayed with me for years.

May Day was really important. Bicycles would be decorated along with your dolly's pram. We had a whole parade. It was an important part of life. We also had a maypole. I've had a maypole put into the school here as a result.

STEPHEN KELLY

I have very few fond memories of my grammar school. It was elitist, trying to ape a minor public school. We were taught Latin but not Greek and did the usual core subjects. We never did anything like woodwork, which was considered the kind of subject you'd learn at a secondary modern school. All the teachers wore gowns. But I will say that the sporting aspect was really good. We would have two PE lessons each week, either in the gym or running around the park – which I hated as I was no good. And then, on a Wednesday afternoon, we would do games. Generally this was rugby. We never played football, which was considered a working-class game. Ironically, one of the boys at the school – Warwick Rimmer – went on to become quite a famous footballer. He had already been capped at England schoolboy level but, of course, the school didn't recognise this. After leaving school he went on to play with Bolton Wanderers for many years and was club captain. In the summer we would do athletics and cricket. The school had Houses – Park, High, School and Birkenhead. I was in School House. And the Houses competed at sports.

I remember the way corporal punishment was dished out. Being caned or slippered was a regular occurrence. Indeed certain teachers seemed to take pleasure in it, in particular the gym teacher, who was something of a sadist. He would make you bend over the high vault and would than leather you with your gym shoe or the climbing rope. It left a nasty mark. On one occasion I was hit over the head with the school bell for talking in line. It left a large lump on the back of my head. But there were one or two teachers who never resorted to hitting pupils. We had a woman teacher in our first year who taught English and she was very nice. And of course we had the resident 'suspect' teacher. He was actually quite a nice man; tall with a clipped moustache and jet black, brylcreemed hair, and always smartly but stylishly dressed. He was also a bachelor and lived literally across the road, with his mother. He would come round and sit beside you and start stroking your hand or leg. We never worried about it; you just laughed it off later with your mates. I don't think you'd be in teaching very long these days if you did that. The art teacher had been in the RAF during the war and used to paint wonderful paintings of aircraft, airfields and battles in the sky. But apart from him and the music teacher, who did instil in me a love of classical music, I don't have good memories of any of the teachers or the way I was taught.

STEVE HALE

I was born in Fazarkeley in Liverpool in September 1945. I was five years old in 1950 and I went to St Philomena's, or St Phillies, as we called it – it was a local Catholic school. It was mixed and went through from five-year-olds to seniors, but I didn't go right through it as we moved. It wasn't a bad school but it had a tough edge to it; the headmaster was an absolute tyrant, everybody feared him. He was very good at giving the cane out, six of the best and all that. All the kids there were well-behaved, including myself. There were a few bad ones but they were soon winkled out. You would avoid the tough kids as they meted out beatings on a daily basis if they didn't like the way you looked, or whatever. I stayed on the right side of the headmaster, Mr Naylor, who was a very tall, slim, smartly dressed man with jet black hair and little round glasses. I stayed on the right side of him. There were a couple of teachers there who were very good and helped me. There was an ex-RAF man called Mr Hart. He was a lovely guy and was actually my form teacher for a while and he obviously spotted something arty in me, even at that age. I was a reader and I liked pictures and he obviously recognised that. So he pushed me along that road.

Mary James

We were in classes of about fifty – how on earth they coped I have no idea, but we got a jolly good education, particularly in maths, and that has always stayed with me. I still have a bag I had to stitch for my gym shoes to go in, and the stitches are tiny. I must have done it quite early on. We used to have to go by bus. I went with my brother. We did walk sometimes; there was what I called a bread and cheese tree. I used to chew on the leaves. David tells me that if we did walk we used to pass a Catholic church and that he used to open the door and go in and say 'Boo!' We went to the Methodist church, twice on a Sunday. I don't remember any anti-feeling about Catholics, but there was something.

Michael McCutcheon

The school in the south of Ireland was basic. It was out in the country, five miles from the nearest town. It catered for all the farmers because everywhere there was farms. Simple as that. There were no school meals; you brought a bottle of cold tea for your lunch, with some bread. It was a very strict school with a very strict head. I think he was an alcoholic. You got the cane, though funnily enough I didn't; he never did much to me but what he did to some of the other children! But it was a good education. He said to me, 'You'll never go to university' but he said he'd teach me to read and write, give me the basic things to get through life. That's all you need; you don't need degrees.

MARY JAMES

I passed the eleven plus but then went to Birkenhead High School, which was an independent school. The classes were very small, smaller even than the local grammar school. I was always amazed that I had passed the entrance exam. When I passed the first part, I thought, yes, I might have passed. But when I passed the second part I was amazed. One of the things the children asked me at school was what I'd had for breakfast in a morning. Now, we always had our breakfasts cooked in the YMCA canteen, so we'd have kippers one morning, bacon and egg the next, and so on. The kids were always amazed. They never had this amazing mixture. The food came up the back stairs from the kitchen to us. So my life was very different from theirs. My father was not earning the income that others fathers were, they were local solicitors, accountants and so on.

I remember going to Liverpool to be measured for my uniform. We had stripes around the arm and collar. We had a summer uniform and a winter one as well; it would have been quite a tidy sum affording all that. I remember my mother using lemon to whiten the straw of my panama hat, which was a hand-me-down from a cousin.

STEVE HALE

I took the eleven plus and I failed it but I later took the thirteen plus and I got through that. Failing was a traumatic experience for me personally. I used to really dwell on that because I was very confident of passing. My weakness was maths and in all the pre-tests we had I was getting enough to get through. They had these benchmarks of having to get a certain per cent, but of course the two big things were English and arithmetic. My English was good but my arithmetic was average, maybe even below. We took an actual exam but I do remember that our form master had us do a pre-test test. Now I was one of the lucky ones because, after that test, I then got put in for the actual test. If you didn't pass the pre-test you didn't get put forward for the actual eleven plus test. It was a kind of filtering system. Now, whether that was his own way of doing things or the official way I don't know, maybe he just didn't want to be seen to have too many failing.

Failing was depressing and I remember it vividly and it did mark me. I remember one day sitting in class and he said, 'Right, we've got the results for your eleven plus and we can tell you who'll be going to grammar school.' This wouldn't happen now but he said, 'I'm going to do it in reverse order. I'm going to call out the people who haven't been successful to the front of the class.' Everyone's faces dropped and their eyes popped. We were all sitting there open-mouthed, trembling and waiting. And of course my name came out – I had failed. You can imagine the absolute devastation on young kids of eleven who mostly didn't come from great backgrounds anyway and this was their opportunity to get on and get out of it. And then you were brought up in front of the class, like 'here are the failures'. It was horrible, absolutely horrible, and I've never forgotten that. My wife says, 'Oh, you're always going on about failing the eleven plus,' but it absolutely shattered me. I've never, ever got over it. I mean, I've done okay in life, I've made my mark as a photographer, but it still rankles. It wouldn't be allowed now, of course.

Joan Wood

I taught in a mixed secondary modern school in a mixed area so they had their problem kids. It was a slum clearance area so it wasn't so good; kid's families in gaol and so on. But there were also some very nice ones. I was very happy there. We had a wonderful head, Mr Garside, a big fat jolly man with daughters our own age. His own daughter came to the school; she didn't go off to some posh private school like some headmasters send their kids to. Our school was good enough for his daughter. He left you to it, he was wonderful, and I've never met one like him since. It was a strict school and there was corporal punishment, though I don't think it was used very much. It was usually left to the head, although one or two of the men had canes.

We had quite a bit of sport. It was a secondary modern – the failures as they were called – it was a very, very good education they got at our school. The girls did cookery and needlework, they made their own clothes, and they did office skills, shorthand and typing. The boys did woodwork and metalwork. And in the fourth year they had an optional period on a Friday afternoon, when the boys could do cooking and the girls could do woodwork and metalwork. My friend and I did domestic science. She did the domestic and I did the science and we did the childcare between us. The pupils went out to nurseries, day centres and got hands-on experience. There were no whizzkids in IT like there are nowadays but they had a grounding in everyday life, well fitted for everyday life.

They had all failed the eleven plus. They all left at fifteen – it went up to sixteen later. If they were bright they did get a second chance at thirteen. There was a scheme of work for the first two years which every school did, so they could easily transfer. They got a second bite of the cherry up to thirteen. Some moved on but I don't know if many of ours did.

Mary James

I went to the Woodland School in Birkenhead after we moved there from Bradford. I took the eleven plus but don't remember any fears about it. I know I had extra tuition, mainly because my father wanted me to go to an independent school. I remember when the results came out and I was one of the few, maybe the only girl who passed the eleven plus. There was only one girls' grammar school in Birkenhead, whereas there were three for the boys. I've always thought that was unfair, it was so difficult for the girls to pass. The vast majority of girls didn't go on to grammar schools.

Trevor Creaser

I went to school at four and a half. I used to go with my older sister; we'd walk there through the ginnels, through the mill and past the tannery. I had a marvellous time at school. It was a wonderful school. It was quite strict but we respected the teachers. I joined the Cubs and Sunday school. Our family virtually ran all the youth organisations in Meanwood. I took charge of Cubs and Scouts.

Mary James

My brothers were at school five and a half days, they went on a Saturday morning. I only went five days but we had a tremendous amount of homework to do, so there wasn't a lot of spare time. I'd go down the coffee bar at the YMCA and there would be people there enjoying themselves. There used to be a machine for making Horlicks. There was a sort of jug with a plunger thing. I liked Horlicks. I had little time to do anything much like going to the theatre or cinema.

Roger Tomes

I was at Jesus College, a very Welsh college – I got an exhibition scholarship for people coming from Wales. Was Oxford an elitist place in those days? Yes and no. Because people were coming back from serving in the war it made it less so, I think, than probably it is today.

One of the things I remember most about Oxford was the first winter I was there, 1946/47, which had been a very hard winter. I was very fortunate in that I had taken digs with a coal merchant. College could be very cold but the summers were marvellous and I celebrated my twenty-first birthday with a punt party – only two people fell in, one took it very well, the other took it very badly. I think what I appreciate most about that time is that there were older people I could relate to, not just my contemporaries, and some of them had a very great influence on my life through the Christian Union. I met some of them again after sixty years last summer, which was very nice.

Oxford rooms had an open fire and an allowance of coal. Of course you weren't in the room most of the day, you might be huddled in the Bodleian Library or attending useless lectures. You'd be there up to the early hours trying to finish an essay. I spent my first year in digs and in some ways I regret not being in college as I would have got to know people better. I was only going in for dinner twice a week, so didn't get a great opportunity to get to know the other people.

NEIL KINNOCK

It was a very close-knit community. I was conscious of the fact that anything I did in that street, that gas-lit street, in the late 1940s and the 1950s was policed by one hundred and fifty households. If I did anything wrong, or any other kid in the street did anything wrong, we would be taken, sometimes by the scruff of our necks, sometimes by the ear, sometimes dragging our feet behind the complainant, to our own front door and we were then admonished heavily by grandparents, aunts, uncles, mothers, fathers.

But I was never hit. My family just never hit anybody because they were very calm and reflective in their temperament, although they were ferocious sportspeople and also the men were physically very strong. And I think that between being civilised and strong they never needed to resort to physical punishment in the way that I saw other kids beaten. But what you knew is that if you produced cause for complaint among the neighbours, the shame the family had to accept would be inflicted on you and it would be miserable, miserable.

But it was ultra safe. I had one little friend when we were in primary school who was killed by a lorry running up the street – that was the only child I ever heard of being killed or seriously injured by traffic. I was sixteen before I was aware that a murder had been committed in the area, and that was a crime of passion. There was no sense of menace whatsoever, so much so that as the dark winter nights came, and as long as it wasn't teeming down with rain, we would play out, swinging around the street lamps or playing football at the end of the terrace. In order to have access to the pit, the gap between two sets of terraces would be 40 yards, which provided a natural play area and some shelter from the rain and wind, and, by definition, because four corners would meet, there would be four street lamps. It would be unthinkable now for anyone to play football in those circumstances but we used to play cricket in November and all we had to do was chalk or whitewash a wicket and goals on the end of the houses. So, it was all very safe.

CLARE JENKINS

I remember the milk; everyone had those little third-of-a-pint bottles of milk, which you'd drink in the morning break. We had dancing and music lessons and some form of exercise and also, in the afternoon, after lunch, we all had a lie down. Now my memory tells me that we had little beds to lie on, but I'm not altogether sure that that was true. Then you'd be woken up after your nap for your milk and then some dancing and then, of course, we had the children's programme on, there was some sort of schools' radio programme on. Before that, there is an abiding memory of being at home. Mum would be listening to Victor Sylvester on the radio while she was doing the ironing in the afternoon. Then, at three o'clock, she'd butter a crust of bread and divide it into three and that would be our little afternoon treat.

My brother John and I used to play together a lot. We played games, we made tents out of sheets, and we'd get cereal packets and take them outside and would invite each other around for tea – because your parents would do that, invite people around for tea. They would have egg sandwiches and tinned salmon sandwiches, tinned fruit salad with condensed milk. That's what they had, so we would pretend to have the same, pretend to be grown-ups, and the teddies would be there as well.

We used to dress up a lot. I've got pictures of us outside some tent we'd made with tea towels tied round our heads. Not sure if we were being Arabs or Jesus, Joseph and Mary from the Nativity play. We did a lot of make-believe games.

If you had parties for your birthday, people would come and all the food would be home-made, all the sandwiches, the jellies, blancmanges and cakes, everything was home-made. We'd have games like pass the parcel, musical chairs, marbles. I loved playing with marbles. Outside our house in Abbey Park there was a grate, and in the grate there was always a little half moon which was an indent for picking up the grate. And that was where we had to get the marbles into. I loved five stoners on your knuckles, cats-cradle with wool, skipping, hide and seek – when we lived in Abbey Park we lived in a lodge by one of the entrances and just outside there was a path with lots of bushes alongside, and we would make dens in the bushes. We did a lot of playing outside.

STEVE HALE

The summers were always great – in the summer holidays, if it wasn't raining, I was told 'Out!' and I'd go out and play. Sometimes I used to wish it was raining so that I could sit in and read my *Just William* books and my comics – I'd get a couple a week. We'd play football in the street, one end of the street to the other, coats down. I would literally spend from half nine in the morning to six at night playing football in the street and just coming home for meal breaks.

I remember the old horse-drawn flat carts coming round. The rag and bone man was just a guy, an old man with a flatcap, and he looked like a bundle of rags with this real old horse and this dirty, flat-back cart. He had these massive black scales on the back of the cart. I don't know what they were for, because nobody ever had anything to give him. He'd come down our street and he'd be lucky if got a pair of holey old socks. He came about once a month, just looking for rags, for anything he could turn round and make a penny for himself. He wasn't a bad old guy 'cos he used to let us follow him down the street. He'd let us sit on the end of his cart until he got to the bottom of the street, which was great. He had this cry which you couldn't decipher and didn't mean anything. It was just like he was making these guttural noises.

The other thing I remember was that on the hot days in summer – and there *were* hot days – we'd go out and burst all the tar bubbles. I used to come back home with tar everywhere and would get a slap across the leg. I'd be kneeling down and there would be tar all over my knees. And that's the other thing; you could go the length of the street bursting all these bubbles. Today you'd be run over flat within two seconds on any street. The other thing we did was play ollies. These were marbles, I don't know if that is a Liverpool term, but we always called them ollies. And someone always had a tenner. There were glass marbles and steel ones, which we called steelies. I used to have a few steel ball bearings because with my dad being in engineering he'd bring them home. And the guys we were always trying to beat were the lads with tenners who had these steel marbles that had smashed ten glass ones. Someone with a tenner was to be feared!

CLARE JENKINS

I often say that my very first ambition as a young Catholic girl was to be a virgin martyr. One of the books we had at home was called *Your Friends the Saints* – I've still got it. The stories were about saints, written for children, and quite a few of them were about virgin martyrs, so, without really knowing what a virgin was (I did know what a martyr was because martyrs were a big thing in Catholicism in those days) I wanted to be a virgin martyr.

Following on from that I wanted to be a combination of all the heroines they had in *Bunty*. I had *Bunty* every week – I think it came out on a Tuesday. I loved *Bunty*. Essentially, I wanted to be an orphaned, crippled, acrobatic ballet dancer, because those were the kind of role models I read about. You were either an orphan or you were in a wheelchair, but then you triumphed over this handicap and became an acrobat or a dancer. One of the games I used to play as a child was to sit in my brother's pushchair and pretend that it was a wheelchair and that I was crippled – you're not allowed to say that word now, of course. Even mum thought it wasn't very nice – and this was way before you had the concept of political correctness.

STEPHEN KELLY

I used to regularly get the *Eagle* comic. It was considered a bit more educational and a bit more upmarket than *The Beano* or *The Dandy*. It had these wonderful cutaway drawings in the centre – ships, destroyers, submarines, aircraft and so on. I also loved Dan Dare and some of the other characters. Years later, I came to appreciate what a brilliant artist Frank Hampson was, and have, ever since, been trying to buy an original piece of *Dan Dare* artwork. Sadly, most of it was thrown away. Later I got *The Tiger*. The front page was devoted to Roy Race, ace goal scorer for Melchester Rovers. What a player!

CLARE JENKINS

A game I loved was The Memory Game, though it's now called Pairs. I've actually got one which I bought in a charity shop. There were all these squares and they all had pictures on and they were blank on the other side. You were supposed to turn them all face-down and you had to pick them up, one by one, and put them back. Because they were pairs, you had to try and remember where the matching one was. Once you had done that you put them to one side. I could play for hours.

Another toy I played with for hours and hours was the Magical Amazing Robot. You had a board and questions on the board or card and a little plastic robot. You put him in the middle and he would turn around magnetically to the right answer. I just never knew how it did that. I could play that on my own for hours. Then the other day, in a gallery in Sheffield, there it was and I bought one! I think the woman I bought it from must have guessed just how old I was when I said the picture of the children on the front could have been me and my brother and sister!

STEPHEN KELLY

Every Saturday morning the Ritz in Birkenhead would have a kids' club. They would show cowboy films, cartoons and so on. It was always rowdy and a bit chaotic – kids running around everywhere and the manager trying to calm them all down. It didn't cost much. They also had a birthday club and, if it was your birthday that week, you all had your photograph taken together, sitting on the steps. And then the following week they flashed the picture up on the big screen. I think I've still got mine (see page 4 of the picture section).

I saw *The Robe* with Richard Burton. There were a lot of those epic, glossy colour cinemascope, quasi-religious films at that time, like *The Ten Commandments*, *Quo Vadis* and *Ben Hur*. I also remember going to see Elvis Presley in *Love Me Tender* and, as me and my mate were underage, we had to get someone older to take us in. This guy said, 'Yeah, I'll take youse in, but I'm not bloody sitting with youse.' So we had to sit by ourselves. Every time the usher came round flashing his torch we ducked under our seats!

Davy Crockett was another I remember. Everyone went Davy Crockett mad and they started selling Davy Crockett hats – they were fur hats with a tail. My mum, bless her, had an old fur coat and she cut it up and made a Davy Crockett hat for me. How kind is that!

HUGH CAIRNS

I went to a Catholic school and we were educated in the faith, English and maths, and all the obvious things. Religion didn't play a big part but occasionally we'd go to Mass. It was a decent education. There was discipline in the primary school but not heavy. Some kids got belted, there was no cane – it was the tawse [a belt with two or three tails to it, used for corporal punishment in Scottish schools], but there was not a huge amount of it. It was a decent school, good fun; we played football all the time. Eventually there was a youth club at the church and when we went there we played football. Football was a second religion. Everyone in Scotland was football mad. If you didn't play football you were odd. There was a good atmosphere at school. I don't remember any animosity with kids from the local authority school. I had friends who were not Catholic and went to the local authority school.

We lived on a very busy street so we had to be careful. The only game I can really remember playing in Shettleston was with a peerie. This was a whip and top. We would scrounge coloured chalk and colour different chalk rings on the peeries so that the colours would whizz around. As I became older and we had a bit more money – and money was always tight – some parents bought their kids bikes. I always wanted a bike but my mother would not buy me one because she said it was dangerous. And so I never had one and to this day I still cannot ride a bike. Swimming was also dangerous, so I never went swimming and to this day I still cannot swim. A lot of my friends went to the swimming baths but I never did. So we had to play in the backyard and we played football with the lads who lived in that part of the tenement, though there weren't many, I can only remember three. So there wasn't a lot of opportunity to play football there. Once we moved to Balanark in the late summer of 1953, we played football there. There was a large field and we played there, even up to half past ten, eleven o'clock at night and all you had were streetlights. Only very occasionally would someone say, 'Let's play cricket,' but it was never very popular. We also played cowboys and Indians; we'd find wood and build dens. I had a tent and we'd make fires, roast potatoes, it was all fairly simple pleasures.

Chris Prior

I was a single child and my dad was working long hours and my mum worked in one or two local shops, so I was left on my own a lot. I was into science and reading, I was an autodidactic reader. I exhausted the local library but a kind librarian allowed me to go to the county library, which was in the next town. I had to get a bus and I'd take six library books out, read them all, and then go back and take another six out. I really enjoyed science at school. I had a chemistry kit at home and I'd buy chemicals and do experiments. I was into Meccano in a big way and I was always making things. That was a winter activity. I always wanted a train set but my parents wouldn't let me have one, they said they couldn't afford it; that was a bit disappointing. I had a clockwork one though. In the summer I was always doing things that involved machine-building or whatever. I remember making little bombs and exploding them in the garden, they were mainly aimed at the neighbours' cat, which was upsetting my dad by eating up his vegetables. I'd watch from somewhere in the garden and when the cat got near I'd detonate this bomb and the cat would jump out of its skin. I had to invent fuses that worked and triggers for them. I had a permanent run of electrical wires around the garden, all slightly buried. I built a rocket that was launched ceremonially with a spider in a capsule underneath, and the capsule would float down with the spider. All this was in response to the space race, Sputnik. I was twelve or thirteen at the time. I don't specifically remember Sputnik, but I was certainly interested in rockets and how they worked.

I used to read the *Eagle* with Dan Dare, and I got *The Dandy* and *The Beano* every week, which liked. I got into photography when I used to visit my dad at work. He would take me upstairs to where the police photo lab was and the two police photographers and they would happily take me in there and let me help them develop prints and show me how cameras worked. By ten I had my own camera and later got the equipment for developing. We'd do it in the kitchen with blackouts. By the time I went to secondary school I could do all that, so that when I got there I helped set up a camera society.

I know we played Monopoly and Totopoly – the horse-racing game – my grandmother loved that. And we played card games, especially canasta. My grandmother would come round after her husband had died, she'd have tea, play games with us, watch TV and then mum would walk her back.

BRIAN HULME

My first school was St Anne's primary, housed in a Victorian building with a perplexing layout for a small child. In 1950 I was in Standard 3, was reasonably literate, poor at sums, and in love with Miss Hopley. She never guessed my devotion, and I kept it especially secret from my classmates. She was tall, elegant, and the only non-Irish woman on the staff. In her class we graduated from pencils to pens – dip pens with squeaky nibs fed from inkwells sunk into our wooden desks. At the St Patrick's Day Concert we sang various Catholic hymns and Irish folksongs. One boy sang so badly out of tune that he was made to mime the lyrics, but did it so convincingly that a grateful member of the audience gave him sixpence for his angelic voice.

From the first class at the age of six you got the strap, but no one took it too seriously; you'd done something wrong, whack! By the end of the fifth year the teachers didn't give it in case you turned on them. There were cases of this – I remember taking a message to a teacher in another class at secondary school, only to find my cousin launching the blackboard at him. It was just a fact of life getting the strap, a sort of badge of war. If you got three or four it was just normal, if you got six and didn't wince in front of the others you were a hero.

IAN RALSTON

I remember a lot about the eleven plus and the thing I remember most is fear. I had a fear of taking exams. I have never thought – even now – that exams are a good way of assessing people's ability. I think there was pressure on me as well because my elder brother had passed and gone on to a grammar school. I can't remember preparing for the eleven plus, or even sitting it, but I remember exactly where I was when I got the result. I was in the Cubs and we had gone to camp and there was one wooden phone box. I remember putting my pennies in and pressing button A, and my mum telling me I had failed. At that time, if you didn't pass, you were a failure – and were destined to be trained for a trade. And that would be seen as failure. My parents never pressured me, they told me to just do my best. Today, when I see parents putting pressure on kids, it makes me feel uneasy. I never had that but I was encouraged. After that I felt a personal sense of failure. Nevertheless, it turned out to be one of the best things that happened to me as it gave me the chance to go to the first ever purpose-built comprehensive school in Liverpool. What I got there, there were teachers committed to the comprehensive principle. It was fully equipped and with the best teachers. In many ways, failing, for me, was probably a good thing. It was not as totally destructive as it could have been.

Stephen Kelly

I remember the eleven plus mostly because it made me ill. In fact, I have to say that I don't remember being overly worried by the prospect and we didn't in fact actually take an exam. But I do remember being called into the headmistress's office one day, supposedly to read to a lady who had come into the school. I can't remember doing much else apart form reading and answering some questions she asked. I guess that was the eleven plus exam. There was certainly no sitting down and being given half an hour to answer questions, as you might have imagined. Anyhow, at the age of about ten I developed a number of nervous ticks. It was rather embarrassing and my parents took me to the doctor. It was decided that I should go to a convalescent home for a month in the countryside, at Thingwall. It's now a very expensive private hospital, where top footballers go for treatment. But in those days it was a convalescent home for kids. I had a horrible time there and, for the only time in my life, I was bullied. We were free to roam about in the large grounds but as I was getting bullied (because I was a bit small and skinny), I didn't want to go out. In the end I feigned illness and my mum and dad went and talked to the staff. The next day all these horrible lads came and sat on my bed and were dead nice to me. I think they must have been told off. After that it wasn't so bad. It was a glorious summer and I played out all the time in just a pair of shorts and had this amazing sun tan. There was another lad there from my school who had had polio, and he was recuperating as well. My mum and dad used to come and visit me every day. It was a huge trip for them as they had to get a couple of buses. Dad used to rush home from work and change, probably not having anything to eat, and then dash out to catch the various buses. They'd bring me sweets or comics, books to read and so on. Being away from school seemed to resolve the problem and the nervous ticks disappeared. Strange, really.

BRIAN HULME

When it came to GCEs, we decided – a group of eight or ten of us – that the teaching at the school was rubbish so we decided to teach ourselves. We bought syllabus books and decided what subjects we were going to concentrate on, so we went to the library a few days a week, we spent our time in Manchester Central Library. We all got the GCEs. Then we went to the grammar schools. I can remember going to St Bede's and knocking on the door of the house, it was a seminary and some of the boys there were going into the priesthood. An apparition appeared in black patent leather shoes with silver buckles, and a black cassock edged in purple. He interviewed us, and it dawned on us that this guy had homosexual tendencies; he kept putting his arm around us. So we agreed that none of us would ever go alone to see this guy. If you had to you'd get the table between you and him and you'd have to do a circle around it. After a month or so, I was threatened with expulsion for skipping games. When the rest of the boys went straight to the games field, I split off, as I had done for years at my previous school, did a runner down an alleyway and went to the pictures with two others. The school never actually carried out the threat – they'd have lost some of the capitation grant I brought to the place. I enjoyed St Bede's. I did English, history and French. I left there at eighteen in 1960 to go to university.

JOHN STILE

We used to have these *I-Spy* books. There was *I-Spy the Countryside*, *I-Spy Cars*, *I-Spy Road Signs* and so. And when you saw something that was in the book you had to tick it off. They were very entertaining, a good way of keeping kids quiet, particularly on long car journeys or on a coach. When you had ticked everything off in the book, you then got a parent to sign it and you sent it in and you received a badge in return. Why wouldn't you cheat, I've always wondered. But I guess in those days you just didn't.

BRIAN HULME

Going to the cinema was a big treat. We had Saturday matinees in a place called the flea pit and it really was. There were Tarzan films, not much fun, dozens of rowdy kids. I used to go with my parents to the cinema as well; films about the war or planes breaking the sound barrier. There was a feeling of optimism; you really felt that. Hilary and Tenzing climbed Mount Everest, there was the Coronation, and British planes breaking the sound barrier. There was also the *Eagle* comic, which was great. It used to have technical drawings – taking a submarine apart, the working parts of a plane or ship, then *Dan Dare* – strange stories, but it also had a serious side. It talked about history and current affairs. My grandad used to get me the *Children's Newspaper* but it was deadly, not much fun, always pictures of English things like Lincolnshire landscapes in the rain. But the *Eagle* in colour was great. I got *The Dandy* and *The Beano* as well from time to time, but they didn't appeal.

IAN RALSTON

I went to Kingsthorne Road County primary school. It's still there. Some of the classrooms had open fires. I don't remember central heating. I distinctly remember the canteen and I can still smell the boiled cabbage and powdered potato. Towards the end of rationing you had those bottles of orange juice as well. The school had a bizarre lighting scheme, with lights that looked like flying saucers. The building looked as if it had been put up during the war and the tables were wooden and with benches. The playing field seemed enormous to me, stretching to the end of the world. I remember teachers and a holiday we went on to the Isle of Wight. We got a terrific old coach once we got off the boat, this would be 1958 or '59.

We played out on the road and we would go to the local park. We were just seven, eight, and we would walk up to the local park. These days that would fill parents with horror. And even though we lived on a major road, there wasn't the traffic as there is today. The traffic wasn't heavy at all, though it changed later on. We would play hide and seek and a game known as Kingy. You had a group of people in a circle with their arms around each other and you would drop a tennis ball and whoever's leg it touched first would be 'it'. That person's task was to chase the others and hit them with the ball. They would then be part of the team. But once there were two you couldn't run with the ball, you had to pass it. The slow kids, like me, were easy meat. That game would carry on until everyone had been brought into the fold, as it were.

Hide and Seek was another favourite. There were lots of closes and roads and footpaths that you could dive down. In the local park or local woods there was plenty of scope for hiding. But it was football and cricket that were most popular. I can remember dad's beautiful garden having a brown patch where we played cricket. We didn't play tennis then, maybe later on, in Calderstones Park.

BRIAN HULME

I rarely took the bus to school, but made the three-mile round trip twice a day, returning after morning school to have my dinner at home. Returning home in the afternoon, I frequently made extensive detours to places unknown to my parents, who didn't seem to question my late arrival. I discovered an area of land beside the railway line which had escaped the post-war building frenzy and now sheltered wild rabbits, field voles – especially under bits of discarded corrugated iron, probably the remains of Anderson shelters, and even water rats in the stream that ran through it.

The stream also contained another curious item – little white balloons. Eventually, one of the older, worldly-wise boys supplied the explanation. We were aghast, and wondered if the Duke of Edinburgh actually did that with the Queen! The problem of royal offspring proved difficult to solve. We eventually decided he must have put his contribution in the balloon, which would then be delivered to Her Majesty by a servant.

Nearby stood the Haunted House, a large abandoned Victorian house that seemed to belong to the local golf club. By the time I was ten, groups of us would scale the wall and creep around the building, disregarding the 'No Entry' signs. The cellars were particularly attractive to us; if you shone a torch in there, you'd be met by dozens of unblinking golden eyes. These turned out to belong, not to midget ghosts, but to toads who had found a plentiful supply of slugs and insects. On an evening expedition, when we found ancient dust-covered armchairs in an upstairs room, we were surprised by the caretaker and his huge guard dog. Me and Ian Coakley just made it down the drainpipe and over the wall, but poor Nigel Norris, who had lost his glasses, was apprehended.

He was released, a poor blubbering wreck, by the caretaker, who was probably taken aback by Nigel's apparently posh upper-class accent. Nigel and his mother had come from the south of England, and Nigel had no dad – a point of great interest to the locals. His clothing was similarly outlandish – he had a yellow souwester and oilskin, like Christopher Robin.

The most important thing was the division of the year into seasons. There was the bonfire season in the autumn, when we got together all the tree branches, old furniture, and anything flammable we could get our hands on, legally or otherwise. All this would be piled up on the canal bank, and we defended it against other marauding gangs. The Ashton Canal was at the end of our street. It was our adventure playground and led to unexplored regions. This canal was still in use in the 1950s; the barges were often towed by cart horses, and there was a store of clay nearby to be used as ballast for the barges. It was also an important source of material for the models I used to bake in the oven of my mother's Yorkshire range. They featured in the model Aztec village I constructed in our garden. The centrepiece was the sacrificial pyramid.

After that there would be winter and the big thing then was sledging and I can remember having all my fingers frozen and be wet through.

Once the winter sport season had finished it was spring – newts and frogs and things like that. Near where I lived, in Audenshaw, there were the remains of the old diggings, where they'd made the railways years before, and there was an old swamp, which was good for catching frogs and newts. We used to spend whole days there trying not to get sucked under, but I remember one lad did and we had to get some adults to pull him out. He was up to his armpits but, as I say, we weren't supervised all day long as kids are today.

After the spring it would be the summer and we really would wander. As I got older we made these bogeys – got the wheels off an old pram, made a chassis and pinned an orange box on the back for the passengers and luggage. We filled it up with goodies, sandwiches, sweets – Spanish, a sort of liquorice – and we'd be off for the day. We'd go off to places like Daisy Nook near Oldham; we'd follow the canal bank. It was dangerous because we'd go through other gangs' territories. There was a pond with crayfish, tadpoles. It was a pretty free life.

When we got older we wanted bikes. We used to do terrible things to get the bikes. There was a stable down the lane and we broke in and found it full of bike parts and we used to go and pinch stuff from time to time – if you wanted a brake or whatever. I remember we were in there one night and a policeman came and he stopped outside for a fag and we could see him under the gaslight and we were frozen until he'd gone. Although we'd been brought up as good Catholic boys, we got up to mischief.

Later, when I had a bike, we'd go cycling, sometimes do a hundred-mile trip, out for the day. I can remember going to see my aunty in Hoylake, or later in West Kirby. I'd go through the Mersey Tunnel on the bike and it was full of smoke and you thought it was fine until you went up the other side and you were puffing and wheezing. But it was great going to West Kirby; that was Shangri La for me.

My birthday present in 1953 was to go with my mother and aunty in a horse and trap to Hilbre Island when the tide was out. We spent all day there and I've been attracted by it ever since.

When I was five my brother was born and, as soon as he could walk, my job was to look after him. He'd come everywhere with my 'gang'. He'd ride in the back of the bogey and we'd get up to all sorts of scrapes. But he was always with us and we would just come in for tea in the evening. It was quite different to how it is now.

There were things like hopscotch and then hide and seek, which was pretty rough. We'd climb into people's sheds. And there was cricket, which we'd play in the street. I was bobbins at sport so I'd always be bowler 'cos I couldn't get the others out and they'd be making scores of 400 not out. We used to make dens all over, in places that no one knew about, in the park, under trees, with corrugated iron. We made a pit in someone's garden once and fitted it out. We collected fag ends and smoked them in there.

Girls were only on the edges of it, though that was partly 'cos there were no girls of our age in our street.

The canal was like a path to adventure for us 'cos we could follow the cinder track. The canal was important to us as there was a basin near us where the barges turned around. I don't know what they were transporting, probably coal from the local pit.

A favourite attraction was train watching. This took on a more active flavour when we discovered that passing steam engines could effectively flatten six-inch nails, which we left on the rails.

PAT TEMPEST

In my spare time I would always have to help my mother doing the cooking, looking after my siblings, ironing, shopping and so on. I used to read a huge amount, play the piano, go to the pictures. There were a lot of cinemas, maybe half a dozen in Douglas, but they would all close bar two in the winter. I went to see *The Student Prince, Three Coins in the Fountain, Seven Brides for Seven Brothers, Sign of the Pagan, The High and the Mighty*; whatever was on we'd go and see it. I loved the pictures and there was also a lot of smoke – which I was used to. It had a very sexy image.

I used to get asked to play the piano – I was good at Winnie Atwell music. I had a blues album as well. I used to go to church with the parents of one of my friends; they were very tiny churches, one was Methodist, one was Church of England. My parents and brothers never came. We'd go to the church then back to my house or Gwen's house and sing songs like The Old Rugged Cross. My piano was something my father had taken for a bad debt. We had this big lounge with a special niche made especially for a grand piano. I never went dancing until I had left school. I was a rotten dancer. It was boys on one side and girls on the other. I was on the Island until the money ran out in 1956. So in 1956 we were taken away and our relationships with all our friends were broken up.

MAX EASTERMAN

I used to read comics as a kid more than as a teenager. I read *The Dandy, The Beano* and *The Beezer*. I had an aunt in London who used to send me the *Daily Express* – that had a lot of cartoon characters. Then there was Dennis the Menace, Korky the Cat and so forth in *The Beano* and *The Dandy*.

Comics were quite a big part of life. I have to say I never really liked the *Eagle*, but if friends had it I read *Dan Dare*. What appealed to me about the comics was the artwork, the caricatures. I can still see the teacher in Dennis the Menace, Lord Snooty and his pals. With *Dan Dare* it was the illustration, it had real character to it. Comics were quite a big part of life.

Brain Hulme

There was a cycle of playground games. For two or three weeks it would be marbles and then it would be cigarette cards then it would be something else, then marbles would come back. I was good at marbles. I had this huge bag that weighed a ton; they were quite cheap to buy. I had about 6d pocket money and you could buy a bag of marbles for a penny.

Pat Tempest

My aunty Peggy used to buy me *Sunny Stories* every week before we went to the Isle of Man, and I used to get *The Dandy* and *The Beano*. I noticed that there were never women in these stories, I was always conscious of that. There was a magazine called, I think, *Heiress*, I used to keep all these. I used to read the *Eagle* – the boys got that – and I would read *Dan Dare*. My grandmother used to get *Woman's Own* and my mother got *The Woman*. I read all those. I'd read anything.

Brian Hulme

From the age of eight or nine, I was a loyal member of the Church Cub Group. We all enjoyed dressing in our green uniforms with a yellow neckerchief held in place by a leather toggle. We all swore allegiance to Queen and country, and studied assiduously vital crafts and life skills, like tying sheepshanks and 'General Health', for which we were awarded coveted badges. We frequently spent days out in the country with Kela – his title should have been 'Akela' but 'Kela' stuck. We'd be off in all weathers to places like Middlewood or Lyme Park, where the train would take us from Manchester. At the age of eleven, I graduated to the Scouts, but left quite soon, after an older Scout showed me how a slipknot works – on my neck!

Chris Prior

I can remember school quite vividly when I was in London. It was a Church of England school and the Church had quite a lot of influence over it. The vicar would come in regularly. There was an infants' school, then you moved into the junior section. I can certainly remember we had a sleep after lunch. There were folding beds and we'd have a half-hour sleep. Then we moved on to the junior school, which was the bigger school. I was friends with the vicar's son. The vicar was very influential. Of all the things that happened at school, such as the smelly, cold toilets and never really liking school lunches – I absolutely loathed ginger pudding – I do remember getting into big trouble and having to go and see the headmaster. In religious education class something had been said by the teacher – I don't know what – but it was something to do with Jesus on the cross. And the vicar's son said something like 'sausages' to me and I laughed and said 'sausages' back. Anyhow, the teacher heard me and pulled me to the front and I got sent to the headmaster and was kept in and given work to do. I was only about six years old – a terrible shock for me – but the vicar's son never got touched. I thought, it tells you lot about how the world works.

Generally, I don't remember it being a terribly disciplined school. I just remember some very nice lady teachers. It was quite a good school in the speed at which it taught you things. When I left in 1954, we moved to Essex and I went to the village school, which was a two-mile walk for me. I did it every day – with my mum to begin with, then by myself. I was coming in at the age of eight – I was a complete outsider and a Londoner as well. It was the beginning of the new year and we were to do joined-up writing. I said to the teacher that I had already done it and that I had a fountain pen because that's what they wanted you to have in the London school, a fountain pen and not a scratchy dip pen. He said, 'Come and show me,' so I did, and he said, 'That's very good. I tell you what, while they learn to do joined-up writing you can go round and help them.' Not a good idea. This little stranger from London who can do joined-up writing and now he's going to teach us. For the first month I was picked on by the kids. They were much more streetwise than me. There were a few playground fights.

We did the eleven plus in Essex. I had to go to one of the schools down town in order to sit it. It was all done in a day, maths things, writing things. There was a clear division of all the kids. So many went to the grammar and the rest to the secondary. There were posh grammar schools and the one which had just been opened, that was the one I went to. But I don't remember anything traumatic about the eleven plus at all. I think the school had already identified who would succeed. I passed without thinking about it. You got no result; you were just told that you'd passed. Some of my friends elected to go to some of the Southend selective schools which was seven miles away and had a much better reputation than the one I went to. I don't know why my parents didn't send me to those schools.

It was a very large school, brand new and they hadn't filled it. They had taken in first, second and third years and were letting them move through. There were lots of technical facilities and it was quite tightly disciplined. Once again you were in forms but it was tightly banded, a selective process. They must have known from the eleven plus results where to put you for that first year. There were seven forms in the first year, that's 240 kids.

I managed to avoid the cane, although it did happen in the school. The headmaster certainly used it and the PE teacher used the slipper, very freely. The main PE teacher was an extremely ill-tempered man. He was a northerner, an angry man who would make you do cross-country. He made us play rugby league although the school was a rugby union school. It was a strange life playing rugby league and then being trained to play rugby union. I fractured a wrist badly in my second year and was in plaster for eight months and then I came back and started playing again and fractured two fingers and that put me out for another year, so I was never going to get into any team, so I gave up any active sport.

BRIAN HULME

I was the first in my family to go to university. There was talk of some distant aunt who had gone to work in the Toblerone factory in Switzerland 'cos she was a linguist. I had an uncle in Ireland who had been the editor of a newspaper, and another who had been a cartoonist. But no one had been to university. My mother had encouraged me partly to get back at my dad. Eventually I got round my dad and made it up with him and we went out for a drink, and he said he was really disappointed when I went to university because he wanted me to come and work in the brewery. He had never mentioned this earlier.

I opted to do French at Leeds University. In those days you usually had to have done Latin to do a language, apart from one or two odd languages, like Icelandic or Russian. I was quite interested in Russia, I'd read a Jules Vernes story about the Tartars, so I plumped to do Russian. All the others had done Latin, so when they talked about genitive cases they were on to that straight away. It took me months to realise. So, I didn't like it at first. I did alright at French. The Vice-Chancellor threatened to throw me out for missing lectures, but he'd let me stay on if I did well in French. I came top in French.

MAX EASTERMAN

I was born in March 1945, so in September 1950 I would have just started primary school, which I recall as being a highly traumatic experience. I hated the first day. Jesmond Road primary school, West Hartlepool, was a big primary school with a very imposing building. I don't remember much about the teachers, but the one I do remember was Miss Gawthrop, who was a nice lady. The school had a big playground at the front and a smaller one at the back, and the desks were not individual but were in rows, so you had two or three people sitting on one bench. The thing I remember most was being taught to write. Of course we were taught to write copperplate, which was highly stylized linked letters; everything was in loops and there was no question of gaps in words. These days I don't write like that. I couldn't write copperplate, I was hopeless. I sat next to a boy who won a national prize for his handwriting, which was unbelievably accurate and pretty but, in retrospect, unbelievably boring to look at. We used a dip pen and pencil. We had a pen monitor as well, who would come around and fill up the three inkwells on the desks. And we had a pencil monitor who would come round at the beginning of the lesson and sharpen the pencils. School was very formal. I never really enjoyed that school because I felt that because I couldn't write copperplate this condemned me for all time.

There was a lot of written work and learning to write was the first thing we did. If you couldn't write absolutely copperplate, you were beyond the pale.

School was pretty strict, although we did play outside a lot, country dancing and so on. There was quite a lot of enjoyment, it wasn't Victorian but it was pretty strict, but not as strict as some later schools I went to.

BRIAN HULME

My parents just let us wander, they didn't supervise us. Frequently, a group of us boys would spend all day in the park. When the attractions of the swings, roundabouts and monkey bars eventually palled, we'd go and disturb the park keeper, a grumpy character in a peak cap and a pair of overalls, who fiercely resented interruptions to his preferred routine – doing the 'pools' in his little office, helped by endless fags and cups of tea. A big source of fun was to get through to the fenced-off stream which ran through the park and make dams across it to cause a flood, then flee at speed when the parkie, compelled to abandon his normal pursuits, charged out of his den in a nicotine- and caffeine-assisted rage. We'd watch from a safe distance while he dismantled our handiwork. Once – I must have been about eight years old – we were greatly intrigued by a speech defect he had suddenly developed. Through swollen cheeks, he revealed it was caused by something he was attempting to eat, something we had only heard of – a banana. On receiving my spends – 6d per week – I joined the queue at the greengrocer, eager to sample this novel luxury.

MAX EASTERMAN

Stanmore was incredibly rural at the time. We could play in the street; we could ride our tricycles and play with our car toys because there was so little traffic. If traffic did come, they were always aware that if they hooted at children all hell would be let loose. A coal truck came down once and the coalman got a bit ratty with some of the kids and one of the parents got the police and the policeman told the coalman the kids had the run of the street and that children played out and it was his responsibility to look out for them.

We'd play games in the street; tricycle races, ball games, play with dinky toys on the pavement, we were very much left to our own devices. Parents only came out when it was time for a glass of milk or whatever. In West Hartlepool we lived with my grandmother and we would go down the end by St Luke's Church and that was almost the end of West Hartlepool. There was a huge field and we'd play down on the field as well. There was a field that had been bombed that was full of craters and things. I'm surprised we didn't set off an unexploded bomb because they were always finding them. One day at school in Harrogate – Grove Road County Primary – this lad came out of a hedge with an unexploded hand grenade in his hand, holding it upside down by the pin. The teacher went mad; I've never seen anyone go green so quickly. 'Put that down boy, carefully!' he yelled. They had to get the bomb disposal unit out. It had been lying under the hedge for nine years.

MIKE PRIOR

I went to the local primary school and went to another school after that which wasn't a local school as all the local schools were Church schools and my parents didn't want me to go to a Church school. So I went to a school in Stroud Green. It was fairly rough, whereas the local Church schools were much more respectable.

I walked to both schools – quite a long way, maybe a mile. I went there for three years and I did the eleven plus. There were forty kids in each class and I think we must have been streamed a bit as I was in the top stream. Of that top class, a third passed the eleven plus. You weren't supposed to use the word 'passed'. A third went on to grammar schools. No one from the other classes passed. I did exams in English, arithmetic, and an IQ test. I remember the teacher coming around when I was doing the exam. She looked down at my paper, put her finger on a word and then walked away. I realised I hadn't spelt it right.

It was a basic education: reading, writing and arithmetic. I don't remember any particular pressure. I think my parents assumed I would pass. The school was becoming ethnic, particularly with Greek Cypriots, who were beginning to move into that area at the time. We played Ball He with them. It's a game of tag. You had to throw a ball at people and if you got hit, you were 'it'. It started off with one person, then it became two and gradually more and more became hit. We would be surrounded by all these Cypriot kids who were good at throwing the ball.

Max Easterman

At Grove Road we went through this series of exercises. It was never explained to us what it was. This went on three or four times and then one morning a whole bunch of us were called into the headmaster's office and he said, 'Congratulations, you're going to the grammar school'. We'd didn't even know we'd taken the eleven plus exam. It was in fact a good approach, as we hadn't been troubled. The Head was a Harrogate Alderman; ex-army, disciplinarian with a gold-plated heart. He could be very fierce. After assembly you marched out to Onward Christian Soldiers, in time. He was quite a character. He lived on West End Avenue in Harrogate, so I would occasionally see him in his garden and he would ask how I was getting on. But he was ex-army and it shone through.

We had caning at the grammar school. To be fair, the head teacher at the grammar school only used the cane in extreme circumstances. I got on the wrong side of him once, he gave me a map of the British Isles and he said, 'I want you to bring that back in the morning with all the Anglo-Saxon tribes marked on it'. So that night I had to go down to the reference library and haul all the books out and find them and do it. When I handed it in, he said, 'Jolly good, you've learnt something'. Funnily enough, my fascination with things Anglo-Saxon probably dates from then.

The thing I remember from my later school years was that the teachers were much more friendly than in the earlier years. One teacher lived on the same street and I saw him regularly. He and my father would chat. There was much more of a collegiate attitude.

We all had to do two practical subjects – music, art, woodwork and metalwork, it was all part of the curriculum. Everybody did it. The first Head was a polymath figure who believed in a broad education. His successor was much more focused and narrow. I turned out to be a linguist. I did French; the A stream did French, the B stream did German, the C stream did Spanish. German was the language of my family, as my father spoke it as well as Yiddish, being Jewish. I also did Spanish later. My father decided I should do German, so he got me private tuition with a German teacher who was an Austrian. By the time it came to A levels – and by this time the new Head had taken over – I wanted to do French, German and Spanish, but he said I couldn't do Spanish because the Spanish teacher didn't have a degree in Spanish. Now the Spanish teacher spoke French, Spanish, Portuguese and Italian fluently. He had taught himself and was fluent in them. So I had to do history instead, which I didn't like and didn't do well in. The teacher would read from some book and then we would discuss it – it was incredibly boring. He was replaced by someone who was young and I am still in touch with him; he had a very different approach, but by that time it was too late.

I was not encouraged to go on to Cambridge by the Head but by another teacher, who knew the senior tutor for admissions at the college. There were two of them who went to St Catharine's. He said, I've got these two boys and I'd like them to go for it in the upper sixth rather than stay on for another year. The senior tutor said fine. I actually had to doorstep the Head and get him to sign the papers on the bonnet of his car one evening, he was so reluctant. He said to my father, 'If you get a place, I'll eat my hat'. So when I found out on Christmas Eve, my father rang him and told him to eat his hat! When it came to my sister, my father sent her to another school. The Head was just not sympathetic to anyone who disagreed with him. I wasn't the first in our family to go to university; others had gone before, although my father had never been. I think he deeply regretted not having an academic background.

Brian Hulme

Teachers at secondary school had different types of straps. The French teacher – a French West Indian – who was a bodybuilder and featured in various types of magazines in skimpy trunks. We used to buy those magazines and read them in the French lesson to embarrass him – he had a special one which didn't hurt 'cos he was such a beast that if he laid into you he'd murder you. And if another teacher said, 'Go and get me a strap,' you'd go to the French teacher for his 'cos you knew it wouldn't hurt.

But I enjoyed prximary school, though the eleven plus was like a big shadow – you knew that it was socially divisive. Those who didn't get to grammar school would resent it and eschew those who got there – who were posh and would be looking down their noses on those who didn't pass. I was no good at maths, so my parents send me round to someone for extra tuition, and I didn't like that. Audenshaw then was an 'excepted district of Lancashire', whose eleven year olds had to sit two exams. The Manchester one would get me to a technical school, but I needed to pass the Lancashire one for grammar school. I must have done well on the Manchester one because I passed and was awarded a prize, but I failed the Lancashire one, so went to St Gregory's Central School. The £10 which I was awarded was big money, so I was able to buy a BSA bicycle, which was my pride and joy.

St Gregory's was a big laugh except for the first two years, when I was a bit bullied, but after that I settled down. It was good for sports but didn't have good facilities. Once every two weeks we were bussed out to the football pitches in Debdale Park, in Gorton. The teachers didn't want to know if you weren't good at football. The worst thing you could be was good at French. And I was good at French. I remember in the fifth year, Michael Delargey in a French lesson smoking a fag at the back of the class, blowing the smoke down a rubber tube which he'd pushed through the sash window. The teacher must have known but he took no notice – he couldn't be bothered.

It was a strange establishment, built around a yard. At one end was a factory with wood off-cuts in bins and the ice-cream man kept his ponies there. You put your bikes next to the factory when you went into school. Carlo Tianni, the ice-cream man, had a little room in the school, where he lived. He got up in the afternoon – he never got up in the morning – get his pony out and would tether it up and bring it round the front of school, and, as you were coming out, his van would be there so you'd buy an ice-cream. Carlo, like the head, Joe Rocca, was a Manchester Italian, and helped to carry the Italian contingent's Madonna at the Whit Walks. The Catholic Walks were held the day after the Protestant Walks. He stored the statue in the entrance hall of the school.

I remember being in trouble in the fourth year, when I was fifteen – coming in drunk. We used to go the pub at lunchtime and we came back worse for wear. It was a geography lesson, but we just carried on singing. The punishment was to sing the 'Banana Boat' song to the whole school at the next morning's assembly. Everyone, including the staff, enjoyed it. School was a laugh, you couldn't take it very seriously. Over the little door which we all squeezed in and out of each day, someone had chalked 'Abandon hope all ye who enter here'. No one bothered erasing it for ages.

MIKE PRIOR

In 1953 I went to the grammar school, but not the one around the corner, which was a particularly good school called the Stationers. They wouldn't send me there because there was an officers' training corps and they didn't like that. They also felt that as my mother had stood as a communist candidate it might impinge on me. Being a communist in the 1950s was not a good idea in a number of respects. It wasn't like McCarthyism, but on the other hand it wasn't like France. You were discriminated against subtlety, for example you were not allowed to have certain kinds of jobs. There was a general sense that you were not good people, so I went to this grammar school that was in Muswell Hill. And it was quite a long trip. There was a funny little train that went from Stroud Green up to Muswell Hill. It was quite a long way to go to this school, which was out of the area but where I wouldn't be quite so marked as the child of the communists.

All grammar schools were very, very different – some had very high academic standards and they often had different sources of funding, some were posher than others, and the school I went to in Muswell Hill was probably about medium level posh. They did things like play rugby rather than football. Playing rugby was a kind of mark if you had pretensions. And most of them had pretensions of adopting the public school system, like having houses and boards with gold lettering, on which the heads of houses were noted, and Tollington School in Muswell Hill was rather like that. It was quite strict with a fair amount of corporal punishment. If you were caught out the master would call you to the front of the class and slipper your hand with a gym shoe. But there wasn't a huge amount; you weren't beaten up in any sense. I was in the top stream there, which meant that I was taught a second language, and that was how you differentiated the top stream, by doing a second language.

Margaret Williams

In 1950 I'd still be living at home but at college in Bingley, Yorkshire, where I did my teacher training. Then I started work in 1952 in Colne, which is next to Nelson. I taught juniors for four years until Frank finished his architecture course, which, at that time, was five years. When he finished we got married and came to live in Denton because we got a flat there. I taught at a school in Reddish and I was very happy there.

Bingley College was an all-girl college then, and it was all residential of course. Some of the staff were residential as well. We had a few men on staff. You were allocated to schools for your school practice at the end of the second term and two practices in the next year. I had one in Bradford and one in Leeds, so you got a training that took you through the age groups to eleven. You did a specialist subject and I did English literature. I had to do a dissertation as well. It was a pretty good course, although it was talk and chalk really, with the emphasis being on children's presentation of work. I was very happy there. I enjoyed it.

Mike Prior

I was badly treated at school when I returned after my six months in hospital. I was bullied. I had come out of hospital after a six-month stay suffering from TB. And because I had had bed-rest for most of that time I had put on an enormous amount of weight. I was twelve and I weighed 14 stone. And as a result I was bullied at school. My mother always felt that it was because of the communist thing and she ever afterwards had an abiding grudge against the headmaster, who she felt had treated me badly, and she was probably right. I was expelled because I was being bullied. I had gone berserk and just attacked all these kids and broken a desk. And for this I was expelled from the school. They must have known about the bullying because I can remember the kids standing in a circle around me, all shouting 'fatty'. The teachers must have known. Anyway, I was expelled and it took some time before they could find another school for me. I remember they were getting quite desperate. They even went to a local progressive school up in Hampstead called King Alfred's, a private school, they were getting so desperate.

But eventually a grammar school in Wood Green took me. Remember, these grammar schools were terribly selective. It was a long way away but the Head took me, for which I have always been grateful. This was a much less prestigious, pretty low-level grammar school. But for me it was tremendous. The discipline was much less rigorous; they weren't so relentlessly trying to ape public schools. And I did rather well there. Basically you learnt facts – exams were based on facts, there was no conceptual work. The only thing I was really weak at was French, because I hadn't practised it. But apart from that I did very well with all of this fact-based stuff because I could gallop through books. So I prospered.

I did my O level GCE. I was in the alpha stream, which was actually the lowest class, but I came top of the school in most things. I got a prize for geography and an English prize at the end of my year for O levels. We did seven or eight GCEs – the standard subjects – I remember how pleased everyone in the alpha stream was because one of them had come top and they were always seen as the thickos.

I went on to do A levels and I chose to do science – rather weirdly because I did much better in English and things like that. My mother had done science so I wanted to do science. In those days if you were left wing and communist, science had a distinctly left wing feel. There were a lot of very overtly left wing scientists, people like Huxley and Joad. There were a lot of left wing scientists and the whole area of relativity and quantum physics had a left wing feel about it. I did four A levels – physics chemistry and two mathematics, and

I did very well. I then went in to do S level, which, if you passed, you got a state scholarship. Normally you got a local education authority grant but this was means tested. But state scholarships weren't. I got a state scholarship. I remember I had to argue with my Head to allow me to do S levels. And I did well. I wanted to go to university and my parents wanted me to as well. At my school people didn't have a clear idea about how you went about it.

At my grammar school nobody went to university. The school didn't seem to know what you did. I applied to Birmingham, Bristol and Durham, and I went to the local library and got their addresses and wrote off for entrance forms. I did it all myself. I also wanted to go to Cambridge, because it was the top physics university. Now, to go there you had to take entrance exams, apply to a specific college and go for an interview, and you had to learn Latin, even though you were doing physics. My school didn't teach Latin – that was how a lot of schools differentiated themselves from the others. The entrance exams were in November and, as I hadn't done Latin, I had to learn it. I had to sit in the library with a Latin textbook because there was no one who could teach me.

So I eventually went up to do the Latin exam and I did okay on the bits about Latin history. But then, when I had the translation paper, I looked at it and I realised I could only do the first word, 'Caesar'. I had not a clue. The books I had read had been useless. I had applied to Downing College. I spent a week there doing the exams – maths, physics, chemistry, and so on, as well as Latin. I was rooming with some kids from Highgate School, a local private school. It was then that I realised that the Cambridge entrance syllabus was totally different from the S level syllabus. These kids had been tutored in the Cambridge exam and I never knew this and my school never knew this. But I must have done reasonably well because I was allowed to stay on to do the practicals at the end of the week. But I didn't get in and I have to say that of all the things I've done in the rest of my life, and I've had ups and downs, the only thing I feel bitter about is that I think I should have been given the chance on equal terms. To go up and do things about imaginary numbers when I had never heard of imaginary numbers before was unfair.

Eventually I was accepted at Durham. I said yes to the first university that said yes to me.

If you didn't have a washing machine it was a case of taking the laundry down to the local washhouse. *(Reflections Photo Archive)*

LOOK DADDY —

just like Mummy's!

When this beautifully finished toy is pushed along, a realistic hum is heard, dust bag is inflated and a small brush is operated that actually sucks up light dust! 24 in. high! No springs or motor to go wrong! Easily dismantled for emptying. A near-perfect replica of the real thing.

HUMS AS IT CLEANS **REALLY SWEEPS**

TOY HOOVER CLEANER

(The word 'HOOVER' is the regd. trade mark of Hoover Ltd. and is used by A. Wells and Co. Ltd. on this miniature cleaner by permission of Hoover Ltd.)

★ Obtainable from all good Stores and Toy Shops or if any difficulty write direct to:—

WELLS-BRIMTOY DISTRIBUTORS LTD.
Progress Works, Stirling Rd, Walthamstow, E17

Why "HIS MASTER'S VOICE" T/V is the finest in the world

The Hallmark of Quality

① H.M.V. Television is designed and manufactured by the people whose researches made possible the world's first public Television Service in 1936 —

② — the people who, since the war, have supplied the High Power Vision Transmitters for 3 out of 4 of the B.B.C.'s Television Stations.

③ — the people who make the Emitron Cameras and Film Channels used in B.B.C. T/V Programmes.

④ — the people who produce the Aluminised Emiscope Tubes which give such brilliant pictures to H.M.V. sets.

⑤ The range of sets offers 12", 15" or 21" Direct Viewing Screens. Bright or Black screen viewing is optional by use of separate filter at small extra charge. All models are available on easy terms from your local H.M.V. Dealer.

69 GNS

H.M.V. "TWILIGHT" TABLE TELEVISION Model 1834

Model 85 GNS. Tax Paid.

THE GRAMOPHONE COMPANY
LIMITED · HAYES · MIDDLESEX

Washing machines, televisions, vacuum cleaners; symbol of the 1950s.

BENDIX

automatically makes washing a leisure

No filling · No emptying · No scrubbing
No wringing · No clouds of steam
You just set it and forget it

BENDIX SOAKS, WASHES, RINSES THREE TIMES, DAMP DRIES
CLOTHES, DRAINS AND SWITCHES OFF *all by itself!*

Look to BUSH for the programme switch to

BUSH TV. 24C. A 12" model with an attractively finished cabinet in walnut veneer. The Bush Auto-control of vision and sound reduces fading effects. **54 GNS.** (TAX PAID)

B.B.C. or COMMERCIAL

When the alternative programmes start this new Bush model will require no modification to bring you whichever programme you want. A simple switch, which has been built into the set, will allow you to tune in to either programme — at a touch. Vision and sound are Bush AUTO-CONTROLLED — this means that any tendency to fade is taken care of by the set itself and does not require frequent adjustment. You can always rely on Bush to bring you the latest and the best at a price that makes sense.

.. and switch to Bush for the best listening value . . .

RADIO MODEL AC 34.
A three waveband, five valve superhet giving a superb performance on the Long, Medium and Short wavebands. Both inside and out this receiver is absolutely up-to-the-minute in design. For value, there is nothing you can beat about this Bush. **£26** (TAX PAID)
MODEL DAC 34 for D.C. and A.C. mains £26.10.0

BUSH RADIO LIMITED, POWER ROAD, CHISWICK, LONDON, W.4.

Terraced streets, bombed houses and gas lamps – this was Liverpool mid-1950s. *(Steve Hale)*

Street games were rarely interrupted by traffic. You could bat all day, hit a century and take half a dozen wickets without ever seeing a car.

Hopscotch was a favourite street game with the girls.

Saturday morning cinema club at the Ritz, Birkenhead.

Servicemen line up for the regimental photo before setting off for war in Korea. Not all returned.

LIVERPOOL OVERHEAD RAILWAY

A ROUND TRIP 13 MILES
GIVES
UNRIVALLED VIEWS
of DOCKLAND
& SHIPPING

FIRST CLASS   THIRD CLASS
1/8   1/4

TRAINS EVERY FEW MINUTES

Commonly known as the Dockers' Umbrella, the Liverpool Overhead Railway ran the entire length of the Liverpool docks but was demolished in the late 1950s. Its passing is still mourned. *(Dewi Williams)*

A christening party for Judith, the newly arrived member of the Jenkins family. Clare Jenkins is the child on the left, alongside her sister Ruth and brother John. Their mother is to the left of Clare.

Former Labour Party leader Neil Kinnock has fond memories of his Welsh childhood.

Below left: Clare Jenkins, writer and broadcaster, in 2011. She enjoyed a childhood of Spangles, Lovehearts, Opal Fruits, Jubblies, Pear Drops, Flying Saucers, Sherbet Fountains and Aniseed Balls.

Below right: Broadcaster and journalist Max Easterman remembers finding an unexploded hand grenade, a relic from the war.

Now an accountant, Hugh Cairns has vivid memories of tenement housing in 1950s Glasgow.

Joan Matthews vividly remembers the first wave of immigration into London.

The King of Skiffle Lonnie Donegan is besieged by fans. *(Reflections Photo Archive)*

'Rock and Roll is here to stay,
it will never die . . .'

Brylcreem, just what every dashing
young man needed.

Knocking-off time at the Cammell Laird shipyard, 1957. Old
industries such as this employed thousands. *(Reflections Photo Archive)*

Most of our international trade was still done by sea. Liverpool docks
is seen here crammed with cargo ships. (Chubb Collection)

The *Empress of Canada* on her side in Gladstone Dock, Liverpool, January 1953. Gutted by fire, she made an unforgettable sight from the Overhead Railway. *(Chubb Collection)*

Labour MP Bessie Braddock on a visit to the North West Gas Board garage. Tom Kelly, the author's father, is on the right, looking more interested in the camera than in Bessie.

Whit Walk in Manchester – a time for dressing up.

It's hard to believe that people went to New Brighton for their holidays, but they did. *(Reflections Photo Archive)*

Liverpool city centre in the late 1950s. *(Steve Hale)*

The author in Santa's grotto at Lewis's department store, Liverpool, early 1950s.

The concrete pyramids that had been built on Britain's shoreline to prevent invasion during the war were still standing in the 1950s. This is Moreton Shore on the Wirral in 1950. The author's mother, Mary Kelly, is on the right with her cousin.

During the mid-1950s the arrival of floodlights brought about a revolution in football, with night-time matches. League champions Wolverhampton Wanderers were pioneers with friendlies against the Russian and Hungarian champions.

The Coronation was a national event with children and families across the country celebrating with street parties as well as parties in community centres, church halls and schools.

CORONATION YEAR

The author's school Coronation photograph, 1953.

Did Bayko sets foster a generation with dreams of home-ownership?

A Hornby Dublo electric train set was the dream of every boy in the 1950s, especially if it was the *Duchess of Montrose*.

Slim hips, suits and pencil skirts were the height of 1950s' fashion.

MARCH FROM
LONDON
TO
ALDERMASTON

Above: The annual CND march to Aldermaston, 1958.

HUNGARY RELIEF FUND

GIVE GENEROUSLY!

Scottish football followers, the most open-handed in the world, are to be asked to support the Hungary Relief Fund.

We know you will eagerly contribute to so worthy a cause. Collections will be made at your ground.

Left: The plight of the Hungarian people in 1956 caught the British public's sympathy with special football matches and appeals for money.

CHAPTER FOUR

ROCK 'N' ROLL LIVES

If the 1930s had been dominated by unemployment, the 1950s were to be the very opposite; an era of full employment. And that brought with it greater spending power. Added to that was more leisure time. Trade unions throughout the 1950s negotiated longer paid holidays and a reduction in working hours. For the first time Britons had money and time to spend it, and much of it went on enjoying themselves. Dancing, cinema-going and sport had been the principal activities of pre-war Britain and this continued into the 1950s. The difference was that it just got better. Cinemascope and stereophonic sound arrived, along with the epic movie and big Hollywood stars, though the likes of Richard Burton and Elizabeth Taylor had been born in Britain. And there was the musical – *Singing in the Rain, Oklahoma!, Carousel, The King and I, Guys and Dolls* and many others. It was an age of optimism.

What's more, there was also a vibrant British cinema offering a diet of Second World War blockbusters such as *The Bridge on the River Kwai, The Cruel Sea, The Man Who Never Was, The Dam Busters, Reach for the Sky* – all films highlighting the heroics of the British soldier, airman, or naval rating. And there were also comedies. The *Carry On* series began introducing matinee idol Dirk Bogarde, Kenneth Williams and Barbara Windsor.

As in the 1930s, the queues for the movies still stretched around the block on Fridays and Saturdays, though audiences were beginning to decline. Cinema attendance in the UK had peaked in 1946, with 31.5 million going each week. Throughout the 1950s it fell steadily; by 1956 it was down to 21 million, and by the end of the decade it stood at just under ten million. The trouble was television. By the end of the 1950s, with television beginning to take hold, cinema audiences had dwindled. For many, however, going to the cinema remained an institutionalised night out, particularly if you were on a 'date'; join the queues, buy some chocolates, sit in the back row, an ice-cream at the interval. It was much more of a social occasion than watching television at home, though television had the advantage of being cheaper, more up-to-date and offered a greater variety of entertainment – not just films, but comedy, sport, music, soaps, news and dramas. In every community there would be at least one cinema. The centre of Manchester boasted a dozen cinemas, Birkenhead had half a dozen, Stockport had fourteen and even Huddersfield had more than ten. Cinemas were even to be found in the suburbs.

What was to primarily emerge from the 1950s, however, was a youth culture. Suddenly young people found a voice and began to stamp their culture on British life in a way that no youth generation had ever done before. And driving that change in culture was music.

When the 1950s began, you would be likely to find the pop charts dominated by American crooners such as Frank Sinatra, Tony Bennett, Frankie Laine and Johnnie Ray. Some of them had been around since the 1940s and the war years. There were women as well, including Ella Fitzgerald, Doris Day and Sarah Vaughan. They sang ballads, often backed by lavish string orchestras such as Nelson Riddle or Count Basie. They would continue to top the charts both in America and Britain and not much changed until November 1955, when Bill Haley and his Comets soared to number one with 'Rock Around the Clock'. Rock 'n' roll had arrived and popular music would never be the same again. For a start it became known as pop music and although Americans would continue to dominate, it wouldn't be too long before Britain was offering up a few rivals of its own.

If Bill Haley kicked off rock 'n' roll, it was Elvis who put it on the international map. Elvis had begun his recording career with the Memphis-based Sun Records in 1954, but it wasn't until January 1956 that he had his first major hit single with 'Heartbreak Hotel', which topped the American charts and went to number two in the UK. Elvis had arrived and neither music nor youth culture would ever be the same again.

At first Elvis was regarded with suspicion. Most of the kids loved him, but their parents, particularly Americans, still stuck in the traditions of the 1940s, were horrified by his suggestive hip movements. He was even banned from the Ed Sullivan Show (an American TV variety show) after his gyrating movements caused an outrage.

Britain was slow on the uptake but at least there was Lonnie Donegan, King of Skiffle. Donegan's career had taken the slow route through jazz and blues but, in 1956, his band of washboards, guitars and doublebass topped the charts with 'Rock Island Isle'. From then on he was to have a succession of hits with 'Cumberland Gap', 'Tom Dooley', 'Does Your Chewing Gum Lose Its Flavour' and many others. For the remainder of the 1950s he was one of, if not the biggest, UK recording artist. Paul McCartney would later acknowledge Donegan's impact on a generation of would-be pop starts, as well as his own development as a singer.

The impact of rock and roll was to be sensational. Suddenly young people had a voice. It was not the middle-aged crooners anymore but young people and as well as Elvis there was Buddy Holly, Little Richard, Jerry Lee Lewis, Gene Vincent, Brenda Lee, Eddie Cochrane and many more. All were under the age of twenty-five and were part of a new youth culture.

The older generation were horrified. The music and the dancing were called 'blasphemous', their attitude was challenging, to say the least, and the clothes they wore were threatening, along with their behaviour. When rock and roll films played at the local cinema, couples got up and began dancing in the aisles. Nothing quite like it had ever been witnessed before.

Whilst Elvis was the American idol, Britain's own teeny-bopper was Tommy Steele, the Bermondsey boy. Steele was young, brash, working class and had a mischievous smile. His first record, 'Rock with the Caveman', shot to number 13 in the charts. But most of Steele's records, as with other UK rock artistes, were cover versions of American recordings. His first big hit, 'Singing the Blues', was a cover of American Guy Mitchell's recording. Remarkably, both records reached number one in Britain. Steele would continue to have chart successes throughout the 1950s, before turning his hand towards acting and later establishing himself as a highly successful singer/actor, particularly in musicals.

Then, in the late 1950s, came Cliff Richard with 'Move It'. Richard, who seemed to be a cross between Gene Vincent and Elvis, with his Teddy Boy looks, quaffed hairstyle and shaking legs, soon found himself at the top of the charts. But eventually he too would follow in Steele's footsteps in the 1960s by leaving rock and roll well behind him.

The followers of rock and roll became known as Teddy Boys because of their style of dress. They wore drainpipe trousers and suits with long jackets. Usually, their suits were a pastel blue with black velvet collars and went with white shirts and bootlace ties. They looked as if they had stepped out of the Edwardian era, hence the name 'Teddy Boy'. And the girls were just as lavish, wearing flowing hobble skirts with petticoats. Later they wore toreador trousers, while their hair was either long or worn in a ponytail. But it was their style of dancing which roused as much comment. They danced with enthusiasm and excitement; gone was the formal, civilised dancing of the previous era. Rock and roll was about gyrating. Girls were tossed over shoulders, and even the men danced using every part of their body. It was rhythmic, in your face and, to many, quite disturbing. They would go to the cinema to see films like *Love me Tender* or *Rock Around the Clock* and would start dancing in the aisles. Everything about rock and roll was loud.

The Teddy Boys seemed to be out to cause trouble. There were gang fights, stabbings, smashed football trains and they generally seemed to be hell-bent on hooliganism. The papers were full of it, reporting riots, fights and anything that seemed to highlight Britain's slow decline into depravity. Much of it was exaggerated. The papers even coined a new phrase 'juvenile delinquent' to describe these unfathomable, crazy, mixed-up teenagers who seemed to have not a care in the world.

Sport had always been the staple diet of the working man and it continued in much the same way after the war, though with greater attendance than ever. Football was the number one sport in winter, cricket in the summer. Rugby union was popular as well, while in the North rugby league was keenly followed. At football matches, attendances reached record levels after the war. Normal league football had been halted during the hostilities, although a league of sorts had continued. But once the war was over, fans flocked back to the dilapidated old stadiums for their weekly fix. And it continued well into the 1950s. There were record attendances at many football grounds in this period, including 62,000 at Anfield, 36,000 at Halifax, and a mid-week record 72,000 on a Wednesday afternoon at Goodison Park, home of Everton Football Club. At Bradford's Odsal stadium in 1954 the rugby league Challenge Cup Final replay attracted a world record crowd of 104,000, though most commentators agree that with so many people clambering over broken fences, it was nearer 120,000.

Floodlights also came into play during the 1950s so that evening games became possible, opening up a new era of European competitions. Prior to that, especially during the winter months, games would have to be played in an afternoon, with a 2 p.m. kick-off so that they did not end in darkness. As a result, if there was a big match, thousands would skip work, either leaving early or simply not turning up for the day. On Merseyside the docks would be deserted.

Football and rugby league were working-class sports, although rugby league was exclusively Northern. Professional footballers lived in the same working-class communities as they always had, being paid only a fraction more than most skilled workers. They didn't have fancy cars or detached houses out in the countryside. Instead they could be spotted in the locality, on the buses and in the shops. They were just like the bloke next door.

STEVE HALE

My nan was a great piano player. She loved music and my mum loved music too. My mum was a great dancer and she taught me how to dance – the old style, no shoes on and me standing on her feet and teaching me the steps in the house. She always had the radio or the record player on. My mum worked on the cooking staff in a school and my nan was always moaning at her. She'd say, 'Lily, not another record!' 'cos she'd come in every Friday night with a record, spent half her wages on a record. Of course she was only young, she was in her early twenties when she got married. Mum loved Glenn Miller, and that's my first memory of music being played on a gramophone. Of course the gramophone was the pride and joy of my nan. She had bought it on the HP from Epstein's old shop in Walton Road. It was a piece of furniture, a beautiful thing. It had a lid on it and it got polished every Sunday morning. It was a proper electric valve job. It was an Eko. After Glenn Miller my mum moved on to Johnnie Ray and Guy Mitchell. My dad was a little bit more smoother, perhaps with going to America on the ships, and he'd heard American music before we heard it and he was into Dean Martin, Frank Sinatra, all those American crooners. And then, of course, there was Peter, who was younger than them even and it was through him that I got into music, that I first heard Elvis and Eddie Cochrane – he loved him. He put me onto Eddie Cochrane as well and I liked him, more than Elvis at first.

TREVOR CREASER

My sister used to keep a book and she'd write all the words of every pop song in this book. There were pages and pages of them. We had a coffee bar nearby called the Del Monico, which was where all the teenagers went, although I didn't go. I had too much on at home. I was the man of the house; I was always making things or whatever. We had a large garden with a lot of grass to cut, which I did with a sickle.

When I got older and was courting, when I was sixteen/seventeen, I used to go dancing at the Capital – it later became the Ace of Clubs nightclub. We used to dance to Jack Mann and his band. Mind you, there must have been several versions of this band as they were still going just a few years back. Initially it was ballroom dancing, but as rock and roll started, it changed. They still had some waltzes and that for the older. But it was a good do, a lot of Meanwood people went. I later discovered that you didn't have to dance; you could take a pack of cards and play pontoon. That's what we did, although we really went for the girls. As for courting, Meanwood was such a small place in those days, we'd walk through the woods, or go to the park; we found lassies all over the place.

Meanwood has always been split: on the one side the decent area, on the other the council estate. There was always trouble between the two. The Teddy Boys came from the council estate side.

They had long jackets with velvet lapels and razorblades under the lapels, drainpipe trousers, and beetle crushers – that's thick crêpe shoes. You didn't see too many Teddy Girls though. The girls generally had durndle skirts. They had separate tops and these skirts like a ballerina skirt. They lifted up when they danced – it was great for us lads. And they wore suspenders as well.

JOAN FINCH

My mother and father used to baby-sit when we went dancing. We used to go to The Barracks on Cross Lane, and on Regent Road there were three or four dancehalls. We went dancing on a Saturday night. The grandparents would take the children to their flat. We always managed to go out together. There was the Palais and the Academy, where we used to go. More often than not we'd go to the cinema. Happy times. Bill was a Glen Miller fan; he had every record of him. Frank Sinatra as well. When we came to live at another house, not far from here, he went to the British Legion, so we used to go with some friends there on a Saturday evening. We never went short of money. He worked hard.

NEIL KINNOCK

My chief occupation was to go places to see girls. This meant going to youth clubs from fifteen, sixteen onwards, dance halls on a Saturday night, but, above all, the Italian café. I had my first cappuccino when I was about nine. The café was owned by an Italian who lived in Tredegar. It had one of those huge steam boilers and you frothed the milk from it. It was owned by this Italian and indeed there were lots of Italians in our communities. They had all come from Italy during the 1860s and, later, from impoverished Italy, looking for work. They brought their cooking with them as well. One of them owned a fish and chip shop. In a way they developed like the Bangladeshi communities have done in more recent times. In the 1950s these cafés became the alternative to pubs. As a result they flourished and the Italians soon became integrated into the community. In Tredegar there were several of these cafés. I used to go to one of them and I remember the owner had a sensationally beautiful daughter called Nora.

In the 1950s there were two important things that happened at the same time – the arrival of the jukebox and the arrival of rock and roll. That meant that you could listen to rock and roll music in a café or wherever. It was instantaneous. I was the first kid in Tredegar to go and see Bill Haley's *Rock Around the Clock*. I went to Cardiff to see it and I took notes! People were jiving in the aisles.

And on the way home on the bus I wrote up my notes. It was like bringing the news of war or something back to the folks in Tredegar. Bill Haley, Elvis Presley, Little Richard – rock and roll became an alternative to religion. It also brought about huge changes in social life and in appearances. Suddenly I became fashion-conscious. There was the arrival of slip-on shoes, drainpipe trousers, tipped cigarettes, cravats – just awful – and all this to a solid rock and roll beat. It enveloped the working classes. Tredegar became a rock and roll town!

Brian Hulme

When I was in the first year at secondary school, music didn't impinge much on me. Much of it was American hillbilly, but in the second year rock and roll came on the scene – Bill Haley and his Comets. I saved up some money and went down London Road, to the record shop, and I bought a 78 of Bill Haley's 'See You Later Alligator', but in the crush coming out of school someone pushed into me and cracked the record, so I went home and had to glue it together on a cardboard disc, so I could play one side but not the other. Never knew what was on the other side. That was my introduction to rock and roll. What got me more was Lonnnie Donegan and skiffle. It was different and it was by someone in England. I went to see him at least twice in the Ardwick Hippodrome. Some of the kids at school were fans of Elvis the Pelvis. I got more interested in him after school. Tommy Steele was interesting because he was the big British star at the time.

Stephen Kelly

I really liked skiffle and was a huge fan of Lonnie Donegan. My mum took me to the Liverpool Empire to see him. It was the first gig I had even been to and I can still picture him on stage in his smart suit. I always thought, years later, that skiffle would make a comeback, but it never did. Me and my mates tried a bit of skiffle. I had an old washboard and one of my mum's thimbles. It made a great sound. Another mate had an old tea chest with a stick through it and a piece of string, but I don't think that worked very well, and someone else had a guitar. Donegan did *Sunday Night at the London Palladium* and he played his new record, 'Does Your Chewing Gum Lose Its Flavour'. By the end of the week it had shot straight to number one in the charts, I think the first time any record had ever done that. Donegan then started doing rather silly records and left the skiffle behind him.

My recollections of rock and roll are a bit limited. I vaguely remember early talk about Elvis but thought it was about a girl. I do, however, recall going to the cinema to see his first film, *Love Me Tender*. I was a great fan of Adam Faith, who had hair that kind of flopped across his forehead. I changed my hairstyle so that I could look like him. I also liked all those other rock and rollers like Jerry Lee Lewis, Little Richard, Eddie Cochrane, Buddy Holly, Frankie Lymon and the Teenagers.

BRIAN HULME

Most of my liaisons were disastrous. I became infatuated with a girl at seventeen, that's when my dad threw me out. If I was seeing a girl I'd go to the flicks, I wasn't much good at dancing. I never went into restaurants until much later. Only posh people went out for meals. I'd maybe go to cafés on holiday, but never restaurants. As for youth clubs, I went to St Kentigerns in Rusholme and one in Flixton as well because there wasn't one near us. They weren't very exciting, but they played records and there were girls.

MAX EASTERMAN

I never got into popular culture, popular music. I wanted to but just didn't like it. There was one music shop in Harrogate and I went there and thought about buying something but I just didn't like it. It didn't appeal. I had been brought up listening to Louis Armstrong and Jelly Roll Morton. I'd go to the old junk shops, of which there were many in Harrogate, and buy old 78s, sort through these huge piles of them. I had started in my early teens buying *Jazz News*, which foundered after a few years. There was an article in it one day about all these records that had been issued in the UK under pseudonyms. I've got dozens of them in my collection now. I went looking in the junk shops for these records. I remember buying Paul Whiteman's 'Mary' – it had 'Mary' on one side and 'Changes' on the other – taking it home and hearing this cornet and instantly recognising Bix Beiderbecke. Just for sixpence. A real find – I still have it. I was a bit of a freak because all my pals were swooning to Connie Francis and Johnnie Ray, Bill Haley, Tommy Steele, the Everly Brothers. Listening to them now, they have a curious period charm. But back then I was not at all interested. When I think about it now, I was listening to music that had been recorded in the 1920s and the mid-1930s. On my tenth birthday, in 1955, I went down to the HMV shop on Oxford Street in London and bought four records. One of those was Louis Armstrong's 'West End Blues', which had been in the catalogue for twenty-eight years and was still being pressed.

IAN RALSTON

And then there were the Teddy Boys. I had some older cousins who were really into the jazz scene in the city. They went to the Iron Door Club wearing luminous socks and the likes. Rock and roll was filtering in then. I remember the greased back hair, drainpipe trousers, white socks, long jackets and thin tie. The women had heavily pleated umbrella dresses – the sort I always associate with Hattie Jacques – that would go out at an angle of about 45 degrees. And the girls also used to wear socks, they were called bobby socks. I particularly remember Chuck Berry. Then it was Elvis on a wind-up gramophone my dad had bought. Then we got a Dansette when 45s came out. You could pile half a dozen 45s on and hope the needle dropped in the right place. And there was Jerry Lee Lewis of course. I remember when my elder cousin wore these luminous socks, her family legitimised it by saying they were safer as she used to ride a bike. National Service was still in then. My dentist disappeared into the army. There was a belief that once they went on National Service, it would knock them into shape.

Dennis Gilligan

Me and the wife used to love dancing. We used to go to Belle Vue. The music was big band music – quickstep, waltz, tango, nice dances like that. I love a big band; I saw Joe Loss at the Isle of Man. There was also the Ritz in town for dancing. I never got into rock and roll or anything like that though. I was shy at first so didn't get up to dance much. The wife lived around the corner, I knew her all my life. She got me dancing. Belle Vue was brilliant, it was massive – one band at one end, one at the other. There was always a fight; there was a Scottish lad and he was a doorman, and he got battered one night trying to stop a fight at Belle Vue, he was never the same again. The only fighting I did was the wrestling. The Teddy Boys were always good dancers. I worked with one, Tom his name was. He was the only one – he used to like a drink, he had an apron, we used to go to the pub and he was always wearing it. He wore tight pants, suede shoes with big crêpe soles, a fancy tie and a good mop of hair, well greased up when he went dancing. But they were good dancers. The girls wore short dresses. There used to be a dance hall at Boughton and we used to walk back through Peel Park at night. You couldn't do that now, but we had no problems. It was a long way to walk. Everything you did was walk, walk. It made you fit. Once I got a car I was less fit.

Joan Finch

Bill was a painter and decorator all his life until he was sixty-five, and he finished then. He was bored to death when he retired. He'd still do jobs for some people though, like family.

He loved rugby league, loved Salford. I hated it, I liked football you see. He'd go and see Salford if he could and it was just round the corner, but he was often working on a Saturday. Before he went in the army we'd go to watch Salford together, but I was bored. We'd go to Wigan, places like that to watch. He liked football – United – I was down there when the disaster happened, Eddie Coleman lived close by. I can tell you where I was when I first heard the news. Diane was nine months old. Janice was in school. I went to the greengrocers on the corner and they said the plane had crashed at Munich. Sad time; I remember that well.

We used to go dancing at Belle Vue as well. A friend of Bill's, his sister met a lad through her brother being in the army. He came from Bournemouth and they met one another in the army. I used to see her at Belle Vue. We used to take the tram and a bus to get there. There was a zoo there as well. It was a big place. It was a day out. I remember my dad taking our girls and then him and my mother used to go to the dogs on a Saturday night, they liked a bet. And there was a racecourse in Manchester as well. My dad used to go there. And he would go to White City as well to watch the dogs.

Bob Greaves

The interesting thing about football matches in those days was the dress of the fans, because people now just assume that you see lads there in the summer and even in the winter wearing short-sleeved T-shirts and very often bare-chested in the freezing cold, walking into the ground. In those days people dressed sensibly and conformed to the weather. You wore overcoats, big shoes, hats, umbrellas even; you just dressed for the weather. And of course there were virtually no women in the crowds in the 1940s or '50s. If you saw a woman it was a novelty, it was 99.9 per cent men.

Steve Hale

My dad was a big Evertonian and all his brothers – my uncles – used to regularly go to Goodison Park. My first memory is an FA Cup game – we sat up in the Main Stand, myself, my dad and three of my uncles. Dave Hickson was playing for Everton then. When they ran out I especially noticed the contrast in the kit. The jersey was a flat blue but the shorts were satin with a big blue stripe down the side – long, shiny, satin shirts. That contrast immediately caught my eye. I remember Dave Hickson going up for the ball and there was a clash of heads and next thing there was blood gushing everywhere out of Hickson's forehead. I said, 'Oh he's hurt, look at all the blood!' And my dad said, 'Oh, he'll be alright once they get the magic sponge on him.' And I said, 'What do you mean?' And he said, 'Well you just watch.' Hickson didn't come off; there were no stretchers or anything like that. He just went to the touchline and leant over and the trainer came along with this big white enamel bucket. This giant sponge came out of the bucket, on his head, rub, rub, rub, wring it out, back in the bucket, back on his head, rub, rub, rub, pat on the head, 'On your way son'. No blood. And there's Dave Hickson running around again. And I thought, wow – that really is a magic sponge; it stops bad injuries, bleeding and all. I think I must have been about fourteen before I realised that it wasn't really a magic sponge, but because my dad had said it was a magic sponge, I thought it really was a magic sponge!

ERIC BARNSLEY

During the old days, they used to have mid-week matches in the afternoon. Those were the days before floodlights, but you still got good crowds. Liverpool always had their games on a Wednesday afternoon, when the shopkeepers had a half-day. When Liverpool or Everton were at home mid-week, the docks used to come to a standstill. There'd be nobody there; they'd all be up at Anfield. You had to think up good excuses though. You had a bad back or a sore throat; they were the best, though some people came up with the most amazing tales. Of course in those days they had casual labour on the docks, so it was fairly easy. You just didn't show up in a morning. Lots of blokes would leave home, pretending to their wives that they were going down the docks to work, and they just didn't sign on. They'd hang around somewhere all morning until it was time to go to the match. Then they'd wander home at five o'clock, telling the wife they'd done a day's work. She'd never know any different. Of course they didn't get paid but somehow they'd manage to cover it up at the end of the week.

GEORGE REYNOLDS

I remember the elation, the slight apprehension and the real fear when coming out of the ground. In those days the only way out of Old Trafford was over the bridge and when you consider there were between sixty and sixty-five thousand people all trying to pour out at the same time, it was quite alarming for someone of my size to be in amongst so many people. But it was something which stayed with me forever. People got to the ground on football specials. Virtually every bus going from Wythenshawe – where I lived in those days – from perhaps one o'clock onwards had 'Match' on it. We all knew where it was going. As far as dress, we all wore grey, we all wore black. There were no club colours apart from scarves and rattles, which made a terrible noise. Flat caps – nearly everybody wore a hat of some sort. If it wasn't a flat hat, it was a trilby. The ground looked a mass of grey-black. There was no colours. The only splash of colour really was the railings around the ground, which were white, which you still see in a lot of old photos. The terraces, behind them, were painted red and the big scoreboard behind, which was there until the 1970s. They call it the theatre of dreams now, which sounds a bit grandiose, but it is believable.

WILF McGUINNESS

Tuesday was a good night to go out if we didn't have a game on the Wednesday. We went to the dance halls, the Plaza. We'd get the all-night bus down to Piccadilly and all stand in the corner like ordinary lads, bit of a snogging session if we were lucky, maybe see them again, and maybe not. I remember going in the odd pub when we won the Youth Cup, I was seventeen, eighteen. It was lager and lime, no drinking really. We realised there was more to life than football. Matt Busby had to pull us up when we got older and said, 'Now lads, I'm hearing stories about you all going into town, drinking and things like this. If you have one drink, by the time the stories reach me, it's eight. So,' he said, 'If you want a drink get out of town, I don't mind you having a drink but go somewhere like Glossop.' So we went to Glossop and we finished up having an all-night party, which did us more harm than going downtown. Somebody recognised us and that was it. When we were a bit older and had girlfriends we went to the Cromford Club, have a meal. It was late night and they had music. Paddy McGrath was a pal of Sir Matt's. It was more the senior players who went there. Bit too good for us then. There was the Continental Club which, for us tearaways was good fun. We didn't get into trouble.

As we got older we got recognised, but people didn't make a fuss of us. When we went training it was on the bus until I got a car. I'd pick my mate Eddie Colman up because he didn't have a car. I was a first teamer, he was a reserve. I'd drive through Salford from Blackely, pick him up and there was a swingbridge, and if we were late we always made the excuse the bridge was closed. All the lads in digs used to come to our house, it was open house, our parents were proud to have us there. Fish and chips on a Friday and then into town for the cinema and back before ten. That was a Friday night before the game. And on Saturday night, if we weren't courting, we'd go into Manchester – either the cinema or the dance hall. Usually, if we were courting, it was the cinema because we didn't need to look for a girlfriend. Then you couldn't use your passes, you had to pay. You didn't want to go in with your pass and pay for the girl, you wanted to be big time and pay for both. Many's the time at the Gaumont, or Odeon as it now is, we'd be in there and all of a sudden you'd hear 'Aargh' and people suddenly standing up. It was footballers with cramp in the thigh or the hamstring. You'd say, 'There's Colin Barlow of City, or 'There's Duncan Edwards, he's in here tonight'. You'd see players standing up with cramp because we didn't have any warm-downs as they do now, so we got cramp.

DENNIS GILLIGAN

When my brother Stanley got demobbed from the army, he started going to the YMCA and went back to wrestling. I used to go with him to watch him. Well, they was short one time and that was it. I got roped in. I started at 11 stone and when I won the British Championship I was 8 stone 13 and a half. It took time to pick it up but when I did I was very good. I wrestled for eighteen years; nine years I suffered and nine years I was top dog. It was the best thing I've ever done. I trained at the YMCA. I started as a novice in the Lancashires, then the Northern Counties Championships, and we used to wrestle in Birmingham. If you won in Birmingham you would usually win the British Championship as well. I was British Champion in 1965, 1967 and 1968.

I was in the Empire Games, as it was called then, in 1958, in Cardiff. I was a novice – I had only been wrestling for five years. I was working until five o'clock and then I'd go to the YMCA until 9 or 10 in the evening. I was getting into trouble at home. My daughter says she never knew me when she was a youngster, because she was always in bed when I got home.

I was the top dog in England, which was why I was chosen to represent my country, but there was a Scottish lad who was the British Champion. So I got chosen for England. I had a white trilby, white blazer, white pants, all worn for the march past, the parade at the beginning and end of the Games. And they had big dances as well. I liked the dancing. The girls were all after me but I was happily married. There was another wrestler, a policeman from Stretford, but we kept away from the girls. I couldn't eat much because I had to watch my weight. One of the other lads had to go home as he failed the weight. I didn't do so well when it came to the actual Games. I won one and got beat twice. I was a novice but the main thing was that I was in it.

I had a fight in Bolton once against France. I wasn't picked to begin with, but I went along. I went for a pint of beer before the competition started, thinking I would be okay. I don't normally drink but then, as I was walking to the stadium, someone said, 'You're fighting, so and so has pulled out'. I was normally a bantam weight and they put me up as a feather weight and I wrestled this Frenchman who looked like Hercules and I pinned him so easily. I was then picked to go to France for the return competition, but I was injured. Later, in the 1960s, I was picked to go abroad.

I would train most nights – Tuesdays, Thursdays, Saturdays, and Sunday morning. I couldn't do it every day because I was working. It was hard. I could have done much better if I hadn't been working. I had to pay for everything; it didn't bother us then though. In wrestling there's no money at all. I was in the union and when I was in the Empire Games the union collected for me. One gaffer gave me a £20 note and I said to me ma, 'He's not given me much

– he's given me a ten bob note,' and then, when I looked, it was a twenty pound note – that was an awful lot of money. I'd never seen one before. You didn't get paid in wrestling; you had to pay for your digs, transport, time off work. When I won the British Championship it cost me around £50.

Geoff Wright

I remember going up to Odsal in 1956, when we beat Wigan by 11 points to 10. We were losing 5-0 and Ken Dean dived under the posts just before half-time at our end. There were fifty-eight thousand there that day, fantastic. When you think of the crowds they brag about today, if they get twenty-five thousand for a game they think they have done well, but fifty-eight thousand at Odsal, and it had atmosphere. That was a great day because Wigan were the Manchester United of rugby league. Mum wouldn't let me go to Wembley so I listened to it on the radio. There was a roar and I heard the commentators say what I thought was 'Palmer' but it was 'Carlton' for St Helens that had scored. The elation and deflation I felt, in the fact that I thought we'd scored but in fact they'd scored. We lost that 13-2. I remember the players coming back from Wembley and they came past the old Ramsdean brewery on Huddersfield Road, we were stood there and watched them in an open-top bus.

The following Saturday they went to Maine Road and I managed to go. We lost that game in the last minute. We had scored three tries to their two and it was 9-8, couple of minutes to go and we got penalised for offside. Colin Hutton, old full-back, kicked the goal and took the championship out of our hands. That was a real sickener. Hull are the only rugby league club that have a song, 'Old Faithful'. We climbed over the fence and went onto the field and they were all milling round us singing 'Old Faithful' and as a twelve- or thirteen-year-old I cried my eyes out, I was really upset.

The crowd that day was probably in the region of sixty thousand – Maine Road was packed, there were no restrictions on the gates then. It was a ticket game but they opened the turnstiles and, as I say, it was really upsetting and going home, the faces on the coach going from Maine Road back to Halifax were rather glum. We weren't happy bunnies at all and my mum didn't need to ask how they'd gone on because she could tell when I walked in the door by the look on my face.

Neil Shuttleworth

The old terrace side at Fartown, home of Huddersfield RFLC, was an amazing sight, with between ten and fifteen thousand guys all looking like clones of each other, all in beige belted macs and flat caps and a muffler. We didn't exactly have a pie store but we had a hot soup stall. Kids went down to the front. In those days it was one and six pence and if boys went behind the posts it was free, or you could get in with your dad for a few pennies more. My dad, fortunately, became a member of the club and a member of the famous Huddersfield Cricket and Athletic Club (HCAC) bowling team, so he was a member and I was able to go in the stand with him on occasion.

But the ground was absolutely full, the trolleybuses ran from the town centre, St George's Square, and it was two old pennies each way to the ground. They used to line up in a big circle, go off to the rugby ground and round in a circuit until kick-off time, then they would park up and start going back to town a little bit later.

As a student later on, I was a conductor of those trolleybuses as I was working my way through college and, if you've ever been upstairs on a bus when you've lost, with forty blokes drawing on woodbines, it was a terrible place to be, believe you me.

Fans were great, their team was their thing. Everybody wore the same knitted scarf that they bought at the market for about three shillings, the famous bobble caps were knitted with the pom-poms on top and, of course, the old-fashioned wooden rattles, which health and safety people, if they saw the size they used to be, would confiscate at the gate now, I'm quite sure. It was terrific, but not too many ladies at that time. Very few ladies because they worked in the mills or they worked in other industries and they went shopping on Saturday afternoons round the market. We used to have a St John Ambulance at one end and the pie and soup stall at the other, and people might have taken a thermos flask of tea with a drop of rum in it at Christmas.

DENNIS GILLIGAN

I wasn't really interested in other sports. My brother did the weights but I wrestled all the time. I used to watch United though. After the war my eldest brother, Wilf, went to United one week and City the next and I went with him. We went on the bikes; we had a big black cape on the bikes. I used to watch the Busby Babes. We'd cycle to Old Trafford and Maine Road and park in a yard for three pence. I didn't buy a car until I was forty-two. It was good going to Old Trafford. It was marvellous football. The atmosphere was good. You didn't worry about the weather. United played at Maine Road after the war because Old Trafford had been bombed. It never bothered us supporting one club one week and another one the next. I was probably a bit more inclined to United. Both were good teams, but United were a better side. I would go to Bolton and Preston to watch either United or City when they were away, but I never went to any of the Cup finals in the 1950s, we never had enough money. My brother got crushed by the barrier one time, so we stopped going. He was a bit frightened and I used to be tired as well after the wrestling.

ERIC BARNSLEY

During the winter, the games would finish up in near pitch darkness. You still had a three o'clock or three fifteen kick-off. So by four o'clock it was getting pretty dark. And when you were standing on the Kop half the time you couldn't make out what was going on down the other end of the pitch, it was so dark. When the floodlights came it caused a social revolution. Everybody had to work a full week; there were no mid-week afternoon games any more, and suddenly we started going to football in the evening. It was an amazing change. The employers loved it. But privately I think the dockers quite enjoyed having the occasional Wednesday afternoon off. It broke the week up nicely.

HUGH CAIRNS

The first time I remember going to a match was in August 1954, when my father took me to Celtic Park. I don't know who they were playing that day. The previous season Celtic had won the double, and the practice in Scotland was that the following season the champions would play their first game at home. Now I remember the day they were presented with the championship pennant. I remember nothing about the game but I remember, as if it was yesterday, the pennant being unfurled. My father said, 'Take a good look son because it will be some time before you see that again.' And the next time I saw it was in August 1966. The old man was right. That's my earliest memory of going to a football match. My next memory was a game against Aberdeen later that season. Aberdeen had won the Championship the previous Saturday and Celtic applauded them onto the pitch. After that, the following season, I started going regularly and then I got to the stage when I was going virtually every week, home and away, with my friends. Sometimes we went on the bus but mainly I walked. Getting the bus was murder as it was so busy. It took about three quarters to an hour to walk there. In all the years I used to go and watch Celtic I never made it to Tannadyce, and only once to Aberdeen.

IAN RALSTON

I can distinctly remember the first football game I went to. It was Liverpool against Huddersfield at Anfield Road and we were in one of the stands near the halfway line. My dad and elders brothers were fanatical supporters and would always go and I distinctly remember Tommy Younger in goal. Billy Liddell was still playing, and Alan A'Court. I think Liverpool won. That was huge excitement. The vast majority of people went on the bus and we took the number 81 to Queens Drive and then walked up.

GEOFF WRIGHT

Norman Bury was a local chap and he edited and published the *Rugby League Gazette*. It was a magazine that covered rugby league, warts and all. He'd get to know things and would put it in the *Rugby League Gazette*. He employed young lads to sell it and we got three pence per shilling, 25 per cent, which was a nice lift on top of your spending money. We used to go to grounds all over: Odsal, Headingly, Oldham, Rochdale, Thrum Hall. We'd go into Lancashire, to Leigh or Salford, sometimes hoping to watch Halifax play at the same time.

One of the bestselling places was Oldham on a Saturday night. In those days, late 1950s, in Oldham town centre, every other place was a pub. You could sell maybe a hundred to a hundred and fifty on a Saturday night in Oldham, which was a good pickup. Alan Davies's, who played for Oldham and Wigan, his dad had a pub and all Alan Davies' shirts and caps were up on the wall. We almost got a free drink in there for selling the *Rugby League Gazette* once.

One of my best recollections was in 1957. Norman went to interview the players for the *Rugby League Gazette* before they played in the final in 1957, and I remember going with him to Headingly and meeting the likes of Geoff Stevenson, Gordon Brown, Keith McClellan, Pat Quinn, Lewis Jones, people who were rugby league gods. I suppose I have an affinity to Leeds Rugby League because of that. You got to meet people and players through being associated with the *Rugby League Gazette*.

OLGA HALON

I've always been interested in sport. My brother was interested and he started taking us. I'm one of seven – the sixth – and he was a bit older than me, so he started taking myself and my sister. I went to United on occasion and there was nobody there – that was before the war. I was going to cricket at Old Trafford as well before the war. We went to Maine Road. I used to go on my bike and park it for two old pennies. I don't know why we went to Maine Road rather than Old Trafford. When I first went I used to stand on the popular side, the old Kippax. There weren't big crowds then. I can't remember what I did in the 1950s when my daughter was young – my husband was working on a Saturday, so I probably dumped her on my sister. I think I've always had a season ticket. It was unusual to see women at football matches, certainly not as many as you see now. I remember going to one match and I was halfway there and it was foggy and the cars were coming back. They'd had to cancel the game, there were no floodlights then. I remember a Cup match against Blackpool and we were winning 3-0 but lost 4-3 in the end. I remember another match which had to be abandoned because of a waterlogged pitch – we were winning and then we lost the replay.

I remember the City goalkeeper, Bert Trautmann. He was a very strong character. And there was Frank Swift, who got killed in the Munich air disaster. I remember hearing about that – I was waiting at a bus stop. It upset me even though I was a City supporter; it was terrible. Everybody was so shocked. All those young players. I remember that very clearly.

I went to both Cup finals in the 1950s. In 1955 they played Newcastle at Wembley and lost. Then the next year they played Birmingham and won. We went by train for the day, a special train from Piccadilly station, and came back straight after the match. I think the train went straight to Wembley and then we walked to the ground. 1955 was first time I had been to Wembley, we had quite a nice seat but I was very disappointed as we lost. But the following year they won. I remember Trautmann breaking his neck, he was on the ground for quite a while and he carried on, but none of us knew that he had broken his neck, he just carried on.

I didn't go to many away games and only for Cup games. I went to see them at Aston Villa and someone sitting behind me burnt my coat with a cigarette. You had to go and queue up to get tickets, you always had to go early. City/United was always the big game of the season and you had to queue up to get in or to get a ticket beforehand.

In the 1950s they didn't have floodlights and the games were in the afternoon. I used to go to all the games. People would take time off work to go.

I used to go to a lot of the cricket matches at Old Trafford to see Lancashire. I think in the 1950s my daughter was at school, so I would mainly go at weekends. I remember Cyril Washbrook and Brian Statham. Lancashire were a good side then. City had a good team as well with Don Revie.

LORD STAN ORME

I'll tell you about one of the Busby Babes – Duncan Edwards. I was chairman of my trade union branch, the AEU (Amalgamated Engineering Union) in Broadheath, and we used to meet every fortnight, on a Friday night. I used to go up and it was the days of no cars so I used to catch the all-night bus, coming back at about twenty to twelve from Broadheath. I remember getting on the bus one particular night and Duncan Edwards was sat there in the corner seat and the conductor was talking to him. Edwards was courting a girl in Timperley and he'd just taken her home. And you know Busby had them all in digs in Trafford with a landlady to look after them. I said to Edwards, 'Big game tomorrow.' And he said, 'Don't let anybody, especially the boss, know I'm on this bloody bus at quarter to midnight, he'll go mad!'

CHRIS PRIOR

My dad would take me to rugby games but I can't think where it was, maybe it was the Saracens, I don't know. But I can remember watching as quite a small kid and not understanding what was going on. My dad would take me to Arsenal, apparently, but I don't remember anything about that at all.

My grandfather on my father's side was a keen cricket fan and a season ticket holder at Essex. He lived in Leyton and he and a couple of his mates were going to watch Essex play the West Indies at South Church Park in Southend. Me and my dad went and we sat and watched this day of cricket and it was when the West Indies had Worrell, Weekes and Walcott – the three Ws. The match was actually won by Essex. I think they were the only county team to beat them. I also remember that one of the men who came with my uncle's mates smoked a pipe, and he had a big box of Swan Vesta matches. Anyhow, he was very excited and as he wriggled about the Swan Vesta matches in his pocket caught fire and he was having to try and put it out. Everybody smoked in those days. My maternal grandad was quite an old man – well into his seventies – and he had whole rack of pipes and he would choose a different pipe for a different time of day. He always smelt of pipe smoke.

DENNIS GILLIGAN

I used to go to the cinema in town, usually the Gaumont or the Odeon. We'd have to queue up for two hours sometimes. I went every Saturday night, loved it. Sometimes there would be such big queues, you'd finish up getting in halfway through the film, so you stayed to see the next performance, then, when you reached the part where you came in, you'd get up and leave.

JOAN FINCH

When I lived in our first house the cinema was close by. It was just four doors away. It was only a little cinema; there was one in almost every street at that time. Bill liked the cowboy films.

HANIF ASAD

On Sundays we used to have the day off. On Saturday we would work until seven o'clock and the only entertainment we had was going to the pictures to watch Pakistani movies and they'd show us two pictures each time on a Sunday. Where Primark is now there used to be a Curzon cinema, and there was a Majestic cinema where Tesco's is and a Cannon cinema across from

Kingsgate. There was also another cinema where the Hindu temple is, and an ABC cinema where Sainsbury's is. There were lots of cinemas in Huddersfield. It was the only way of socialising because everyone would come and we would go for a coffee or a cup of tea afterwards.

MAX EASTERMAN

My father would take me down the West End to a news theatre, which would have Pathé News and lots of cartoons, this was the big treat on a Fridays. Then we'd go to a friend of his who owned a café near Kings Cross – he had one of these big coffee machines which I always thought might explode. That was what I remember most about the school in Stanmore, going on the bus down the West End.

JOAN WOOD

Occasionally we'd go to the theatre and orchestral concerts. My husband was keen on classical music. We weren't into opera very much. We'd go to the Free Trade Hall to see the Halle orchestra, Barbirolli was conductor then. That was about it – cinema occasionally as well and a few orchestral concerts. There was the Opera House and the Palace in Manchester, and the two main cinemas were the Odeon and the Gaumont.

PHILIP LLOYD

In my leisure time I was involved with Chorlton Methodist Church. I was a regular churchgoer from an early age. I used to go to Sunday school and then church when I got older. In the 1950s I'd be going to church in the morning, coming home for lunch, then Sunday school in the afternoon and finally back to church again in an evening; three times a day on a Sunday. We also had a youth club. It was restricted to those who went to the church. We tried once to have an open club, where anybody could come, but it was a failure as we got so many people just intent on wrecking the place. Normally we'd have a bit of music, a few folk dances, country dancing, billiards and snooker. We also had a darkroom, as one of the leaders was interested in photography. I was never interested in modern music or jazz. I liked musicals, Gilbert and Sullivan, that kind of music. I used to go roller-skating on a Wednesday afternoon when the shop was closed. I used to go to Levenshulme roller-skating rink and then, later, ice-skating at Derby Street. I also used to go to Belle Vue occasionally, to the zoo. There was quite a big acreage of ground at Belle Vue, including the zoo and a funfair. There used to be firework displays, and there was the greyhound track and speedway as well, and boating on the lake and a circus as well. And there was the Kings Hall. When the Halle was bombed out of the Free Trade Hall, they went there. I think that was probably where Sir John Barbirolli started before the Free Trade Hall was rebuilt. I remember Isabel Bailey – she sang with Kathleen Ferrier. She had started life in the Methodist church nearby so she came twice to our church for fundraising or something. I've still got an autographed programme. We had a choir at the church, it was about fifty-strong and we'd put on things like Handel's *Messiah*.

Win Hindle

We used to go to Belle Vue for old time dancing and there was shows – Ted Heath, Jack Parnell, Slim Whitman, and firework shows. In them days there was the lake and they re-enacted battles on the lake. And then there was the wrestling at the Manchester Hippodrome as well. Every Saturday night we'd go to the wrestling. There was Jackie Pallo, Farmer's Boy – oh he was gorgeous – and Mick McManus. Oh, he was a right one. He was dirty. Billy Two Rivers, he was fabulous. He'd start getting annoyed and when he got annoyed he'd start doing an Indian dance.

We used to go to speedway as well. And there was a big zoo and a circus every year. George actually worked in the aviary at Belle Vue. George had to look after the dingoes. He almost got attacked by them. He stayed behind one night catching rats in the bird house. There was a woman called Winnie Smith, who had reared this tiger since it was born. Well it was poorly and one night she had gone back home, had a bath, and came back to look after it. She had put different clothes on. It didn't recognise her smell and it attacked and killed her. The tiger then realised and they had a job getting her away from it as it was cuddling her. The tigers were screaming.

I loved old time dancing we had some laughs. You needed kneepads, every dance was a tango. When rock and roll started, you had dresses with all this material sticking out, it was lovely. I loved jiving, I loved it. My baby sister came over from Australia recently and I said, 'Come on, let's have a jive'. George couldn't dance but for the last waltz we'd shuffle around. George didn't know one dance from another. I liked everybody – Jack Parnell, I loved. Slim Whitman was good. I liked Howard Keel. I met Albert Pierrepoint, and oh he was a gentleman. He was a very nice man.

We went to the cinema a lot. I used to go to the Manchester Hippodrome and there was a little picture house around the corner – they used to come round with a spray to get rid of the fleas. I used to go and see Sherlock Holmes. There was a cinema on Hyde Road and it was five pence and you could go in at five and stay until ten at night. I liked the musicals, *Tarzan* films, *King Kong*. There was no TV, so if you wanted entertainment you went to the cinema.

ANTHONY HANBURY

I used to go to the Free Trade Hall. That was great fun, I really enjoyed it. We went to an opera at the Palace, lots of intervals and we would rush to the bar. I would go and see the Halle at the Free Trade Hall. Barbirolli was the conductor then. He was very popular with the fans, they loved him but I'm not sure how popular he was with the orchestra. When Barbirolli was conducting you could hear the difference.

JOHN HECTORBALL

I used to go out cycling on a Sunday. I was in the Manchester Spartans cycling club. We used to cycle to Buxton, Chester, Derbyshire, sometimes as far as North Wales. We'd go touring. I've been to Lands' End and back. I had a lightweight bike made of Reynolds 531 tubing with ten gears, drop handlebars. It was an L H Brookes bike and a Pennine, I had two bikes. We used to go out all year round. It was a way of life; people didn't have as many cars in those days. There'd be fifteen to twenty of us go out every Sunday. I used to race too, in the towns around Manchester. I did one or two time trials, then I did mass starts. I used to go to the Fallowfield cycle track on a Monday and Thursday. It was an open-air track and quite popular. It was a steep, concrete track and if it was wet the tyres would slide and they'd fall off. Sometimes we'd see Reg Harris when we were out cycling because he lived in Macclesfield. He was a star, very famous. My other favourites were the French and Italians, people like Louison Bobet and Fausto Coppi, they were my favourites. I saw the World Championships when I was on holiday in Holland in 1959. There were ten of us and we hired these yachts and went round the canals of Holland and we got to see the World Championships. We saw Tommy Simpson, he was in Holland at the time and we were cheering him.

I had a girlfriend who was in the cycling club as well. We'd go to the cinema in town once a week, usually the Odeon. I remember the Coronation, we all got the day off. There were parties in the street and there was one in a street near mine, but I didn't go. I never went dancing – I didn't get the hang of it. I liked jazz, Gerry Mulligan, Milt Jackson, the Modern Jazz Quartet, Charlie Parker, I liked all those. They had concerts at the Free Trade Hall and about every six months someone big would come and we'd go and see them. I saw Count Bassie there, and Gerry Mulligan, west coast jazz, he was my favourite. I saw Dave Brubeck as well.

MARGARET WILLIAMS

We got married in 1956 in Manchester. We were at school together. We went out before university, then it fizzled out a bit but picked up again after that.

We were cyclists and walkers, that was our main activity. Nelson is on the border of Yorkshire and we would go off into Yorkshire, sometimes to the Lakes. We went hostelling, sometimes you went with friends. I think I went from school with some of the teachers. That was very good. I had the job of booking the hostels, it was very cheap and the food was basic, but it was good fun. There were sometimes things in the evening – games or whatever. Hostels are rather different today.

I had a Dawes bike, my first real bike. It had three-speed Sturmey Archer gears. Not like today's bikes with twenty gears. And it had drop handlebars. We wore capes when it was raining, which were so sensible as they covered you completely. We had a saddlebag as well.

We were riding up the A6 one Sunday – nothing like it is now. We went fairly early because of the traffic. We used to ride in twos in a file. A cat ran across the road. The first person ran over the cat and we all piled up. I sailed over my bike into the saddlebag of the chap in front. He had his sandwiches in the saddlebag and when we stopped for lunch his sandwiches were a parallelogram, all squashed up.

Another time we had been hostelling and had left the hostel early. We came to a junction and there was no traffic so we shot across. Unfortunately, there was a policeman sitting in his car and he was obviously bored, so he stopped us 'cos we hadn't stopped at the white line. He laboriously took all our names. When he got to me you could hear the sniggers 'cos my maiden name was Lockwood, I was Margaret Lockwood, which was the same name as a rather glamorous film star. So when he got to me – I was a fifteen- or sixteen-year-old in shorts – anything but glamorous – I told him 'Margaret Lockwood'. He said, 'Don't be cheeky young man'. I had a flat cap on as well and he thought I was a boy. Everyone was laughing and he was annoyed. In the end I said, 'You can phone my father if you like'. Yes, we had lots of good fun.

We went dancing mostly in Nelson, at the Co-op rooms. We used to have live bands. We did all the swing things, quickstep, foxtrot and so on. We went to the theatre in Burnley occasionally. And yes, the cinema as well. We would see the Pathé News 'cos there was no television.

Ian Ralston

We'd go for days out or for picnics. We went to the local amateur theatre as well, which included a certain Rita Tushingham, who lived just up the road from me. I played in a play with her once as well; that's my claim to fame. We'd go with my mum to the local drama group; my dad wasn't into that. We'd go the park, see the cousins, and we'd also go to the cinema. This was the period of the great British black-and-white movie. I remember going to see *Reach for the Sky* because I threw up. I saw that in Allerton, where cinemas were places of splendour, with fountains, marble floors, beautiful booking halls. I saw *Cockleshell Heroes* as well, all those war movies. Also films like *Genevieve*. And Westerns – I would go with my dad to see Westerns, *The Man from Laramie*, *High Noon*, and then they would be on the television every New Year's Day.

CHRIS PRIOR

An old lady lived opposite us, though she probably wasn't that old, maybe in her fifties. She was a very cultured lady – whether she did this for other people or just my mum I don't know, but she gave me piano lessons and elocution lessons. My mum was very concerned about me getting rid of this north London accent and I remember taking at least two exams in elocution and having to go to some cold church hall and recite a poem, speaking properly. But this lady was also a member of the Royal Zoological Society and she had one these magic passes that she could let other people use. Because she rarely went to the zoo she would let my parents use it, and, quite often – at least two or three times a year – we would go to Regents Park and look at animals. I loved it; you could get in at times others couldn't, like a Sunday morning, when it was guests only.

MAX EASTERMAN

We used to go to the cinema a lot. I used to go on a Saturday morning. It was a mixture of cartoons and I remember *Brick Bradford*, which I enjoyed. What I do remember about the cinema was the organ. The organ would rise out of the pit before the programme started. Of course the wonderful thing was that you got two films – a B film before the main feature and then the main feature, the A film. Some of those B movies were absolutely fascinating. They were either so bad that you couldn't believe them, or really good. I remember one at the Odeon in Harrogate that was about a girl who fell in love with an American serviceman. She had come from the slums and the American was much wealthier. You thought it was about class but in fact it was about race, though you didn't find this out until late in the film. It seemed tacky. Some of those B films are classics now – Norman Wisdom's are indeed classics, more so than the *Carry On* films, which were rubbish. I saw *Kiss Me Kate* in 3D, wearing red and green glasses. And there were those religious films like *The Robe*, *Spartacus*, *The Ten Commandments*. In later years we got more critical of these things. I saw one called *The Crimson Pirate* with Burt Lancaster. It was shot on such a low budget that when there was a shot of a pirate on the rigging, there was a cruise liner in the background.

The other thing we did a lot of was to go to the Repertory Theatre in Harrogate (the Rep we called it) to see the White Rose players. I went with a group of friends from school every Monday night. I loved it.

CHAPTER FIVE

THE WORKING MAN (. . . AND WOMAN)

1950s Britain was dominated by heavy industries, most of which had been around since the early years of the twentieth century. It could broadly be divided into half a dozen categories – coalmining, steel, textiles, shipbuilding, shipping, and manufacturing. They were the industries that had made Britain 'great', helped create the Empire, and set in motion a bustling economy. By the end of the decade the picture was pretty much the same. The heavy industries still existed although, by 1960, many of them would be under increasing threat.

In particular textiles were changing. New man-made fibres such as nylon, bri-nylon and plastic were on the market and taking the place of cotton and wool. In Lancashire and Yorkshire the mills were beginning to face closures and in the 1960s would begin to disappear. It was the same with shipping and shipbuilding. Trade was changing from West to East. The old ports of Liverpool and Glasgow were about to find themselves facing in the wrong direction. Europe was now demanding more of our goods than India, Africa and North America. Containerisation was also on the horizon, while airfreight was on the increase.

For centuries Britain had built ships, including some of the most famous names of all time, from the great Cunard liners to the naval ships that had ruled the waves. By the end of the 1950s, however, British shipyards were being challenged by countries such as Sweden and Japan. They may not have been able to build better ships but they could certainly build them cheaper and quicker, and that was beginning to count for more than quality. One by one, in the 1960s, the great shipyards of Britain would gradually close.

Coalmining and steel, however, remained dominant and whilst shipbuilding and textiles were under threat, our manufacturing base was thriving. New goods were pouring onto the market. Britain had taken its cue from America and was now producing its own television sets, vacuum cleaners, washing machines, refrigerators and, of course, cars. Car factories had long existed in the UK, principally at Trafford Park in Manchester, where there was a Ford plant, but then in the 1950s major plants elsewhere rapidly increased production and employment. The Ford plant at Dagenham in Essex had been in operation since the 1930s, steadily building a trickle of new cars, but in the 1950s, as demand increased, there was massive expansion and 50,000 were soon employed on the new assembly lines. Over the decade car ownership doubled. Wages in the car factories were good, conditions were better than working down the mines, and thousands moved south to Dagenham and elsewhere to take up work on the assembly line.

In the old heavy industries health and safety remained a major issue. The high level of deaths continued, particularly in coalmining, where eighty miners were killed in a disaster at Cresswell Colliery in Derbyshire in September 1950. Within a year another eighty-one had died at Easington in Durham, and in 1959 forty-seven were killed in a pit disaster in Ayrshire. In all, 321 miners died in serous pit accidents in the 1950s. There were also the miners who died of pneumoconiosis and other bronchial related diseases, all still unrecognised as a killer disease at that time. In shipping, Liverpool dockers went on strike over having to handle asbestos, much to the outrage of the press and employers, who insisted that it was not a problem.

Trade union membership during the 1950s soared to an all-time high up to that period of over 9 million, comprising almost half the workforce. Prior to the war, in 1938, there had been only 6 million members. In most of the large industries, being a member of a union was the norm. In industries such as coalmining, print, shipbuilding and the railways, a closed shop existed so that everyone was obliged to join their appropriate union. Union members were overwhelmingly male; few women joined, partly because of the nature of their work, much of which was part-time and in non-industrial sectors. But perhaps more importantly, the male-dominated unions saw little reason to encourage female recruitment. The unions had little to offer women and issues such as equal pay and equal rights had been barely considered, let alone taken up as campaigning issues. The Transport and General Workers' Union was by far the largest union, with a membership in 1956 of 1.2 million, followed by the Amalgamated Engineering Union, with 860,000 members. The National Union of Mineworkers had 673,000 members, while even the National Union of Railwaymen boasted 369,000 members. Those figures in themselves paint a fairly accurate picture of industrial Britain in the 1950s. There were also more than 600 trade unions, many of them small craft unions, such as the delightfully named Colne and District Power Loom Overlookers' Association. They had few members and would soon begin to disappear or merge with larger and more powerful unions. Indeed, Colne in Lancashire actually boasted four separate registered trade unions, all associated with the cotton industry. Workers were proud of their unions, supported them and gave of their time to be involved.

Most workers had to clock on, that is placing your time sheet or card into a machine, which would then record what time you had started work. Sometimes you simply had to sign in. Often you had to repeat the process when you finished. Anyone who was late would generally be docked half an hour's pay.

Those at work also tended to live close to their place of employment. There was little commuting. Cars were rare and although public transport was generally good, few would travel more than ten miles. Most people lived less than two or three miles from their workplace and either hopped on a bus or cycled. Look at any photograph of workers leaving their factories and the one thing that strikes most of all are the sheer numbers. They pour out in their hundreds, if not thousands. Major factories such at Metro Vickers at Trafford Park or a shipyard like Cammell Laird would employ upwards of 10,000 workers.

Industry was booming and, along with it, employment. As Britain emerged out of post-war austerity there was full employment by the end of the decade. Astonishingly, most trade unions also paid an unemployment benefit to their members, a good indication that unemployment was low. Indeed, throughout the 1950s unemployment rarely rose above 2 per cent, which was the standard level for an active, fully employed economy. Anyone out of work would be sure to find alternative employment in a matter of weeks, making long-term unemployment something that belonged to the 1930s. School-leavers never had to wait around for a job to appear, there was always three or four opportunities.

But despite booming opportunities in the British economy, many looked abroad for a new life. Australia, New Zealand and Canada all offered financial incentives and the prospect of better opportunities. And the British seized the chance in their thousands. Sailing from Liverpool, London and elsewhere to the new world and beyond was all made possible by the £10 passage. It was a new life – sunshine, better homes, a new culture, more opportunities. For many it worked out well, for others it was not so easy. They missed Britain, family and friends, and soon returned.

But while many thousands emigrated, many more thousands came to Britain to find work, often to fill in where there were now shortages. Hospitals, transport, the mills – all cried out for workers and offered a far better way of life than currently experienced in their own third world countries. They came initially from the West Indies, the first ship, the *Windrush*, arriving at London's Tilbury docks in 1948. But of course Britain was not the land of milk and honey that they had imagined or even been promised. There may have been jobs but accommodation was not always easy to find. At first they were welcomed but as numbers grew, so attitudes began to change, and racism soon reared its ugly head.

For women, however, work was often very different. During the war years women had been employed on assembly lines at munitions factories, had served in the armed forces, had run hospitals, and so forth. But once war was over, there was a return to 'normality'. Many women might have gone on to higher education, and those who did generally settled into teaching. But once they began a family their occupations took a back seat. There was little or no nursery provision in those days and indeed many employers frowned upon women with young families being out at work. Teachers, for example, were not allowed to work once they were pregnant. And for many husbands, a wife at work was not the kind of status symbol they wanted. It looked bad, as if you couldn't afford to keep a wife. And certainly once they had a family many husbands did as much as they could to persuade their wives to remain at home.

Very few people went on to university – as little as eight per cent of six-formers. Most of those leaving school and entering employment in the 1950s started life with an apprenticeship. This was a five-year attachment to a trade, such as electrician, draughtsman, fitter or plumber. It provided a solid grounding in the trade and often with night-school classes leading to an official qualification.

The whole white-collar area was also beginning to mushroom. There were more office jobs, particularly in clerical and administrative work. And for women this was an area of huge potential and in the 1960s, as attitudes changed, women would pour onto the job market and particularly in the office as secretaries, typists and clerks.

NEIL KINNOCK

My father and grandfather worked down the mine, and all my uncles, on both my mother's and father's side, were all, at some time, miners. My father was the elite – he was a coal hewer, a face captain, and he worked in the pit for twenty-seven years. He had to leave because he had industrial dermatitis and it nearly broke his heart. He thought that to be a coalminer at the front of the face and leading the men was the finest thing a man could do. He was furious when I applied for a mining management apprenticeship – I never took it up because of the scale of opposition from my parents. For him, being a coalminer was a wonderful endeavour and a real profession, but he would have closed the pit rather than let me go down there. My uncles, with one exception on my father's side, all escaped the pit mainly because of the Depression, when Tredegar experienced 65 and 70 per cent unemployment in the late 1920s and early 1930s. Two of them went off to become prize-fighters and ended up as steelworkers in Lincolnshire, in Scunthorpe, and one became an electrical engineer in Welwyn Garden City. The youngest one, Billy, was the only one who managed to get to college, teacher training college. He volunteered for the forces in July 1939, when he left the teacher training college and went through the ranks and ended the war as an officer in the army in India. Other than him ours was a typical working-class family with a diaspora that produced wonderful Christmas reunions, utterly dependable, flawlessly honest, tough men and, in a way, much tougher women because, of course, they bore the brunt of everything. But they were gentleness itself in their conduct. They were solid steel, they really were.

PHILIP LLOYD

Most people worked at Trafford Park, many at Metro Vicks and all the other factories there. Or, if they were office workers, they'd go into Manchester. We had one coalminer nearby, probably from a mine in North Manchester or East Manchester, I'm not sure exactly where. His wife and family came to the church. Trafford Park was a huge industrial estate and, of course, was one of the main targets during the war. They made aircraft and munitions there and so forth. After the war they converted back to building civil aircraft, electrical goods and installations. We used to get huge boilers being driven from Trafford Park through Chorlton. They had to choose a route where they didn't have to go under railway bridges. When we went to church early on a Sunday morning you'd see these things crawling along at about three miles an hour.

Ian Ralston

My father, like many at that time in Liverpool, worked in the shipping business, for Coast Lines, and he was a clerk in wages or accounts. My mum, like most mums, did not work, at least while we were in the early stages of growing up. But she did go back to work when my youngest brother was ten or eleven. She worked as a comptometer operator, a job that has now entirely disappeared. She had been a teacher in a comptometer school and then worked for a construction company in Speke. Our house was a semi-detached with a garden, which was my dad's pride and joy. It seemed to be a comfortable time, though money was tight for them. The aspirations were there but not necessarily the money.

Bobby Charlton

I lodged in a big house close to the ground. It was no more than a mile from Old Trafford. Of course in those days none of us had cars, we went everywhere by public transport, so our digs had to be near the ground. Most of the time we would walk to and from Old Trafford. There were twelve of us in this house. Remember that I was an amateur at first. I couldn't turn professional until I was seventeen, so I had to get myself a job. I worked as an electrical engineer in Altrincham for eighteen months, then I turned professional.

Old Trafford was very different then. There was only one end that was covered and that was the Main Stand. The Stretford End and the City End were both open and there was just a small covering on the North Stand. I used to train at Old Trafford every day. We had a little hut outside the ground where we would go for treatment – that's how basic it was in those days. Then I would go to The Cliff to train on a Tuesday and Thursday evening.

Being a footballer then was not like it is now. The fans and the media were not as intrusive. We had to travel everywhere by bus but you didn't get hassled like players would now. We could go anywhere. I'd go to games at Maine Road, Bolton or Birmingham, get a ticket and stand on the terraces. No player could do that these days. We just mixed in with everybody. Of course we didn't have much spare time. I worked from 8 a.m. to 5.30 p.m. and then went to train. We didn't have much money either. But we would occasionally go to the pictures on a Monday or a Wednesday evening, down town, or to some coffee bar. But because we didn't have the money we didn't have a lot of choice, usually just the pictures.

STEVE HALE

During the war my dad was a ships' engineer in the Merchant Navy, working down in the engine rooms. He was with Cunard for a while and then on another line. He had been to South America and done the Archangel run during the war, bringing all the supplies back. I remember, years later, him telling me how lucky he was to be here. He had been on a convoy going out to Archangel and on the way out it was discovered that he had chickenpox, which was very contagious, so they put him off at Archangel and he spent three weeks in hospital there, but the ship he came on got torpedoed on the way back and everyone on board was lost.

When he was with Cunard he was on the *Queen Elizabeth* and he brought all the yanks over for D-Day. I didn't see him at times after the war as he was still away so my mum and nan brought me up. When he came back to Liverpool he had a hard time finding a job, but eventually he was offered a job in Rugby, so we moved down there. There was a lot more work in the Midlands because of the car and engineering factories, so we went down there and lived in a little two-up two-down terraced house for a short while. Then I got scarlet fever. It floored my mum. She was looking for any excuse to come back and my having scarlet fever gave her a good excuse, so we came back to Liverpool.

At the beginning of the 1950s my dad worked in a bakery. I remember the smell. He had problems getting a job in engineering but he got this job fixing machines in a bakery, the Mothers Pride bakery. It was night work. It was the only job he could get at the time. I think that's what led to him to go off to Rugby to get work, because there was so little up here. When we came back from Rugby he got a job at a firm called Connolly's, and he was there for the rest of his working life. It was a big wire-manufacturing company, copper wire, heavy duty wire for cables that go under the sea.

DEV SINGH UPPAL

My grandad came in 1937, my dad came in 1954, and I came in 1958. I was only eighteen years old when I came and I started work in John Cotton, Mirfield. We all lived in Huddersfield but worked there because my uncle worked there. We would get the bus then. Not many people had a car and I would work twelve-hour shifts. After that I went to a foundry and worked there, on the fitted shop floor The reason I left John Cotton was because the shifts were long and it took time to get to Mirfield, but I did return to John Cotton as the shifts went down to eight hours but I got paid for twelve. I eventually had to stop because I got injured. You had to put oil in a cylinder and mix it with water and spray so the wool doesn't fly about. You'd spray them so they would fold. The cylinder had oil in it. It went to three or four machines and someone put more water in it and forgot to turn it off. The oil spread on the floor and I slipped. I couldn't get up. I was off for a few months and then that was it.

ANTHONY HANDBURY

I finally got my big chance and went to work for a polishing company, making polish for dance floors, parquet, wood flooring. Quite a lot of places like churches and dancehalls had parquet flooring. Places like the Ritz. We used to supply the Ritz because they had a massive dance floor there. We didn't put the polish on, we just supplied the tins of it. I used to make the polish to a secret formula. There were a few dancehalls around Manchester but the Ritz was the biggest. There was one on Plymouth Grove, where they played orchestrated jazz. Stan Kenton was the big name then. I didn't go to dance, just to hang about and listen to the music. I couldn't dance. I didn't particularly like rock and roll. It wasn't my kind of music.

I worked at the polish job for about two years. After that I got into selling – selling things for offices – typewriter ribbons, carbon paper – I did that until about 1970.

JOAN WOOD

I was teaching at a school in Stockport called Avondale Secondary Modern. It was a local authority school, mixed. I was teaching science. I'd been to Manchester University, where I met my husband. He'd been in the RAF and then gone to the university and we met on the teaching diploma course. I had done physics and chemistry. People think that was unusual in those days but it wasn't so unusual, there was one girl there doing engineering. In fact there were quite a lot of girls in the science department. In those days you got a free place if you were bright.

We got married in 1949. I was teaching until 1952. I had a baby then. I stayed at home with my two children. It wasn't altogether unusual for women to go back to work, if they could get somebody to mind the kids. Before that I think women used to have to leave when they got married as teachers. I think it probably changed during the war. No, I don't think husbands liked to see wives working. I think most of my friends thought mum should stay at home and look after the kids.

MARY JAMES

Coming to Birkenhead from Bradford was a huge change. My father had been very ill in Bradford with a duodenal ulcer. We were living in this lovely area in Bradford. I remember coming to see Birkenhead and wondering what it was going to be like, how was I going to make friends. Birkenhead itself was rundown, the YMCA was very rundown, the whole place, and I was going to live in the centre of town. I was going to a school that was close but it was so different. The YMCA had only been built in the 1930s but I think it had had some bomb damage. Birkenhead YMCA was clearly failing but my father turned it around. He did it. We were living in the building and when I looked out of the window of my old bedroom I could see the lights in the distance of Bradford, it was beautiful. The Birkenhead flat was small, albeit four-bed. There was no garden; we used to have a vegetable patch in Bradford as well as a garden. My mother did build a garden on the roof of the YMCA but it was very different. My brother had got a place at Bradford Grammar School and had even bought the uniform but then he had to go to the Birkenhead School. It was a tremendous difference. The only plus side initially was that we had beautiful views of Liverpool and the Liver Building from our sitting room. At New Year all the boats would sound their sirens to welcome in the New Year. We had some involvement with the Cammell Laird Shipyard in Birkenhead, which was originally Gilchrist Cammell Laird, and the Gilchrists were a part of our family. We would go there when ships were being launched. They were a huge employer

The other thing I remember when we first went was an old chap who was the night porter. He always brought tea in the morning for the family. I thought he was a great old bloke but he had this thing on the side where he was selling space to anyone who was homeless. My father had to deal with that.

There was this old Irishwoman who was in charge of the hostel. The curtains weren't up properly apart from the room of Patrick York, who was a gentleman and paid for about three rooms. The other rooms were pretty awful.

JOAN FINCH

During the week my main job was sewing, I was a raincoat machinist at Greengate and Irwell and then we went on four days a week as no one wanted any raincoats. My daughter Janice was born in 1954 and then Diane a few years later, in 1957. I stopped working when I had the children. I did some evening work, sewing, but Bill said I had enough work with the children.

PHILIP LLOYD

At the beginning of the 1950s I started working at the shop. It was a stationery – fancy goods, greeting cards, toys, games and a sub post office, although at that time I wasn't working in the post office. The shop was owned by my father and before him my grandfather. My grandfather had opened it in 1909, when it was built. I continued to work in the shop having left school the previous summer, in 1949, when I was fifteen. I worked there from then until I finished in 1990.

The shop was quite busy in those days and it wasn't always easy work. Down the years we had lots of problems, particularly in the war years. Things were picking up in the 1950s though. Quite a lot of people would shop locally rather than go into town. In the small row of shops here we had a shoe shop, a baker, bank, dairy, hairdresser, Boots the chemist, a butchers, grocers, sweet shop, haberdashery, almost everything. No mans outfitters' though, you had to go into Chorlton for that. We sold newspapers as well, and cigarettes. We sold many more papers that you see today. The *Daily Express* was the most popular. *The Mail* was popular as well and the *Guardian*. We sold a few *Daily Heralds* but not a lot – not many labour people here then, mainly liberal or conservative.

My grandfather had lost both his legs through disease. He couldn't get upstairs to the flat so he went to live in a ground-floor flat not far away. He came in on a motorchair through the back and went around the shop in his chair. But he was a very jolly sort of person. I worked in the shop throughout the 1950s and just had three years away in the Air Force, from 1952 to 1955.

Once I was back in Civvie Street it was back to working in the shop. In the meantime my grandfather had died. My father and I worked together then until well beyond the 1950s. As I was over twenty-one, I then worked in the post office more. We used to get some of the footballers from Manchester United come in. It wasn't that far from Old Trafford. Matt Busby lived in Chorlton so he had to pass the shop on his way home, and we were probably the nearest post office to Old Trafford anyway. Matt and his son, Sandy, came in with parcels to send off. I didn't know the footballers as I was not interested in football. After they'd gone the assistants would say, 'Do you know who that was?' and when they told me I'd say, 'Oh really!'

MICHAEL MCCUTCHEON

I went back to Northern Ireland at twelve, in the mid-1950s. I can't remember why I went back for the love of me. Two of my sisters moved to the seaside with their jobs; that would have been the mid-1950s. They demolished all the old houses and we had new ones with more room. Dad was a wagon driver, making new roads, he drove for a contractor. I went to another Catholic school to finish off. But I had to go out and earn a living when I was fourteen. In the summer I'd be dodging school, picking potatoes in the fields to earn a few bob, but the school never bothered much. At fourteen I got a position in the Co-op, the Northern Ireland Co-op, filling bags. Everything was loose in those days; I was filling up paper bags with sugar, tea. I should have stayed there but the money was lousy. If I had stayed I might have got to work in the shops. I then went to the brickworks just out of town; they made bricks, pipes for drainage. I stayed there for a few years, but that ran down, bringing in plastic and so on, and I was made redundant. That's when I took up decorating. I knew a decorator so I went with him. I'd be about sixteen and a half. I went with him for three years. He was another one fond of the booze. We did a lot of work in pubs and he'd drink while he was there and there'd be no money left. But I learnt a lot.

JOAN MATTHEWS

I was born in 1929. I graduated in 1950 when I was twenty-one. I had a London degree, which I had taken at Southampton University. I moved back to my parents' house in Farnborough and it wasn't long before I got married. I did teach for a term and then took a new exam for the London County Council (LCC). I had the option of working for the Civil Service or the LCC. I chose the LCC because I did not want to leave London. They were excellent employers. I started with a one-off job, helping to produce proof of evidence for a public inquiry. It was an inquiry into the purchase of land in Hertfordshire where the LCC wanted to build a big housing estate. And indeed when they did eventually build this housing estate, the very interesting thing about it was that there had been a gentleman's agreement before the war about the purchase of this land. Well, as you know, gentleman's agreements are not necessarily written down but this was well understood to be a gentleman's agreement and so the contract went through. My life was maps and talking to surveyors and people like that.

The job was very interesting. The big question mark was the edge of the estate, where it faced onto a big road, and on the other side of the road were some very expensive houses and those people objected to the council estate most of all. So the LCC agreed to build a certain number of what they called higher income group houses so that from the road it looked a bit more upmarket than the rest of the estate. I was told when I first went into the office to do this work that I ought to get to know a bit about the background to LCC housing, because, under the terms of the 1936 Housing Act, only the LCC and Birmingham City Council were entitled to purchase land compulsorily. All other authorities had to negotiate with the vendors.

But the LCC could purchase compulsorily so it was a rather special situation. For example, the Dagenham Estate was on compulsorily purchased land and the first thing that the person in charge told me to do was to read through a big volume of applications for houses. It really pulled the heartstrings because there were hundreds of letters from very poor people living in the most appalling slums hoping to get a home. I remember an absolutely typical one: 'I am a train driver with four children and I earn ten shillings a week and I promise faithfully that I will never miss the rent.' And the interesting thing was that people did not falter with the rent, but there was a lot of malnutrition. I suspect people paid their rent before they fed their children.

After that I moved into the housing department. I didn't have to go there but I wanted to. I went to the office in Bethnal Green, which was called the Eastern District Office, where we dealt with applications and tenants and housing problems in Stepney and Bethnal Green and Hackney. That was very much a working office. There were an awful lot of bombsites in the area. When we compulsory purchased land in East London, all that happened was that a surveyor went out with a pole with a notice on saying 'This land has been compulsorily purchased. If you are the owner or know the owner apply for compensation at County Hall. Land value £20'! Unfortunately, the houses that did remain were all those awful Peabody buildings. They were strong enough to stand up to the bombs. They have now been very much gentrified. I remember we had a big gentrification programme in a block very close to the City and they have become luxury flats now. Any rate, that was my first job and I really, really liked it.

TREVOR CREASER

I finished school in 1957 at sixteen. I got an apprenticeship at Greenwood and Batleys; they built all sorts of machines – turbines, ammunition, armaments and employed 4,700 alongside the canal. I was on an engineering apprenticeship that lasted five years and I worked in every department. I had a marvellous time but I couldn't get in the drawing office because in those days it was not what you knew, it was who you knew.

JOHN HENDERSON

I played at Wembley in 1956. We got £4 because we lost, can you imagine that? People just don't believe it. We went in the big hotel in Oxford Street in London and what I got paid didn't pay for my round of drinks that night. If we had won I would have got £9. I got £52 when I played with Workington in 1952 and we won Featherstone. We lost against St Helens in 1956 and it was £4. At that time, it's hard to say this, but we really weren't in the game for money. It was OK though, a nice little lift, you could work as well as you weren't full-time professional and if you got that added work pay it wasn't too bad. But you had to train Tuesday and Thursday night. We were not as fit as they are now, obviously they train full-time, in gyms every day.

I did all sorts of jobs. I had to have a job where I could get time off to go training, so I worked for Halifax Corporation, labouring actually on houses and crawling about on roofs with slates. I could have gone to a gym and trained everyday and done it that way, but money was not the sole thing then that you played for, you played for your town. Not a lot of transfers went on because all the teams paid more or less the same wages, so there wasn't a lot of point in upheaval and going to play for another club unless something happened and you fell out. You weren't consulted as much as you are now. The offer came in and you were told about it. There were no contracts then, or agents. You just signed on for the club. You were there for life once you signed that, there was no two, three-year jobs, that was it.

I went on the 1954 Great Britain rugby league tour to Australia and it took four days flying and we were absolutely shattered. In those days you went in March and you came back in August. Took three weeks to get over it. We weren't ill but it took three weeks to get back to full steam. I'd never been on a plane in my life, never, not a great lot of people had in '54. The captain said to us, 'Now, Rome is our first stop.' Well Rome is nothing now – two or three hours. He said, 'When we take off, it'll be just like a car, the engine will appear to stop at a certain point but don't worry, it'll pick up again.' I've not been so bloody scared in my life. I had forgotten what he said when the engine stopped and of course your heart's in your mouth isn't it.

We stopped in India, Pakistan, Thailand, Singapore – you name it. We came back the other way, via Fiji, Hawaii, San Francisco, Chicago and back across the Atlantic. Up down, up down. That's what knocked you up, the buffeting – it wasn't the flying itself.

JOAN MATTHEWS

I didn't have any problems as a woman in work but I think there was a little bit of suspicion, not because I was a woman but because I went in at a senior level. It was the first year they had graduate entry. Before then people had taken the standard Civil Service or LCC exams and moved up. So I went into the office in Bethnal Green and I was the only graduate there, but not the only woman. There were quite a lot of women. The LCC really looked after its staff. We had two women who had been badly injured during the war. They had been severely disfigured. They kept their jobs and they expected us all to help them along. A lot of the porters were ex-servicemen who had been injured in the war.

There were cellars under County Hall with baths. On a Friday all the girls in the offices used to flock down there, have a bath, have their hair done, and then go up to the West End.

JOHN HECTORBALL

I was born in April 1937. I left school in 1953, when I was sixteen. My father had twins by another woman, so he left home. It was very difficult for my mum; she got £4 a week for her maintenance and £1 for me. She managed quite well until I left school, and then she only got £4 a week and nothing for me. Divorces did happen in those days. They got divorced many years later; however, she was bitter and wouldn't allow a divorce for a long time. Financially it caused problems. I was at Burnage Grammar School, I passed the eleven plus. There were about six hundred at the school. It wasn't very strict; I got the strap a few times, a leather strap. Before that I was at Birchfield Secondary Modern. After school I got a job in textiles at a company called Barlow and Jones, in a big building on Princess Street. My job was humping – humping pieces and sending out invoices. It was not an apprenticeship. I was there for about four years. I didn't enjoy it. I wasn't good at it and there was no future in it. It was boring, no prospects.

My father later wrote a letter and I got a job at Metro Vicks in Trafford Park – an engineering company – and I was taken in as an apprentice in mechanical engineering. It was a huge company, twenty thousand in the main works and ten thousand more scattered around Manchester. They had facilities, it had a good name. We were making generating equipment and steam turbines and electric motors, transformers. I enjoyed my time there. I was there five or six years.

I joined the Communist Party but my workmates thought it was odd, they knew it wouldn't get anywhere. Jimmy Reid was another apprentice; he was an engineer in shipbuilding. He was a good orator. I knew some people from Liverpool, Ken and Joe Bush. I was in the engineering union, later in the AESD (Association of Engineering and Shipbuilding Draughtsmen) union. I later trained in the drawing office and was a draughtsman. I wasn't very good though. This was at Metro Vicks. After my apprenticeship I went into the drawing office.

JOHN PALMER

When I got back from the army I went down the dole office and the only job they offered me was working down the mines. Of course I could have gone down the mines rather than go into the army in the first place. I got on my bike and went round the factories. I was riding down the Dagenham Road and I saw the fire station and there was this guy sweeping up outside and I thought, I know you. So I stopped, asked him how he was, what he was doing and so on, and we got talking. I said, 'I'm looking for work'. He said, 'Why don't you come and join the Fire Brigade?' He told me all about it and I said it sounded interesting. 'I'll get you a form,' he said. We went into the office and got a form. I filled it in, had a written test and a few other tests, then they got this 60-foot turntable ladder to make sure I wasn't worried by heights. You hook yourself on and then they shoot you up 60 feet. When you look down, argh! It's swaying as well. Anyway, they brought me down and it was satisfactory. They run a school in Dagenham so I had some time there learning stuff. It paid £5 five shillings a week. It was quite well paid, same as the police. It was a good job, it was like a family, and we all looked after each other. There were always Christmas parties, parties for the children.

WIN HINDLE

I was born in September 1931 in Gorton in Manchester. I was nineteen in 1950. I was working at Thomas Hope and Sankey Hudsons in Manchester. They were printers and they made writing pads, envelopes, books for schools, and jigsaws. I was going out with George, who worked there as an apprentice. My job was putting the covers on the writing pads, using the guillotine, glueing and packing. Hundreds worked there. It was very old-fashioned and we had a very old-fashioned supervisor. You were not allowed to breathe. If you went to the toilet you'd come back and she'd be saying 'Quick, quick, quick,' and clapping her hands. You had to clock on in a morning when you arrived and when you went. You had a card and you put it in the machine and pulled a handle and it recorded the time, so if you were late you were docked some of your wages. Sometimes I sneaked in.

After that I went to Kirkham and Pratt – they did books for education – all education stuff, it was another printers. I was there for the Coronation. After I was married I came out with about £3 four shillings a week, it was about 21 pence an hour – it was quite good that. Eight o'clock in the morning to five thirty at night.

I left school at fourteen and went straight into work. My mother met me from school and we went down to the labour exchange. I got five shillings and my mother gave me two shillings. Your money did seem to go further. You did seem to have more. You didn't want for things as much then.

My dad used to say you put makeup on only if you were ugly or, if you put perfume on, he'd say it was 'cos you smelt!

Mike Prior

Dad was a shop steward. My parents were both active communists. Both had been born into humble circumstances and both had bettered themselves by going to evening classes. Dad had left school at fourteen and gone to work in the local Co-op. Mum had won a scholarship to the Latimer School but had to leave at fifteen because her father was unemployed, and, though she had a scholarship, she had to go out and earn money. Both had educated themselves at evening classes. Dad became a certified accountant. When he came back after the war he took up teaching at the Regent Street polytechnic and taught students. My mother took a science degree at Holloway Road, then Northern Polytechnic. In the early 1950s she trained as a teacher and taught mathematics in a girls' school. So by the 1950s both were teachers.

Dennis Gilligan

I was born in 1930 in Salford and was living there in 1950, when I was twenty years of age. I've lived there all my life. I first started work as an upholsterer, in Eccles. I was there about twelve months, then I went somewhere else after six months to get more money. I was told you'll never make an upholsterer; anyway, I did it for sixty years. I must have been okay. It was about making furniture. I loved it, making three-piece suites – I was very good at it. And that's got a lot to do with it, enjoying your work. But I had no problems. I also worked for myself for twelve years in Ancoats. The firm I was with was in Salford and in Manchester. It was a big firm, a Jewish firm. I loved it there.

Steve Hale

I started getting into photography when I went to St Swithins. I'd been pigeonholed, I guess, and they were pushing me at what I was good at, the arty stuff. A teacher there – Mr Connor – recognised things in me and he just brought a camera in one day and I got interested in it. He was a great guy and he said. 'If you look after it, I'll let you take some pictures with it'. Then one day he said, 'I've got something for you to do. I want you to go outside, look around to see if there is anything interesting that catches your eye. and take some pictures'. And I did, it was only black and white. And the next time I remember he let me take the camera home but made me promise to look after it, and if I broke it my parents would have to pay for damages. But I did look after it and I took some pictures and that was my first introduction to photography. I then persuaded my mum and dad to get me a camera for my birthday and I've still got it, it's a 127 Brownie Kodak and it was 17/6d (in decimal currency this would be 75p). It makes me quite emotional thinking about it. It's because of that camera and Mr Connor that I got in photography. My dad used to say, 'All his pictures come out.' He never used to say, 'He's a good photographer,' it was always, 'He's good with the camera, they all come out.' You know, when you took pictures then, half of them didn't come out. Anyhow that's what set me on the road to becoming a photographer.

MARGARET WILLIAMS

I went to a school in Colne. It was a junior school. I enjoyed it very much as it was my first effort at earning a living. I have always been interested in the countryside and there was a hill behind us and if I felt like it and I felt the children had earned it, I would down tools and take them up the hill. There were Roman ruins up there. It would also get rid of any high spirits that the children might have. It was much freer then. We didn't have a national curriculum then, which in some ways was bad as we didn't cater for everyone's needs, but I think the children were happy. They were mostly children of mill workers – mainly working class, although some had shops. We also had a good number of gypsy children who came in the winter and then went off with their families in the spring. They were lovely children. We had quite a mix really. I think it was quite a popular school.

JOHN STILE

The overhead railway was a great favourite. It was commonly known as the Dockers' Umbrella because it was used by dockers going to work and back. It ran the entire length of the Liverpool docks, from Bootle to the Dingle, about seven or eight miles. It really was fantastic and was called the overheard railways because it was at a height of about 100 foot or more. If you ever go to New York you can see that the subway in parts is a bit like the overhead railway. There were stops for every dock. Unfortunately, when the docks went into decline, people stopped using the railway and it fell into disuse, so they pulled it down. What a sad day that was. I remember going on it once in the early 1950s, when the liner the *Empress of Canada* was lying on its side in Canada dock. It had caught fire in one of the docks and capsized onto its side. It was completely burned out. This massive liner was just lying there in this dock on its side, smoke coming out of it, and when you went on the overhead railway you had this spectacular view of it. They later had real problems in righting it and I think they held a competition for someone to come up with an idea about how to upright it.

BRIAN HULME

My father disapproved of wives who went to work, but my mum eventually rebelled and got a job in the ladies' underwear department of Kendal's Department Store – a supposedly high-class establishment in Manchester. He went ballistic, but it didn't stop her – she made her bid for freedom.

From the age of fifteen I worked in the summer holidays, at first on the market gardens of Ashton Moss, doing manual work to earn pocket money. When I went into the Sixth Form in 1958, I worked in the Christmas holidays too, at Lewis's in Manchester, in the poultry department. People would order a turkey in advance, to be collected before Christmas. It involved going into large cold-rooms, then being horribly obsequious to prize a tip out of the customer, for example by jangling loose change in your pocket and saying 'Happy Christmas!' in a jolly, confidential voice.

VERONICA PALMER

In 1950 I would have been seventeen years of age. I was living in Hornchurch in Essex with my parents and I was working in a tailoring factory. I had left school at fourteen and I went straight into the factory. I was a machinist, making skirts, suits, and things like that. It was very nice. It was a brand new factory. In those days most factories were a bit grim, but this one was all bright, and we had music and it was all young people. So I was fourteen when I went there and I stayed most of the time until I got married at twenty. The music was always fast music so that we didn't slow down while we were working; it was all beautiful music from the shows, like *Oklahoma!* and that kind of show. It was a nice place to work. Many people had bad experiences at work in those days but I didn't. I worked from eight in morning until six at night, five days a week, and on a Saturday from eight to twelve noon, and even though I was only fourteen, I never thought it was terrible. You wouldn't dream of letting a fourteen-year-old do that today. I think I got £1 25s a week, I gave my mum a pound and I had five shillings to myself. My mum didn't ask for any money, I was just delighted to give it her. She wasn't well-off but she never asked, ever, for any more. I worked until I was twenty and got increasing wages, but I doubt I ever got more than £3. It went a long way in those days.

JOHN STILE

Work conditions were improving in the 1950s and it was certainly better than it had been before the war, but they still weren't great. Every morning I had to clock-on. By that I mean I had a time card and I had to insert this card into a machine with a clock on it and it recorded the time I had arrived. Then, in an evening, I had to do the same again. At the end of the week I handed my card in so that they could see how many hours I had worked. If I had arrived late any day I would have half an hour's pay docked from my wage packet. I'd be working on average about forty, maybe forty-four hours a week. Then, some weeks, there might be overtime on top of that.

I also remember that there were a lot more accidents at work then. I remember a steel cable from a ship, which tied it to the quay, snapped one day and took three or four blokes out. All dead. There was also asbestos. It was imported by ship and docker's were expected to unload it. There were no safety conditions and at first nobody thought asbestos was dangerous, but then when it became apparent that it was, dangerous docker's were *still* expected to unload it. They went on strike at one point and were heavily criticised. But it wasn't until they started doing that that the people began to think, yeah maybe it is dangerous. Nowadays you wouldn't go near asbestos unless you were wearing a massive protective suit and helmet. And then it would only be done by a specialist company. It was pretty strict at work as well. You'd get shouted out and so on. No bullying charges were allowed then! They started time and motion studies as well. Someone would come around with a stopwatch to see how long it took you do a certain job. They'd stand over you clicking this watch and writing stuff on a clipboard. It made you feel like you were being spied on.

GEOFF WRIGHT

All the players worked in local jobs. Alvin Ackerley – he was a drayman for Whitaker's brewery. [Alvin Ackerley was a Halifax and Great Britain rugby league player of the 1940s and '50s.] When we were going to school Alvin would be there on the dray wagons and we'd see him in the streets. Les Pearce, Ronnie James, Jon Thorley all came from Wales but they married and made their homes here and they became local people. Because they worked locally, you knew them; you saw them in the street, you looked up to them and you maybe aspired to be one of them. They were part-time pros but they played in big stadiums, played at Wembley; what a fantastic thing to play at Wembley or Maine Road, Manchester, when you could get fifty, sixty thousand for a Championship Final yet they were working alongside you, they worked in engineering shops. I never actually worked with any of the players but I knew Charlie Renaldson very well because he came in the pub. We watched *Match of the Day* on a Saturday night and his wife Thelma and my wife Val they'd be in one corner having a natter and we'd be in the other corner watching *Match of the Day*, cursing and swearing at the television.

Malanka Salivic played for Bradford and Wakefield but he had the chippy down road, then he bought a milk van and he was my in-laws milkman. This guy had played in two Wembley Cup finals and yet he's delivering milk. They were part of the community; you could rub shoulders with these people.

VERONICA PALMER

I stopped work when I got married. Married women never worked. If a woman did work it didn't look good. When we had three children and we didn't have a lot of money, I said I'd go back to work but John said, 'No don't go back to work, 'cos if you do it'll look like I can't keep you. It'll look bad.'

Things were different for women. It was better for my generation than it had been for my mother's. I was lucky enough in that I had John. He wasn't a drinker, he was good with the children and he would never sit down while I was doing things, he would always be helping. But not all families were like that. In the average family the man would come home from work and his dinner would be on the table, but John was never like that. He'd come home and would help me.

OLGA HALON

My husband had the gents' outfitters at the time, so bringing up a family in the 1950s was not difficult for me. There were four brothers. They had twenty-seven shops at one point, had them all over the country – Shrewsbury, Newcastle and Manchester. They had four shops in Manchester at one time, one on Oxford Road, one on Deansgate, one on Portland Street and one in Church Street. They were all called Halon. Now there's just one son who has one in Shrewsbury.

JAMIL AKHTAR

I lived on Bradford Road. I think there was six people in three bedrooms – two to a room – the toilet was outside and there was no bathroom, so you'd have to go to the baths to have a bath. It was quite overcrowded. If you went to the toilet you'd have to put Wellingtons on, because it really snowed in those days. So it was quite a harsh life. Obviously there was no jobs in those days, they did not accept qualifications from Pakistan, the only jobs were on the buses or the mills, there was no other jobs anywhere. I went into the mill as a trainee designer of textiles, but I left there and then came to the buses as a conductor. There was a shortage of drivers in those days, so they made me a driver. I would start at five o'clock and finish at one o'clock at night – and the wages you were paid! I went to a union meeting and they said, 'Why don't you stand, if you think you can do the job?' and there was an election, somebody proposed my name and I became shop steward. When I stood in the 1970s for secretary, some inspector said that they would leave the job; they would not accept any instruction from a black person. That was where the racism was. When I was elected, obviously I was surprised, never mind anybody else. I think I was probably the first Asian secretary in the North of England, and the transport workers union was in those days the largest union.

CHAPTER SIX

THE BOX IN THE CORNER

If you had to pinpoint a specific date on which British television came of age it would have to be Tuesday, 2 June 1953, the day of Queen Elizabeth II's Coronation. Television may well have been introduced to the UK before the war but in reality, only a handful of sets were ever available and you not only had to be fairly wealthy to be able to afford one but also live in London, close to the BBC transmitter. The development of television was delayed due to the war but once hostilities had ceased, the BBC began to slowly progress output. The range of transmission, however, was still limited, usually to just London or the Home counties. So while television may have continued to grow after the war, it was slow. What's more, there were far more important goods needing to be produced than televisions.

The 1948 Olympic Games had been shown on television, which in itself was a landmark event and which, incidentally, cost the BBC a mere £1,000 for transmission rights. New outside broadcast vehicles were used for the first time along with an innovative range of cameras, each with three lenses. In all, more than sixty hours of coverage was devoted to the Games, though limited to athletics, boxing and swimming. But despite the BBC's massive input into the Games, only 50,000 homes were within range and able to receive pictures. The technology was there to manage the transmission but two essential ingredients were still missing. First, the ability to transmit the pictures to far corners of Britain and, second, a television set in every home. By 1953, however, all this was beginning to change. What was needed was another major event, like the Olympics. The Coronation provided just such an event.

Manufacturers responded to the challenge and a welter of sets was produced for the UK market. A new 17-inch television was introduced and television licenses increased from two million to three million during the year. But before the Coronation there was the FA Cup final, and although it was not the first FA Cup final to be shown on television (they had in fact been shown since 1937), it attracted by far the largest live audience to that date. What's more the appearance of the great Stanley Matthews, playing for Blackpool against Lancashire rivals Bolton Wanderers, promised a sporting event of such importance that the combination of this and the Coronation had thousands rushing to the shops to purchase their first television sets. Neither event would disappoint. At Wembley on May 2nd, Stanley Matthews finally picked up an FA Cup winner's medal. Three goals to one down late into the second half, Matthews inspired his team-mates to a memorable 4–3 victory in what has often been described as the greatest Cup final ever.

The Coronation proved to be even more spectacular. Many interviewees in this book vividly recall watching the Coronation on television, not least because of the length the coverage lasted. It began at 10.15 a.m. and went on until 11.30 p.m. that evening, when a firework display rounded off the day.

Initially, Prime Minister Winston Churchill and his Cabinet had been strongly opposed to the BBC's request to show the event, arguing that it would be enough of an ordeal for the young Queen without all the lights, cameras and paraphernalia of television. But when Churchill relayed his Cabinet's decision to Her Majesty at one of their weekly meetings, she politely reminded him that it was she who was being crowned and not the Cabinet. She wanted her people to see the event, and they would.

But of course, many people did not have televisions and could not afford them. The solution was simple. This was an event of such importance that those families with televisions flung open their doors to friends and neighbours. A steady stream passed through most houses where there was a set, enjoying a cup of tea, a sandwich and slice of cake whilst watching the dramatic pictures being beamed from London. For many people this was the first time they had ever watched television. Coverage, however, was not universal. In large parts of the nation, such as Northern Ireland, Scotland and Wales there was no coverage, with no transmitters able to relay the pictures.

By the end of 1953, Britain was well on its way to becoming a television-viewing nation. Over the remainder of the decade a steady stream of unforgettable programmes would be unleashed on the British public. Initially there were many American imports such *I Love Lucy*, *I Married Joan* and the inimitable Sergeant Bilko. But gradually the BBC built up a stock of its own comedy masterpieces, with comedians like Tony Hancock, Benny Hill and Harry Worth. There were also outstanding dramas that would include *The Quatermass Experiment*, *Dixon of Dock Green*, *Fabian of Scotland Yard*, and, direct from the Whitehall Theatre in London, *The Whitehall Farces* with Brian Rix.

The BBC also gave us a wealth of memorable children's programmes such as *Muffin the Mule*, *Lenny the Lion*, *Billy Bunter*, *Educating Archie*, *The Flower Pot Men* and, towards the end of the 1950s, *Blue Peter*. Children's television was in large part educational as well as entertaining, with shows like *All Your Own*, where young children would show off their talents at singing, playing an instrument, building a tower out of matchsticks or other bizarre but clever products that they had made. It was hosted by Huw Weldon, who later went on to become controller of the BBC. But there was also children's drama, with a regular Sunday evening classical serial and programmes like *Robin Hood, Ivanhoe* and American imports including *The Cisco Kid, The Lone Ranger, Lassie* and *Champion the Wonder Horse*.

Sport has always been at the cutting edge of television, ushering in many technical innovations, from outside broadcasts to international and satellite coverage. Sport was always high on the BBC's agenda of programmes and the 1950s had more than its fair share of memorable sporting occasions. Fortunately, many of these were captured by BBC cameras, often live. In those days there were no multi-million pound transmission rights, so sport came relatively cheap. Cricket was covered live including one of its greatest moments, in 1957, when England spinner Jim Laker's 19-wicket haul at Old Trafford single-handedly defeated the Aussies. There was athletics as well and with British middle-distance running on a high there were memorable encounters between the British stars Christopher Chataway and Derek Ibbotson taking on the indomitable Emil Zatopek and Vladimir Kuts, often under the spotlight at the White City, ironically now the home of BBC Television. Although there were no rights to show league football, the BBC was able to show friendlies and internationals. The installation of floodlights at football grounds in the 1950s allowed for matches to be shown live in an evening. It fitted perfectly into the TV schedule with those epic Wolves friendlies against Moscow Dynamo, Honved and Red Banner under the Molyneux floodlights, topping the list of outstanding games. Plus there was always the annual England *v.* Scotland international, the Boat Race, Wimbledon and the Olympics to be enjoyed by television viewers.

Television sets were often pieces of prized furniture, housed in stylish wooden polished frames. In the early 1950s, screens were small but became larger and the sets generally became more functional and less like pieces of furniture as the years progressed. You also had to switch them on well beforehand and allow them to 'warm up', a process that could take as long as ten minutes. Gradually, the fuzzy light in the centre of the screen would become sharper and larger until you were able to decipher a picture. Reception wasn't always good. There was interference, particularly from the next door's vacuum cleaner, and always a fear that one day the set would explode or get too hot if it was on for too long and burst into flames. Parents were also concerned that children should not sit too closely to the screen because television was not good for their health. And there were other concerns about what television was doing to us.

For half of the decade the BBC had a monopoly on television coverage, but then, in 1955, ITV waded in to offer a new range of programming along with commercials. It was novel and although the diet of programming was pretty much the same as the BBC, it did offer a great many more American bought-in programmes as well as TV's first soap – *Emergency Ward Ten*. There was also *The Army Game, On the Buses* and Arthur Haynes, and, of course, commercials for a variety of offerings such as sweets, cigarettes, washing-up powders and detergents. Some regarded ITV as down-market and would only watch the BBC, but others enjoyed its lighter touch and in particular the adverts. ITV was also regional and for the first time viewers were able to identify more with their own area.

By the end of the decade we were well and truly a television-viewing nation. Not every household, of course, could boast a television set and not everyone was able to receive pictures, but most had easy access to viewing via a relative or friend. While all this was taking place on the small screen, radio continued to pour out the nation's favourites. No Sunday lunchtime in Britain would have been complete without the smell of roast beef drifting from the kitchen and *Two Way Family Favourites* playing on the radio. Indeed, Sunday lunchtime listening was a must for every family – *Round the Horne, Archie Andrews, Life with the Lyons, The Billy Cotton Bandshow, The Navy Lark* and so on. Sunday lunchtime listening, as so many testify here, was an essential and still evokes strong memories. Joan Finch even had a record played for her husband who was in the army.

And then there were the evening programmes – *Dick Barton Special Agent, Journey into Space* and *The Goon Show*, while daytime offered *Woman's Hour, Workers' Playtime* and *Mrs Dale's Diary*. Sport was covered as well with commentary from the likes of David Coleman, the memorably moustachioed Raymond Glendenning, and the gentle Irish brogue of Eamonn Andrews commentating on world heavyweight title fights or presenting *Sports Report*.

It even catered for children with *Listen with Mother* cropping up every afternoon. 'And when the music stops Daphne Oxenford will be here to speak to you . . .' And on a Saturday morning there was Uncle Mac with his familiar, 'Hello children everywhere . . .' The show was a mixture of music and record requests, with evergreen favourites such as 'Sparky's Magic Piano', 'Big Rock Kandy Mountain' and 'Nellie the Elephant'.

When the 1950s began radios were also housed in large, elegant wooden cases. The reception was not always perfect and portable, and cheap they were not. But by the middle of the decade smaller radios had become commonplace. They could be carried around from room to room, although they would still have to be plugged in. Later on the transistor radio arrived, run off batteries, meaning that it could be used outside of the home or simply carried around the house. It was a major innovation. Teenagers could also listen to rock and roll beneath the bedsheets.

When it came to music the BBC barely catered for young tastes. There was little or no popular music to be heard, although every Saturday evening television's *Six Five Special* came down the line with its mix of rock and roll, skiffle and country music. Teenagers instead re-tuned their sets in the direction of Luxemburg and Radio Luxemburg, which pumped out all the popular music you could ever wish for. An entire generation listened as the sound faded in and out, sometimes to a crackling background, though, as one interviewee recalls, that was part of the attraction; you thought you were doing something furtive and that it was from another world.

Another favourite was *Workers' Playtime*. This was a programme which visited factories all over the country and played music in the canteen. There was often a comedian as well and many comedians who later became well known honed their skills in this arena. Then there was the inimitable Wilfred Pickles with *Have a Go*. This was another programme that went out and about visiting local communities. Pickles was a hugely popular star, a Yorkshireman who would invite members of the audience onstage and ask such questions as 'Are yer courting?' He would then ask Mabel, his wife, 'What's on the table, Mabel?' Mabel would reply, 'Well, there's a nice fruitcake baked by Mrs Winston, a bowl of fruit and half a crown.' The contestants would then have to answer some questions and the winner would receive the fruitcake or whatever. But even if they failed they still won something.

Just as many memories are linked to music, so they are also linked to television and radio programmes, fondly recalled many years later. Almost everyone interviewed could vividly remember some of the programmes that shaped their childhood or adult life and each programme could spark off a litany of memories associated with that particular programme.

Radio was still capable of attracting an audience of millions but by the end of the decade radio's best days, despite the technical innovations, were behind them as television audiences increased weekly. The price of television sets was declining and soon became an essential household item rather than a luxury, so that by 1960 most households boasted a TV set in the corner.

Professor Peter Hennessy argues that as a nation we shared our culture. For half of the 1950s we had just one television channel and, for the remainder, two channels, while at the same time everyone listened to the Light Programme on the radio. That shared culture meant that we all had focus points for discussion and developed our culture alongside each other, unlike today where there is a multiplicity of cultures.

STEPHEN KELLY

I vividly remember sport on television. My first sporting memory was the 1953 Cup final, the Stanley Matthews final – Blackpool against Bolton. I watched it at my granny's on her new television. It was a black and white picture of course and the screen was about 12 inches by 12 inches. You also had to switch the TV on ten minutes beforehand because it had to warm up. It would start with a dim bubble of a picture in the centre of the screen and gradually it would get bigger and stronger, although it was never that clear. It was nearly always out of focus. Anyhow, various men came down to watch the game with my dad, uncle and myself. I have a more vivid memory of an event that took place a few years later. It was Jim Laker's ten wickets in the second innings against Australia at Old Trafford. He'd taken nine wickets in the first innings and broke just about every record in the book. I remember that I was watching it at my granny's. My uncle was there, I think he was getting ready for work, and every time Laker took a wicket I dashed into the kitchen yelling with excitement, 'He's taken another wicket!' My uncle would then wander in, but of course in those days there was no action replay. This went on and on, me racing into the kitchen every five or ten minutes.

I remember watching the 1958 World Cup final between Brazil and Sweden on my mate's TV, and this teenager called Pelé. They all had strange names like Pelé and Didi. Also in the 1950s there were those great athletics matches under the floodlights from the White City – GB against the Soviet Union or GB v. East Germany with long-distance battles between Vladimir Kuts and Chris Chataway or Derek Ibbotson, with the spotlight picking out the two as they came into the home straight.

Eamonn Andrews was one of the most famous sports commentators, he did boxing mainly. I remember getting up in the small hours to listen to him commentating on the world heavyweight fight between the great American champion Rocky Marciano and the British challenger Don Cockell, which took place in America. Marciano won. Andrews also presented *Sports Report*, the five o'clock round-up of the day's sport. It still goes today. There was also Raymond Glendenning, a heavily moustached man, who commentated on football. David Coleman did athletics and Peter Dimmock introduced a mid-week sports programme on BBC television.

JOAN FINCH

I can remember when we got our first TV set. In the little house that we had you could put it on the shelf. We had a little radio. My brother had got a TV so we decided to get one. We had to pay weekly for it – that was the only way we could afford it. A lot of people had Rediffusion – that was very popular. We always had the radio. I listened to Mrs Dales' Diary every day when I wasn't working. Bill always liked the radio, then we got a radiogram where you had a radio and a record player, it was a nice piece of furniture. We had that for years; television in one room, radio in the other. I liked Billy Cotton and *Two Way Family Favourites*, that was my favourite. In fact I sent in a request when Bill was in Egypt. It was Dorothy Squires and they played it. He was in a tent in Egypt at Suez and someone heard it and shouted to him. There was no message, it was just the song. It said all I wanted to say.

Anthony Handbury

I liked *Dick Barton Special Agent*. I can remember the music. I was a big *Goons* fan. I was secretary of the under-17s team at St John's and the captain of the team was a keen *Goons* fan and all the lads in the team would be mimicking the voices, Neddie Seagoon, Hercules Grytpype-Thynne, and they'd be shouting to each other in these daft voices. Because of that I started listening to it. Tony Hancock, Sid James – they were very funny as well.

Clare Jenkins

Dad came home one day with a box and told us to guess what was in it. We knew it was a white good of some kind, and we children thought, oh maybe it's a television. But it wasn't – it was an electric kettle. Mum was quite excited but we were disappointed. I can't remember when we did get a TV but I do remember some market researcher from ITV coming up to me and Ruth in Abbey Park. She wanted to ask us what we watched and we said *Jane Eyre*. Mum told us off later because *Jane Eyre* had been on BBC and this woman was from ITV.

We would listen to the radio; there was *Children's Hour, Uncle Mac* and *Listen with Mother*. For reading we had Ladybird books. They were among the only books that we actually had – our Aunt Molly used to buy them for us for birthdays and Christmas. We went to the library quite a bit rather than buying books, which were expensive.

Mary James

We were one of the first in Bradford to have a television. I remember Dixon *of Dock Green* and *The Groves. Dixon of Dock Green* started with the blue lamp outside the police station. It was about a policeman and what happened to him and his family, but there was never anything violent, it was very gentle. I think there was a woman called Nancy in it who was a real down-and-out. I was always amazed when I met someone called Nancy and she was beautiful – I just assumed that all people called Nancy must look like down-and-outs!

I think television started at about five in the evening, it was not on during the day. *The Groves* was a soap about a family. I can't remember much else about them but we would watch it regularly. But what I do remember is that when television finished at night, the National Anthem was played and my father always stood to attention. As we got older we would be rather rude about this but he would turn the sound up and still stand to attention. They had a test card before the television programmes began but I'm not sure what the purpose was. We got the news on TV as well, with the tower and something going round it.

I remember listening to *Listen with Mother* when I was younger. I think it came on at two o'clock. 'Are you sitting comfortably, then we'll begin'. We also watched *Muffin the Mule* – I can still remember the song. I had a puppet from that. There was *Andy Pandy*, and Sooty with Harry Corbett. That ran for years and years. There wasn't daytime TV or anything like that and there was only one channel until the mid-1950s. I don't remember watching much other than BBC. I don't know whether it was that we could not get other channels.

JOHN STILE

The television set had to warm up, so you'd switch it on ten minutes beforehand. Gradually a picture would emerge. But it was never that clear and the reception would vary all the time. Then it was the same when you switched it off. The picture would slowly fade away to a small circle of light in the centre of the screen, and then 'pop' it would be gone. They'd also not got their timings right so frequently you would go to the test card or the potters' wheel just to fill in the odd minute or so. TV's were also housed in these large wooden frames. They were rather special pieces of furniture. Some even had doors on them. In time, however, the furniture aspect disappeared and they were just TV sets, which you plonked on the table or on a cabinet. The screens were also small to begin with and you could barely see them. In the mid-1950s we got ITV and had adverts. People used to go around singing and humming the ads, they loved them, although plenty didn't. At first ITV was considered a bit down-market compared to the BBC and many people wouldn't watch it, mainly because of the adverts.

The night ITV started, the BBC put out a spoiler by having Grace Archer killed in a fire at her stables in *The Archers*. Amazing to think that the BBC was so competitive at that time. Bit of a nasty trick that.

STEPHEN KELLY

There was a programme called *What's My Line?* which was on every Sunday evening. It was a light-hearted panel game, hosted by the sports' commentator Eamonn Andrews. On the panel were Isabel Barnett, Gilbert Harding, Barbara Kelly and David Nixon. The panel had to guess the occupation of a guest who came on and gave a brief display of what they did. I think the panel then had twenty questions to guess it. It was an enormously popular show. There was another very popular programme called *In Town Tonight*. It began with a shot of Piccadilly Circus and all the traffic zooming around it and in the background there was this Eric Coates music. Then all the traffic would suddenly stop. The programme was about the stars who were in London and they would come on the programme and be interviewed as to why they were in London, usually film stars, singers and so forth.

PAT TEMPEST

I had a portable radio, although it was huge. I used to listen obsessively. But then we all did. My father was fond of dance music and he had all these 78s. We had a massive radiogram and people would come up to the house and we would play all these records, open all the windows. It was a good job we didn't have any neighbours.

We had a telly from 1953. We used to watch *Sunday Night at the London Palladium* because my father liked that. When TV finished at ten we had to go to bed.

PHILIP LLOYD

I used to be a great radio listener. I liked *ITMA* (*It's That Man Again*) with Tommy Handley and there was *Monday Night at Eight*, which was a mixture of things such as music, humour, sketches. *Much Binding in the Marsh* and *Round the Horne*, both with Kenneth Horne, were great favourites. We didn't have a television so when the Coronation was being shown we went to my grandparents. As my grandad couldn't get out because he had no legs, he bought a television to compensate.

Michael McCutcheon

I didn't see my first television until about 1959, 1960. It was black and white, fantastic. That was coming into the music era when everyone had a gramophone, a wind-up; we all listened then to Radio Luxemburg, they played all the pop music. They didn't show much on the telly. We didn't get to see that much any rate because they didn't have proper transmitters. We were lucky if we got the BBC and sometimes some Irish channel, but we never got ITV.

On the farm in Ireland there was a radio. It was battery-operated as there was no electricity on the farm. It had big batteries which had to be charged. You had to take them into town to someone who had electricity so they could be charged up. The radio was only used for the weather forecast, because weather dictated farm life. We used to listen to the weather forecast at night and the next morning, because it was so important, and occasionally Irish music. You couldn't use it too much because the battery would go down.

Trevor Creaser

The only comics I saw were those passed round at school and then they'd be about a month old. There was *The Beano* and *The Dandy*, and *School Friend*, which I tried to get for my sisters. I liked listening to Paul Temple on the radio, and there was *The Goon Show* and the *Black and White Minstrel Show*. On Saturday morning I'd listen to Archie Andrews. And there was Radio Luxemburg as well in the evening. We couldn't afford the cinema. We later found out how to get in through the toilets. One of us would pay to go in and then he'd open the toilet window and we'd all climb in. That was until they cottoned on.

Win Hindle

I listened to the radio as well; *Saturday Night Theatre* was a favourite. *Lost in Space* was another one. *The Man in Black* – he used to tell these ghost stories on the radio and I used to be frightened to death. When we finally got the TV it was small and black and white and we'd invite people around to watch *The Black and White Minstrel Show, Sunday Night at the Palladium,* those kind of shows.

I don't remember watching the Coronation. I don't remember anyone who had a TV then. I also used to love *Frankenstein Meets the Wolf Man.* It frightened me to death. When I got home we had to put a penny in the meter 'cos it had gone. I struck a match and it was just like someone had blown it out. I shot out of the house.

Hugh Cairns

We never listened to the radio much and if it was on it was usually after I had gone to bed. I feel sad about that because I missed out on a lot of good programmes. They might seem a bit naff now but they were of great quality. One I do remember was *Two Way Family Favourites*. The world stopped for that. I would listen at my grandmother's. We had no one in the family who was in the forces but we still listened. It was good to hear people's stories and the good wishes to the family. When I did listen to the radio it was at my grandmother's. When I was a teenager, I started going down to my gran's because she still lived in that same close at Shettleston. I can remember going down, doing her shopping, having a bit of lunch and listening to the radio at lunchtime. There was *Life with the Lyons*; that was a variety comedy show. I loved it, it appealed to my sense of humour. But the radio was not on much at home.

We moved to Barlanark in 1953 and I remember a family over the road who always gave the impression of being a well-to-do family. The kids had been over playing at our house and I asked them if I could go over and watch their TV and they said, 'No, no.' I later mentioned it to my dad and he was furious, considering the hospitality we had given them. He said, 'That's it!' The next I remember we all went to the Kelvin Hall on the west side of Glasgow to the Ideal Home Exhibition and buying a television. This was in 1956 or '57.

One of my early memories was in October 1957, because we listened to football commentaries and it was Scottish League Cup final day. We pasted the Rangers 7-1 that day and I couldn't wait for the television highlights that evening. I watched the first half and they announced that they couldn't show the second half because the cameraman had forgotten to take the cover off the camera!

My first memories of television were a year or two before that. My Uncle Tommy had a television and we were invited there on Fridays and holidays. Susie, his wife, was a wonderful character – she always wore a hat in the house. If someone came to the house she would answer the door in the hat and if she didn't want to see them, she'd say, 'Oh, I'm just going out'. And if she did want to see them, she'd say, 'Oh, come in, I've just got in myself.' But if you were invited in it was your lucky day. Anyway, we were invited down to see their television and we were huddled around this little square box with a tiny glass screen that was grey but you could just make out the images on it. I was reasonably impressed but I was never enamoured by it as some people were.

I can remember *Andy Pandy, The Flower Pot Men*. I hated *Rag, Tag and Bobtail* and I hated Charlie Drake-like slapstick. But I really remember *The Six-Five Special*. It was absolutely great. It was Pete Murray and Jo Douglas. I actually remember that intro with the train going down the track – that was wonderful. And I can still sing the song. There was Kenny Ball and his Jazzmen on it. People were dancing in the studio. If I was in on a Saturday night I'd always watch it. If Celtic was at home I'd be back in time to watch. I remember *Juke Box Jury*, and there was *Robin Hood*.

Ian Ralston

We were one of the first to get a TV. During the war my dad had been a radar technician in the RAF. He was a brilliant electrician. Why he didn't do that as a job I don't know. Maybe he just wanted to escape being working class. We had this TV; I think it was a Bush, with an 11-inch screen. You had to switch it on fifteen minutes before so that the valves could warm up. If it ever went wrong dad would get the blueprints out and repair it. We had it for about twenty years, we were praying for it to bite the dust but it never did. When ITV started in 1956, I recall going to see it with these two old Scottish spinsters who lived a few doors away. The first programme I saw was a Roy Rogers and I was disappointed, as I had assumed it would be in colour but it was in black and white. When we harangued dad he finally bought one of these boxes which he connected onto the TV, so we still had this old TV but could at least switch to ITV.

What sticks more in my mind was radio. On Saturdays we would sit down for tea, listening to *Sports Report* and the football results, and always eating corned beef and lettuce. Listening to the radio is always associated with doing things. Sunday lunchtime was always *Two Way Family Favourites*. I used to always wonder what this BFPO was. That was followed by *The Clitheroe Kid, Beyond Our Ken, Round the Horne, The Navy Lark, Hancock* – though he may not have been on a Sunday. But those were the programmes I distinctly remember. Ted Ray I remember because my dad was a big fan, and there was Arthur Askey. And that awful programme in a morning called *Workers Playtime* with some of the worst comedians ever. Frankie Howard I enjoyed and *The Goon Show*, of course, although my sense of humour was more Kenneth Horne than the *Goons*.

There were bits of news I remember as well. I remember a radio broadcast about Cyprus, about a British officer called Moorhouse who was a part of the Moorhouse jam-manufacturing family, who had been killed by EOKA. I can remember bits about Suez as well.

I've always thought radio was a much more imaginative medium than TV. My dad would get these second-hand radios that people were about to throw out. They were works of art and he would get them going again. I had one in my bedroom and I'd be trying to tune in to Radio Luxemburg. The choice was either BBC or Luxemburg. I loved the BBC but you didn't hear any music on it, whereas you did on Radio Luxemburg. On *Children's Favourites* you might get one record, but there was something about Luxemburg as it played different music. Listening in to British music from the continent and it's fading in and out, a sense of distance. I think that's what Radio Luxemburg did.

JOHN STILE

I listened to *Journey into Space* and *Lost Planet*. It was the beginning of the Space Age and I can recall exactly where I was when I first heard of the Sputnik and Yuri Gagarin.

I used to rush home from Cubs on a Monday night to listen to *Journey into Space* on the radio. Space travel had not even begun then, this was the mid-1950s, and Sputnik had yet to be launched. Anyhow, I can still recall the four characters in the show. There was Jet, who was the captain of the spacecraft. He was played by someone who went on to become a Labour MP. Then there was Doc, who was a medical man, serious and intent; Mitch who was also quite serious and the technical person, and then Lemmy, who was a bit of a fool, always being cheeky and messing around. In a way they were like the four Beatles! Anyhow, they would go off on these space journeys and I can remember how they had to close the airlocks on the spacecraft. You'd get 'Open airlock one', and there would be this noise. Then 'Open airlock two', and you'd get the same noise. It was really exciting. I loved *Journey into Space*.

Later in the 1950s, on television, there was *Quatermass*. I remember being quite scared by it. I had a party at my house – I was a young teenager – and we watched *Quatermass*. They'd found this object under the ground whilst they were drilling a new tube line. But they couldn't work out what it was. As they dug more its size was enormous and the material from which it was made was as hard as anything they had ever come across. They couldn't make out what it was. Then at night there were these strange sounds down there, which seemed to come from the object. Someone did a bit of research in a library and it seemed the building on which the tunnel stood had a long history of ghosts and spirits. Strange beings had been seen as far back as the tenth century. Wow, were we scared! The girls were petrified.

Veronica Palmer

We got our first TV when Michael, our son, was about two. He was born in 1955 so it would be about 1956, 1957. We were the only ones in the flats with a television. All the little children used to come in and watch *Andy Pandy*, *Watch with Mother* and all the other children's programmes. I think it used to stop for two hours after that so you could put the children to bed. It was very expensive to buy or rent a television.

Mothers in those days never left their children with anyone, they never had babysitters. I've had three children but we would never hand them over. Today mothers do.

We used to like *Beat the Clock* with Bruce Forsyth. There was *Sunday Night at the London Palladium*, the *Black and White Minstrel Show* and the *Billy Cotton Band Show*. We never thought of the *Black and White Minstrel Show* as being racist.

We used to listen to the radio but we never got one at home until I was about ten. We always listened to the news on the radio. There was *Dick Barton Special Agent* and John liked *Journey into Space*. I liked *The Goon Show* and comedy like that.

Chris Prior

I was a radio listener. I went to bed at seven o'clock when I was eight or nine. My parents bought me a portable radio with an opening lid. I'd go to bed at seven and listen to *Journey into Space*. But I can't remember much about it. I do remember *The Goon Show*, but that was a bit later. The only thing I can remember the family listening was to *Two Way Family Favourites*, then there was Archie Andrews. On Saturday morning there was *Children's Favourites* with Uncle Mac. My father's father was very keen on radios, he had worked for the Post Office and he was very keen and always had a very nice radio, I think dad got it from him. I would listen to *Listen with Mother*.

I remember the first television we had. It was a rental – an Echo set – they were actually made in Southend, that must have been just into the 1960s. I know my grandparents before that had a television and we'd go round there on a Saturday evening and watch. We'd watch *The Billy Cotton Band Show* and the *Black and White Minstrel Show*. I went to see Billy Cotton once at the London Hippodrome. It must have been for my fifth or sixth birthday. And my parents must have sent a message onstage because Billy Cotton said, 'And now I'd like to send a message to little Chris Prior and his favourite song is "I've got a lovely bunch of coconuts"' – and they played it. And they threw these paper balls at the audience and they threw them back.

MAX EASTERMAN

I used to listen to *Children's Hour* and *Listen with Mother*. My mother's brother was an electronic engineer and his attic in West Hartlepool was full of electronic stuff. So we had a radio with all the valves showing and I would tune this in and listen to programmes. It was rather dangerous. He actually built a TV from scratch for my grandmother with a little 8-inch screen, which she had for about thirty years.

I also used to listen to music programmes. My uncle was a jazz pianist and I wanted to become a jazz pianist. He had a collection of records so I was brought up with swing and jazz. I used to like listening to the music programmes – *Sam Costa's Record Requests* on a Sunday – I was allowed to stay up for that. My mother used to listen to *Mrs Dale's Diary* and early editions of *The Archers*. Later on I listened to more adult programmes like the news and *Letter from America*. The radio played less part in my teens than the TV. The radio became a Sunday lunch thing – the *Billy Cotton Band Show*, *Round the Horne*, *Two Way Family Favourites*, things like that. I remember *Housewives' Choice* and the signature tune. Radio was the background to daily life, whereas TV was an evening thing and wasn't on in the day.

We bought an expensive TV, Kolster Brandes – we bought it because they had them on the *Queen Mary* and the *Queen Elizabeth*. I particularly remember the early TV dramas like *Dixon of Dock Green*, *Tales from Soho* and things like that. My original introduction to television had been on my grandmother's television. I would often watch children's television on her set because we didn't have one at that point. I would watch the drama serials. Two of them were serializations of the books published by my father's company, Bodley Head. And of course there was *Crackerjack* with Eamonn Andrews, and *All Your Own* with Huw Weldon. At weekends the whole family would go to my grandmother's to watch TV and stay up late watching *Café Continental*.

CHAPTER SEVEN

HEAVEN AND HELL

A theme that recurred time and again in interviews was religion. In a way the 1950s marked a watershed. It marked the end of subservience, churchgoing and an acceptance of the Church's rulings.

At the beginning of the decade churchgoing was still important with many families regularly attending church together on a Sunday morning. It was as important a family activity as any in the immediate post-war years. Parents regarded it as an essential element in bringing up children with the right ideals, attitudes and beliefs. On a Sunday morning or afternoon most children were packed off to Sunday school The Church of England stood at the centre of British life, with the Archbishop of Canterbury a major figure. By the end of the decade, however, much of this had been challenged. Church attendances were on the slump, particularly at the Church of England, whilst some new evangelical religions were making themselves heard.

The popular American evangelist Billy Graham arrived in Britain in 1954 and took the capital by storm with his new brand of straight talking, high octane religion. Most of his preaching was at the Harringay Arena in north London, but he also preached to massive crowds in Hyde Park, the Royal Albert Hall, at American airbases, before the royal family at Windsor Castle, as well at Stamford Bridge in the half-time interval. Accompanied by the American actor cowboy Roy Rogers and his wife Dale Evans, the tour ended with a massive rally before 120,000 at Wembley Stadium and another 67,000 at the White City stadium. In all, more than two million were said to have listened to the American evangelist. The Church of England may not have necessarily seen it as competition to its own brand of religion, but it nonetheless saw it as challenge. Graham employed new tactics of rabble-rousing, tub-thumping eloquence coupled with skilled marketing. It was all-new and clearly had an appeal to many who were coming to see the Church of England as outdated and outmoded. At a time when everything American had an appeal, so too did Billy Graham.

But it wasn't like this everywhere. In Northern Ireland and in Scotland the Church remained fundamental to life, but it was just as divided as ever. On the one hand the Church of England or the Church of Scotland and on the other hand the Catholic Church. The divide was massive.

Schools remained religious and for many young people it was the norm not to come into contact with someone of another religion until you had started work. Your home would be in a Catholic community, your school would be Catholic and your friends would be Catholic. It worked the same way for Protestants. In Glasgow the religious traditions were even a part of sporting life, with Glasgow Rangers representing Protestantism while Glasgow Celtic was the club of Catholics. Neither club recruited players or employees from the other religion, and fans naturally aspired to the club of their own religion.

But there were notable exceptions. Hugh Cairns was born into a Catholic family in Glasgow but recalls that he was not ghettoized in the way that many Catholic families were, particularly in Northern Ireland. Employment in Northern Ireland was also often dictated by religion. The shipyards, the print industry and other sectors of the industrial economy were often out of bounds to Catholics.

Catholicism, however, in the 1950s was strict and unyielding. Veronica Palmer's experiences as a child at the hands of nuns and Catholic teachers bordered on abuse and left her unforgiving and scarred. Elsewhere in this book others have testified to the punishment, particularly to boys, doled out by priests. It could be brutal and was often for the most insignificant of misdemeanours.

In Wales the dominance of the Chapel was drawing to a close. As Neil Kinnock testifies, he would go to chapel most Sundays but as the years went on, the congregations visibly shrank and the magnificent gothic chapels of the Valleys were closed down, boarded up and placed up for sale. They had been a crucial focus for the community, but community life was beginning to change and by the 1960s and '70s, community life as he had known it had all but disappeared. And once the coalmines disappeared the Valleys were unrecognisable from their grandest days.

For the most part in the 1950s Sunday was sacrosanct, a day for relaxing, the family and worship. Few people worked on a Sunday, only those in the emergency occupations, and shops, apart from newsagents, were closed. Streets were quiet, particularly in the city centres, and on a Sunday evening people saw family rather than venture out for entertainment. Many local railways stations were closed and there was always a less frequent rail service on a Sunday. It was the same with buses. Pubs were allowed to open but not in many parts of Wales, where they remained closed all day long, such was the stranglehold of Welsh Presbyterianism. Nonetheless, there were loopholes and it was often the case that a pub might be closed in what was known as a 'dry' area, but down the road in a 'wet' area they were open. In England, however, the pubs were open, although sometimes they closed earlier. Indeed, in England a Sunday lunchtime drink followed by Sunday roast dinner at home was something of a tradition, although it was always the wife who was left at home to cook the roast.

Holy days were also strictly kept. On Good Friday people always ate fish, usually went to church and, in keeping with the day, stayed at home or with family. In the Catholic Church there would always be a Mass on specific holy days. And then there were the Whit Walks, more likely to be found in Catholic areas like Manchester or some of the northern towns like Warrington. Young people would march from their churches into the city centre and would always dress their best, often in new clothes bought especially for the occasion.

And of course there were the Orange Lodge parades held every July, when Protestants marched in memory of King William of Orange and his victory over Catholicism at the Battle of Boyne in 1690. Again these annual marches varied from area to area. In Northern Ireland they were especially large and more often than not ended in violence. In Glasgow too, thousands participated with sporadic outbursts of violence, whereas on Merseyside the parades were largely peaceful and numbers were beginning to dwindle.

Attendance at church services varied, with Catholic churches always more likely to attract larger numbers than the non-Catholic churches. But there were distinct signs by the end of the decade that churchgoing was falling.

Apart from Oswald Mosley and what was left of his blackshirts, the Jewish population – largely centred in north London, north Manchester, Leeds and Glasgow – generally lived without fear. Memories of the Holocaust meant that attacks on Jews were few and far between, though this did not stop people openly referring to them in such racist terms as 'yids' or 'nebs'.

The churches were also involved in a variety of youth organisations, from the Scouts to the Boys' Brigade. They ran their own youth groups as well, often on a Saturday or Sunday evening, with table tennis, music and, in the summer, rounders, football or cricket in the park. Indeed, many professional football clubs, such as Everton, owed their very existence to the churches. In Glasgow, the Boys' Brigade boasted the largest football league in the world, with 200 teams competing regularly on a Saturday afternoon. The Scouts and the Girl Guides were also heavily involved in Christianity, with regular church attendance and religious ceremonies, and, like the Boys' Brigade, were founded on a basic Christian ideal and held close links to the Church. In the 1950s, the majority of young people would, at some point, have been members of the Cubs, Scouts, Brownies, Girl Guides, Boys' Brigade or Sea Scouts.

CHRIS PRIOR

I went to a Church of England school but don't remember going to church with my parents in London at all. When we moved to Hockley, some distant relative persuaded my mum to let them take me to this church, where they were the stalwarts, so at eight years old off I went with them. It was very high church, Anglo-Catholic, and I was invited to join the choir. I went into the vestry with the vicar and was given this surplus to wear and they lit up the incense and there were all these Latin prayers. It must have been 1955/56, and some of the prayers in the church were in Latin as well. I didn't know the hymns. Anyhow, after about four weeks I told my mum I didn't want to go anymore as the incense was making me sick. She said, 'Well you've got to go,' and I said, 'I don't want to,' and I stamped my feet and I never went again.

STEPHEN KELLY

Religion was always thereabouts. People were much more religious and went to church a lot more. Living on Merseyside, there was also the religious divide, which doesn't exist so much now. Every year there was quite a big Orange Lodge parade through the streets of Liverpool. My best friend was a Catholic, whereas we were Protestants, but it didn't matter to my parents or to us. With a lot of people it would have mattered and you would not have had a Catholic in the house let alone as a best friend. For a while we went to a Church of England and then we got in with the Baptist church, partly because it was nearer, but there was also a nice bunch of people there. There was a youth club, with lots of girls of my age, so you can guess why I went. We even had a vicar who was known as the 'Rock and Roll vicar' as he tried to introduce popular music into his service with his guitar. I always remember, with some amusement, that he baptised a rather luscious redhead from the congregation who was a good few years older than me. The baptism pool was at the front of the church and me a group of teenage lads sat at the front just so as we could see her rising from the pool in this soaking wet, white gown. It was a bit like a wet T-shirt competition! Anyhow, some months later the vicar left the church. It seems he had been having an affair with her and had left his rather dowdy Welsh wife and four kids for a life of passion with this redhead! Such are the ways of God.

ANTHONY HANBURY

More people went to church in those days. There used to be the Whit Walks. There'd be lots of people in the procession and many more watching from the sidelines. I'd go to church on a Sunday at eleven o'clock Mass. And they would be Latin Masses. My dad was the choirmaster at the church and we'd have a rehearsal once a week. The church would be fairly full, but not completely. It was much more important then. These days people don't go to Mass like they used to. My wife and myself wouldn't miss Mass. These days people prefer to watch telly or go to football, they don't put Mass first any more.

MARY JAMES

After church we had to discuss the sermons at lunch. My father used to take notes of the sermon in shorthand. We didn't have to really discuss the sermon; it was more a bit of dad-baiting. Whatever he thought of the sermon we would take the opposite view. My father was a Methodist and my mother was brought up an evangelical. My father was not into music apart from hymns. Music was not of interest to my mother either.

STELLA CHRISTINA

For Whit Walks the kids all had new clothes. They would have been saving all year so that they could show them off. The walk was from St Wilfrid's into Manchester, along Oxford Road and into Albert Square and into the church there, St Mary's. It was quite a long walk for little children. I can't say as I enjoyed it. It seemed a stupid thing to do. Hundreds went on it and thousands would come and watch, they'd come quite a distance to see. It was much bigger then, in the 1950s and '60s.

WILF McGUINNESS

People used to say Manchester United was a Catholic club but I didn't notice this. Matt was a Catholic, Jimmy Murphy was a Catholic, but Les Olive wasn't, nor was Walter Crickmer, the directors weren't either. Certainly we used to get a lot of priests at games, and Davyhulme Golf Club on a Monday had Catholic priests there. We used to mix with them there. But we also used to pal out with the Jewish lads as well. We used to go to coffee places like Lyons or the Kardomha and drink coffee, or Lewis' for a few hours, chat up any gorgeous girls. We mixed in with everybody. Nobody thought of religion or race being different.

NEIL KINNOCK

The 1950s marked the end of chapel. When I first started going in the early '50s, usually with my aunty, the chapels were full, everyone was there. But as the 1950s went on you could literally see them emptying. I don't know what the actual figures were but you didn't need statistics, you could see with your own eyes. There were less and less people attending each week. And by the end of the 1950s there were chapels all over the Valleys closed, up for sale or boarded up.

Some of the chapels were magnificent buildings – ornate and with magnificent pews, all highly polished, wonderful polished brasses and so on.

There were clubs that I would go to and, of course, later on there were girls and that's why I continued going to the youth clubs.

HUGH CAIRNS

My father had previously never worked on a Christmas Day until he was working at the station. We would all go to Mass on Christmas Day, including all the extended family, though someone would stay at home to cook the dinner. It was a day of great jollity, great excitement, partly because it was a religious day but also because it was a day of presents. The Christmas Day my father worked was quite traumatic. It broke his heart, it broke my mother's heart and it created a tension because he had to work. He didn't stay in that job very long but then got a job as a buyer in a construction company. They were on the other side of the city at Maryhill and that meant a bus into the city, and then another one out. He stayed there until he was sixty-four, when he had a stroke.

Religion was very important and, unfortunately, there was a big divide. We were all Catholics. Two of my grandmother's sisters, my great aunts, had married non-Catholics so had effectively left the Catholic faith. In those days if you married someone from the other side they 'turned' – a phrase I hate – but I think the family was amicable toward it. But I have no idea how it was taken at the time as it was before I was born. I suspect it was not taken well at the time. By the time I was conscious of things, there was never any hint of animosity in the family.

I can recall a conversation that this man called Jimmy and my father had when we were in a car going to watch Celtic play. Jimmy's wife had converted before they were married and that hadn't gone down too well with her family and he always felt not 100 per cent welcome in her family's home. There was a time when he needed some money but had not gone to his father-in-law and his father-in-law asked him why. He said, 'Well, I didn't think you were too keen on me and thought you wouldn't help.' And his father-in-law said, 'No, we would have done; you're family now.' And with that he thought that maybe the barriers were coming down.

I think there is still great bitterness in Glasgow and that's very sad. The bitterness wasn't overt, a lot of it was covered. Glasgow is not like Belfast or Derry, where there are Catholic areas. Glasgow may have areas where there are enclaves but they are not the same as in Northern Ireland. There might be areas which were more pronounced Catholic or Protestant but not wholly, like in Northern Ireland. There were some professions that were closed to Catholics. It was, for example, virtually impossible to get a job in the printing profession, and very difficult in the newspaper industry. I remember when I was eighteen there was a lad I had gone to school with and he got a job as a printer and I can remember my mother asking how he managed to get a job in printing. I think someone his father knew had helped.

If there were Catholic jobs they were the more menial jobs. I think the shipyards were okay. People like Billy Connelly started in the shipyards. I don't think the shipyards were as bad, but there were occupations were you just couldn't get a job and if you did there was then a glass ceiling. A sad state of affairs.

We would go to Mass on a Sunday morning. There were no evening masses or afternoon masses or anything like that in those days. Generally the last Mass anywhere would be at twelve. Then there were holy days of obligation during the year including the annunciation, the Immaculate Conception, Easter Sunday, Good Friday, and so on. Certainly when I was in Glasgow Good Friday was not a holiday. Some churches had youth clubs but there was none at St Paul's in Shettleston.

ROGER TOMES

Religion in those days was stronger than it is now. I think what I noticed particularly is that most people had some kind of church background, even if they were not churchgoers at the time. I don't know that there was a great deal of success in persuading people to come back to church if they had stopped. But at least in Yorkshire most people had been to Sunday school in their youth. I would probably have up to fifty on a Sunday at congregation, but the membership of the church was about seventy. It was a small church. There were other weekly activities which weren't particularly flourishing, but I managed to co-ordinate them into one, on a Wednesday evening, called Open Night and the various interests were catered for. I wouldn't have said it was a flourishing church from the point of view of activities reaching a wider clientele.

Were people more tolerant? Well, yes and no. I recall visiting the parents of one girl who came to our Sunday school and they had never actually married. They were living together and they said they wouldn't come to church because they wouldn't be accepted, which was probably true. On the other hand we had a paedophile in the church and the toleration there and understanding and hope for the man would be difficult to find today. I had to go to court several times to speak on his behalf and he was given a lot of rope. I can't recall coming across homosexuality during that period. I think we were still used to bachelors and spinsters.

Hugh Cairns

I don't recall ever having seen a Catholic parade. I'm not conscious of my parents having anything to do with them. I can remember the Orange walk passing the top of our street in Barlanark. I've heard people shouting abuse as they marched past but I never participated in any heckling. There were some people who lived down the road from us who were heavily involved in the Orange Order.

Brian Hulme

I went to church on a regular basis. At primary school you went to benediction on a Tuesday before school ended and then on a Sunday you went to Mass in the morning. There would be Midnight Mass at Christmas and we'd go to that. That used to be fun because a load of drunks would roll up. Religion was taken for granted, though I knew my dad wasn't keen because he'd been brought up a Methodist. It seemed like it was a matriarchal society to me. My mother and her family were religious, so I had to go to church. I can remember at secondary school and there was a kid who was one of the only real English kids – most of them were Irish, or part Irish, some had Italian or East European names. He was quite shocked to discover that I had Protestant friends.

The Whit Walks exemplified this divide. One day there would be the Protestant Walk, which we had nothing to do with, and then there was the Catholic Walk. There'd be walks all over Manchester, but never on the same day as the Protestant one.

Ian Ralston

Technically speaking I came from a Protestant background. Hunts Cross was predominantly Protestant. In the Dingle it was a predominantly Catholic area. There were no Jewish families up our way. There were Catholics and you knew they were Catholics and there was this division in schools, even at primary school. The Catholic kids were not allowed in for the service in the morning. They'd come in after, it was almost as if these kids were different from you. They'd be le led in and led to the back! It was aspiring middle-class

Protestant where I lived in Liverpool. There were never any religious-inspired hostilities. But you knew who they were.

Brian Hulme

The school prepared its pupils for the religious rituals expected of good Catholic children. There was first Holy Communion, when we wore white sashes and had a celebration breakfast in school, having fasted from the previous evening; Confirmation, when the bishop asked us questions from the Catechism and smeared our foreheads with Holy Oil, and, every Tuesday afternoon, Benediction, my chief recollection of which is the trickles of warm pee which would proceed from those who, overcome by the solemnity of the occasion, had overindulged in Vimto.

Veronica Palmer

I was brought up a Catholic and we got married in a Catholic church but I got disillusioned. Growing up I was very, very fearful – my mother wasn't a Catholic but my father was a convert, but, to be honest with you, they didn't know much at all about the Catholic religion. I know the Catholic Church is different now, but I was brought up in a Catholic school and everything was considered a sin. On the Monday morning my school would have a mass register. All those who went to church on the Sunday had to put their hands up, all those who didn't then had to put their hands up. It was no good lying 'cos they said you can lie to us but you can't lie to God. They said to lie to God was a mortal sin and that it would leave a black stain on your soul and if you were ever to have an accident on your way home from school and got killed you would go straight to hell. So you were terrified and you owned up. And when you owned up what do you think happened – you got the cane. No way could you win. I was always terrified at school. If you were late you got the cane. I'm not saying that didn't happen at other schools but the nun's seemed to find any reason to cane you. In a line at school in the playground, someone nudged me. 'Veronica Palmer, outside Sister Mary's room, now!' I had done nothing but it made no difference. 'You wouldn't be here if you did nothing,' Sister Mary said. 'Hand out!' I was given the cane. I lived in fear of the cane.

I went to another Catholic school. It was thick snow and one lunchtime we were told that anybody who hadn't got footwear could stay in. I had clogs with a slit in them and I thought I could stay in. 'All those who didn't go out I want outside my door,' said one of the nuns. There was a long queue. 'What's your excuse?' she asked and I told her. She said, 'You could have gone out.'

Whack! I had a little sister and they caned me in front of her – she was five and she had to watch me being caned.

When I was ill I went to a Catholic convalescent home run by the Sisters of Mercy. They had absolutely no mercy. I was there six months and I have never seen such brutality in all my life. They cut your hair. I had long hair but they cut it. I told them my daddy wouldn't want it cut, he liked my hair, but they said I couldn't have long hair. Any child that wet the bed got the slipper. I was there for an illness but I still got the slipper. I could go home at night but a lot of the kids were orphans. If you wet the bed they'd put the wet sheet around your neck so that everybody knew you had wet the bed. What they didn't realise was that we didn't think the *children* were terrible, we thought the *nuns* were.

I got married in a Catholic church to please my parents. John had to take six weeks religious instruction as he was not a Catholic. In the car after we'd got married I said, 'That's the last time I'm going in a Catholic church'. And it was. I had done my duty to my parents and I never set foot in a Catholic church again.

When I had my baby in hospital the Catholic priest came around, as they do, and he said, 'Are you a Catholic?' And in those days I still was and so I said 'Yes'. He said, 'Oh, where's your baby being baptised?' and I said, 'St Albans'. And he said, 'That's not a Catholic church.' I said, 'I know.' He said, 'But you are a Catholic.' I said, 'I know, but my children are not going to be.' He said, 'If you don't have your baby baptized in a Catholic church you are doomed to damnation.' I said, 'Well, now I *know* that I am doing the right thing.' I know they wouldn't say things like that nowadays, but they did in those days. I've not been sorry.

OLGA HALON

I am Jewish. Personally I never had any problems in the 1950s and it never affected me. I remember Oswald Mosley here at West Didsbury spouting his anti-Semitism. I didn't get involved though. We never got involved in politics at all. I go to a synagogue every week now but in the 1950s we never went as much, but I used to take my daughter. We'd keep all the Jewish holidays – New Year, fast – and we'd have the meals for Passover and so on. We weren't strict but we did have kosher meat. There was a Jewish butcher close by on Burton Road, but now you have to go to north Manchester to find a kosher butcher.

CHRIS PRIOR

We lived in Harringay in north London, where there was a significant Jewish population. My memory is that the Jews and non-Jews lived in parallel universes and never had anything to do with each other. The Jews would walk up and down their street and go to their schools and we'd walk up and down our street and go to our schools. The only time we had anything to do with the Jewish community was if we went to one of their shops, otherwise nothing.

MAX EASTERMAN

I didn't suffer any overt anti-Semitism as a kid. One of the girls in my class in Harrogate was Orthodox and when we were having Bible classes the teacher would involve her and get her to tell us about her religion. She would bring Matzos in. My father would also bring some back from a Polish Jewish bakery in Bradford when he visited there. My family largely abandoned Jewish religion mainly because the senior brothers were all members of the Communist Party, and the Communist Party in those days would not allow you to have a serious religious affiliation, it was very much Moscow line when they signed up in the 1920s and '30s. My father never joined but he claimed to be socialist. We used to eat a lot of Jewish food. My friends knew I was Jewish. In the immediate post-war period the things that had happened to the Jews were still very much in people's minds. My father was not at all religious, indeed he was violently anti-religious. But because he was away from home at the end of the war he couldn't stop me being christened. Once he was back home, though, he would not allow me to go to church. My mother was brought up as an Anglican. I don't think she had much faith even back then.

CHRIS PRIOR

When we lived in London we were only about 500 yards from the Harringay Arena, which was a centre of big events. It was used as an ice rink and every winter there was a show put on. In the summer there was a circus – Tom Arnold's Circus – and they would bring animals. And every year there was the Horse of the Year show – that was the great show jumping event. Harringay Arena was a massive oval arena, built in the late 1930s. Because we lived so close to it, not only would we go to all the events but we would go in the afternoon and have a look around as things were being set up, see the animals in their cages, see the horses at the Horse of the Year show. I had my photo in the *Evening Standard*, me and the little girl who lived three houses away meeting a Welsh pit pony. I looked incredibly scruffy. There we were meeting this miner with his helmet on and his ponies; very exciting when you're that age. I remember Foxhunter and Harry Llewellyn. My mum would tell me he was the best rider ever. There might have been boxing there as well – I wouldn't have gone – but my uncle would have done.

The thing I do remember about Harringay Arena was in 1954, when Billy Graham had his first great crusade there. My mum went to it and she actually walked up the aisle when he said, 'Come to me.' From our house we could hear the singing and the preaching, and the applause. But despite walking up the aisle it didn't seem to turn my mum to religion especially. She was impressed by Billy Graham but not a lot more. It was the first great crusade. Up to then he had been a small-time preacher in the USA, but the London Crusade turned him into a star. It went on for weeks and hundreds of thousands of people came to hear him speak.

OLGA ATKINS

By the time I got here from the West Indies there were people I knew who went to church, they didn't give up because they weren't welcome, they still went to church. When I go to church I don't go because of a person, I go because I want to worship God. So if people didn't even speak to me I would still go to church and I would praise my God because that's what I go for.

Yes I wanted to be with people, I wanted to talk to them. I wanted to say I'm a human being, I'm me. We might eat different, we might have a different accent, but deep down inside we are all human. There were things that I accepted which I probably wouldn't have accepted back home. I accepted it because I was here, it was home but it wasn't home, so I had to do my best to make it my home. I missed home, the warmth, the friendship. The West Indies is a small country, you're never lonely, you never feel isolated, and you never feel alone because someone will be passing along the road.

CHAPTER EIGHT

A 'SUCCESS STORY NATION'

People tend to remember not major political happenings, but rather those events which have been personal to them and impacted upon their own lives. They will remember music, films, school life, games, but rarely political or historical events.

But of all the major political, economic and social events of the 1950s the one that was remembered most was the Coronation on 2 June 1953. Since the death of King George VI in November 1952, at the early age of fifty-six from lung cancer, the Coronation had been eagerly awaited. But again the Coronation was recalled not because of what it represented but mainly because of the street parties and the fact that it marked the first occasion when many watched television. Trevor Creaser had the distinction of actually being in Westminster Abbey as first reserve choirboy and was able to watch from a unique vantage point behind the Coronation throne itself. He may not have had the chance in the end to actually sing, but it left an indelible memory of an occasion still revered in recent history. In London it poured with rain as the Coronation coach made its way towards Westminster Abbey and then back to Buckingham Palace. Elsewhere the weather was brighter and many had to be satisfied with street parties, bunting and cakes or squeezing into someone's lounge to watch a flickering black and white television set, alongside most of the occupants of the entire neighbourhood. For most it was the first time they had watched television and it was to launch television into the modern era. It was a major outside broadcast operation, the first of such size that the BBC had undertaken, and its success was to shape the direction of British television.

Major wars are normally events that remain forever in people's memories. And yet the Korean War, which began in 1950 and ended in an armistice three years later, was barely recalled by anyone, apart from Steve Hale whose uncle was sent off to fight. More than a thousand British soldiers were killed but the events seem to have impacted little on the general public. Perhaps this was because it was many thousands of miles away, in an inhospitable, undeveloped country, and seemed to be at the behest of an American government rather than a British initiative. Korea was a long way off and unless you were personally in the fighting it faded into the background. There had been no general call-up and not all conscripts were sent to the front. Surprisingly, the Suez Crisis of 1956 loomed larger in people's minds, perhaps because there was a partial call-up accompanied by major demonstrations in London, a division of opinion in the British press and a major split with the United States. Palestine, Egypt and Israel were places the British public could relate to in the 1950s. Show them a map and ask them to point to Korea and nobody would know precisely where it was situated. They knew nothing of Korea, its history, language or culture. But Suez was different and the British army had long been involved in that area of Middle East politics, having occupied Palestine since the early 1920s. British Prime Minster Sir Anthony Eden had also painted President Nasser of Egypt as a fervent nationalist, describing Nasser's seizure of the Suez Canal as an act of appalling international defiance, not dissimilar to Hitler's seizure of the Sudetenland. It was a view that helped shape public opinion, well for some time at least. What concerned people more was whether the British invasion of Suez and subsequent recapture of the canal might escalate into a third world war. Memories of the Second World War were still fresh enough for many to be fearful. Fortunately, such views proved to be exaggerated, but the Suez Crisis nonetheless certainly heightened the Cold War and even, for a time, seriously damaged relations between Britain and the United States.

But of all the events of the decade the one that stood out most was the Munich air disaster in 1958. Like the later assassination of President Kennedy in Dallas, Texas in 1963, many people could remember precisely where they were when they first heard that a BEA Elizabethan flight carrying the Manchester United football team back from a European Cup quarterfinal game in Belgrade had crashed on take-off at Munich Airport after a refuelling stop. Eight members of the famous 'Busby Babes' team, who were league champions, were killed, along with eight journalists, two crew members and two other passengers. Manager Matt Busby lay critically ill in hospital, his life hanging in the balance for a number of days. Team captain Roger Byrne was among the dead, along with centre-forward Tommy Taylor, both England regulars. Duncan Edwards, another England international and perhaps the brightest young talent in British football for many decades, was fatally injured and would die in hospital a few days later. The tragedy rocked the nation and anyone who was a football fan retained vivid memories of the disaster and the moment they heard the news, particularly those who lived and worked in Manchester.

Perhaps it was the fact that the players were all so young which caused so much grieving. Certainly all those people interviewed here who were living in Manchester at the time have vivid memories of the disaster. Among them, journalists Bob Greaves and David Meek recall the hectic hours following the crash, notifying the families and trying to put together the details of the story. For them it left indelible memories, though in the case of David Meek, it ironically opened up a new career as a sports' journalist after he was drafted in to takeover from Tom Jackson, the *Manchester Evening News* reporter covering United, who had been killed in the disaster.

People also recalled the 1951 Festival of Britain with its celebration of a brighter future, though few were able to recall much beyond the Festival's iconic Skylon tower. Many thousands visited the South Bank exhibition site, enjoying its glimpse into the future. The World Trade Fair in Brussels in 1958, also known as Expo 58, with its iconic atomium landmark, was similarly remembered.

For many the early days of the space age are a distinct memory, with the Soviet Sputnik orbiting the earth every ninety-six minutes. Launched in October 1957, the Sputnik would emit its memorable beep-beep over the next year or so, until it finally burned out. For many young people it ushered in an exciting new scientific era that made *Dan Dare* and *Journey into Space* a reality. Dogs followed into space and other animals before, finally, in 1961, Russian cosmonaut Yuri Gagarin was launched into orbit. Suddenly the Moon and space exploration were within our grasp and who knew what benefits it might bring and where it might all end.

Of course there was another angle. It accelerated the Cold War with worries of what military potential it might all have. The Cold War was always there, always threatening. There were fears that any minor conflagration might suddenly escalate into full-blown war. The Soviet Union and its Eastern allies were the enemy, China remained largely unchartered and unfathomable. Stalin and then Khrushchev were communist demons. Governments built nuclear bunkers, set up regional seats of government, installed warning sirens, and developed their own deadly weapons amidst much talk of a nuclear holocaust. In the end it all amounted to a nuclear stalemate. Nonetheless, it cast a shadow over a generation.

Most surprising of all the major events and conflicts that littered the 1950s was how the 1956 Hungarian revolution impacted on so many of those interviewed. At least three interviewees had personal experiences of the revolution and its aftermath. Britain admitted refugees and raised money for those affected, while the Communist Party suffered its biggest division to date as thousands resigned in anger at the brutality of the Soviet invasion. Many were disillusioned and never returned to a belief in old style Soviet communism.

Steve Hale

I remember the Korean War well. Life was plodding along nicely in Liverpool and I remember getting up one morning and there was this strange hush in the house and my Uncle Peter had got his call-up papers to do National Service. He was only eighteen. I later learnt that it was expected. It was more or less given that he would do some training and would then be put on a ship and sent out to Korea. And that's exactly what happened. The barracks of the old Kings' Regiment are still there on Townsend Avenue and he walked up there to sign in and from there he was taken in an army lorry to the camp at Altcar, near Formby. He did six weeks solid training there. He then came home for two nights and we had a great big shindig. It was a big party and all the street came because he was, at the time, the only lad who had been called-up and was going to Korea. Everyone in the street, at some point during the night, came to the party. So he had two nights at home and was put on a ship and it took six weeks to get to South Korea. That was the last we saw of him for two years. I remember asking my mum why my nan was crying. Nan feared that he'd not come back because he'd be right amongst it all, fighting.

He was changed when he came back. Whatever he'd seen or been involved with, he was very quiet about it. He was very introspective and had started smoking. Nan was very strict and against smoking and she wouldn't allow it in the house. He talked about it later on, but it was a *lot* later on. Nobody pressurised him to talk because they knew he didn't want to, and he didn't for quite a while. We got letters off him but they never came on a regular basis because they'd be going all over the place and they took a long time to get here. And they were always on those blue airmail letters that you had to carefully open and then fold out. I used to run downstairs when I heard the postman to see if there was anything from him. If it was a blue airmail letter then we knew it was from him. Other than that we just got bills like everybody else.

When it was all over we'd had a letter off him to say that his unit was being taken out of the front line and that he was going over to Japan with a few mates from his unit, because he had some 'r and r'. He said he'd be gone for a couple of weeks and when he was back he'd write and tell us which ship he'd be on. So he went over to Japan and visited Tokyo and I know he visited Hiroshima because he talked about what he'd seen when he came back. He was very keen to go and see what this bomb had done to a complete city. He said he couldn't believe the total annihilation of a city by one explosion. He'd taken some photos as well, tiny little black and white pictures, and he was trying to explain about a monument, I think it was a church that was left standing. I think it's still there. Anyhow, whether he forgot or whether it got lost we didn't get the next letter to tell us which ship he was coming home on. We found out that the first ship was coming into Liverpool with the King's Regiment soldiers on board, so we got up early one morning at about five-ish to get a tram to the pier head. And we waited hours and hours, literally until the last soldier had come off the ship, then my nan just burst into tears because he obviously wasn't on it. She went to see somebody immediately after the last soldier had come down the gangplank and she asked if this person if her son was on the ship and he said no, but he might be on the next one, that there will be three or four coming in over the next few weeks. So we didn't go down again even though my nan kept tabs on when the ships were coming in. But then there was a knock on the door one night, it was April, either a Thursday or a Friday, and I answered the door and there was Peter standing there in his uniform, with his kitbag slung over his shoulder. I stood mesmerised for a minute. My mum was shouting from the kitchen, 'Who is it?' And I said, 'You're not going to believe this.' She said, 'Don't tell me,' and I said, 'Yes, it's Uncle Peter!' And she just flew out of the kitchen, through the living room and into the hall. My nan was upstairs and she near broke her neck coming down the stairs. The next thing my dad came home from work we heard him coming in the back with his bike and mum said, 'Hey, there's someone here for you and it's a big surprise.' And of course it was Peter. Next thing, my dad jumps back on the bike, goes off, and ten minutes later comes back with a crate of brown ale on the back of his bike. Then we knocked on neighbour's doors and they were invited in and within the hour there was another big party going on to celebrate Peter coming home. The community was like that then. Maybe lives were duller at the time and for someone to have survived that and come home gave them a good excuse to have a good time. My nan was on the piano banging away and everyone was singing. I'd been sent to bed then to try and sleep but what with the excitement of Peter coming home and all this noise going on downstairs I didn't get to sleep for ages.

Next morning, when we got up, Peter was delving into his army kitbag, bringing all this army washing to give to my mum to do. When he got to the bottom of it he pulled out this brown paper bag and in the bag were two things: a satin bomber jacket with a tiger on the back that he bought for me in Japan, and a little tin fire engine. Of course I was straight out in the street with my jacket on and my fire engine. I was everybody's best mate in the street for a while 'cos of this jacket with the tiger on the back. Of course I wanted to go to school in it but I wasn't allowed because it would have been ripped off my back by the older guys.

Phillip Lloyd

I went to the Festival of Britain in 1951, in fact I went twice. I saw the Skylon, which was like a cigar floating in space. That's the best description of it. There was the Festival Hall, which is till there. There were all the science exhibits as well. I saw CCTV for the first time when I went there. I went in and you saw the screen ahead of you 'That's me!' Wow – it was the first time I had seen anything like that. Things we take for granted today. I went a second time to see more of it. I had an uncle who lived in Edgware so I stayed with him. I went to Battersea Park on my visit as well, that was a funfair, a bit like Belle Vue back in Manchester only much bigger and much better.

Mary James

We went to the Festival of Britain – that was quite something. I don't remember much about it except that it was on the South Bank, which I think was built for it. My brother Peter had to wear David's school hat in order to get in free as you had to be of school age, fortunately he was quite tall for his age. I was impressed by all these new buildings on the South Bank.

Roger Tomes

I did spend one day visiting the Festival of Britain though I don't remember a great deal about it. It was nice to be optimistic about Britain and its place in the world, though most of the colonies had not rebelled then. There was a sense of optimism. It was before there was any great unemployment. Not so many people expected to be employed. It still wasn't common for married women to have a full-time job and I don't recall many part-time jobs being available either.

John Palmer

We went to the Festival of Britain. There was the Skylon and always something going on. We went on a boating lake. Before we were married we used to go to London regularly to see all the London shows. We went to the Palladium, all the musicals in Leicester Square. We'd go to a café, have a meal. We lived in Romford then and it was easy to get into town. We went up there on a regular basis.

MARY JAMES

We went to Brussels for the Exposition, I think it was 1958. There are photos of me in my school uniform. There was this giant atom as the emblem of the exhibition. We camped and we had waffles, which I'd never eaten before. It was very French. We had coffee in bowls for breakfast and large chunks of bread. It wasn't long after the end of the war. It makes you realise how quickly things recover.

TREVOR CREASER

In 1952, the year the King died, I was in Leeds parish church choir and I was picked out of thirty choirboys to go to Westminster Abbey, along with another lad, to sing at the Coronation. I was his understudy in case he got ill. Anyhow, he didn't get ill or anything but I still sang in Westminster Abbey. I sang at the practices but not actually at the Coronation itself. During the Coronation ceremony I was in the choir vestry at the back in case anything happened, listening to everything that was going on. It was very exciting being at the Coronation. I stood there, in the background; I saw the Queen and everything.

JOAN MATTHEWS

I think we had a television in 1937. Living in London meant that we could get television pictures. We were allowed to watch *Monday Night at Seven*. I heard Neil Kinnock talking about television recently and saying how they all managed to get a television for the Coronation in 1953. I remember the 1953 Coronation. I remember 1952 when the King died more than the Coronation because it was the day I went to hospital for a pre-natal examination – I was expecting Josephine – and I remember somebody standing at the bottom of the steps by the railway and saying, 'He's dead, he's dead,' and I said, 'Who's dead?' And he said, 'The King's dead.' I was astonished. When I went home there was nothing on the radio apart from stately music. And then of course there was the Coronation the next year. I went up to London with three of my college friends and we sat out in the road and watched. It was the first time that I had left Josephine in the charge of her father. I was convinced I was going to come home and find her ill. We sat in St James' Street to watch it, which is fairly close to the Palace. We chose it particularly because it is narrow and we thought we'd get a good view, but it poured and poured with rain. In the morning, when people and carriages started making their way to the Abbey – the whole place was police lined of course – it was such a dull miserable day that anything that walked down the road got cheered. The men sweeping the road got cheered and a dog wandering down the road also got cheered. And one or two men who must have been lords or something, they got cheered and looked very embarrassed. It was quite funny really.

It was pouring with rain and the poor old Sultan of Zanzibar was sitting in the same carriage as the Queen of Tonga and he was looking so miserable and there was this huge, great lady next to him gracefully waving in the pouring rain. After Elizabeth had been crowned we went to Buckingham Palace and watched it all. I'm not a royalist but it was a spectacle.

STEPHEN KELLY

I have a very vague memory of the King's death. We had to stand up in class for a minute's silence. Presumably that would have been for the funeral. But that's all I remember about that. I do have some stronger memories of the Coronation. We didn't have a television, in fact we didn't have one until about 1960, but my granny bought one for the Coronation, or rented, I don't know which. She lived at home with three of her grown-up children, none of whom were married, but a couple of them were working, so they had a little bit of spare money. Anyhow, it was a whole-day event. We arrived early enough to see the future Queen emerge from Buckingham Palace in her carriage to make her way to Westminster Abbey. I have a suspicion it was raining as well. We stayed at granny's all day. Neighbours and friends were piled into the house and would come and go. I vividly remember that we had lunch, sandwiches and cakes in front of the telly, and then more tea in the afternoon and more cakes later on. And so it went on, all day with granny and my aunts popping into the kitchen all the time to make more pots of tea and produce more sandwiches. But what everybody was talking about was the Queen of Tonga. She was a rather stout lady if I remember, who smiled and laughed throughout the proceedings despite the pouring rain. She made a rather cutting contrast to our own sour-faced royal family. We also got a commemorative Coronation mug. I think we were given it at school and I think my mum bought a book with the order of the Coronation service in it.

BRIAN HULME

At the Coronation, at least three families were in the front room watching the telly. It was a hot day, and by the end it, I hated royalty. The neighbours were all trying to show off, and ended up just bickering. People painted their houses red, white and blue and there were street parties, but there wasn't one in our street.

JOAN WOOD

We didn't have a television until 1960. I don't think we even saw the Coronation until we went to the pictures. We listened to it on the radio; our Janet was six months old. I remember the King dying. It was rather a surprise and poor young Elizabeth on holiday in Africa was suddenly called back. There were street parties for the Coronation and everybody came out. There were trestle tables down the middle of the road and everybody shared their food. They had one recently, they sealed the road off, but each little family had their own table and their own things. It was not very communal like in the past. I think people had more fun in those days, they shared things. Of course they'd gone through a war, when they *had* to share things.

MARY JAMES

I remember the Coronation well. At church we had a pageant and I was Queen Elizabeth II! My mother made all the clothes and was very involved. And we had a street party. We were one of the few, maybe the only people in the area to have a television. My father was always interested in new things. We were the first in the area to have a washing machine as well. David, my brother, was a great supporter of the missionaries and he got out his missionary box and made people who came to our house pay to watch the Coronation, and he made some money for the missionaries. Then we all got dressed up and had a street party. I was a Welsh woman, all dressed up, and one of my brothers was a herald. Everyone was dressed up.

JOAN FINCH

I remember the Coronation. I remember her getting married in 1947 and the year after she had Prince Charles, and then her father died in 1952. She had Charles and she had had Anne by the time of the Coronation. I remember more about her getting married than the Coronation. We had a holiday. People were upset when the King died. I preferred him to his wife. I think I watched it on television. I don't think we had a television then but mum and dad did. We had a street party. There was always one every bonfire night as well. There was bunting up in the street. Everybody had a little flag outside.

Veronica Palmer

Unfortunately John, my husband, was ill in bed at the time of the Coronation. The children next door were all dressed up because they were going to a street party, so they came in and showed us. I went into a neighbour's house and I watched it on this small screen, about 9 inches square, almost pitch black. The house was full of all our neighbours. It was fantastic. When I saw her she looked like the crown on her head was weighing her down. That would be the first time I had ever seen television. We were living in Essex then. There were loads of street parties but I missed all that because John was ill. At that time anyone who had been near us had to have injections, like the children next door and so on. The doctor said to me that they thought that I would get tuberculosis as well but I didn't. When I was a small child I had a lung infection and had to go to a convalescent home. They called it catarrh of the lungs. Later they said there was no such thing but thought it might have been TB-related. At any rate, it protected me and I didn't catch it off John.

Max Easterman

I very clearly remember watching the Coronation – Richard Dimbleby commentating. It was a whole-day event, with the whole family gathering around my grandmother's TV set. It brings back very vivid memories. We were given a book at school called *Elizabeth Our Queen*, which I discovered in a pile of my mother's stuff after she died. And there was a brochure as well showing you where everyone was sitting. It was what sold TV to the British public. The sale of television sets prior and immediately afterwards went through the roof. My father was teetotal so we had relatively little alcohol in the house, but on Coronation day I remember lots of alcohol being drunk. On Christmas Day we would have a bottle of Graves with the chicken. That was the only time we had wine in the house.

Chris Prior

On Coronation day, the whole family went to my aunts, my mother's sister. She was the only member of the family who had a television. They had a tiny house with a tiny television set. I don't really remember watching it though. What I do remember is that we had cold lamb with mint sauce. The cat got so agitated by all the people there that it ran up the chimney then fell down and there was soot everywhere. The Coronation to me is cold lamb and mint sauce and the smell of soot.

ROGER TOMES

Our local MP in Yorkshire was a man called John Edwards – he was a Labour politician. I was always happy to meet and talk with him. I did a session at one of the elections as a poll clerk, which was interesting. There were a few Asian families and I was struck at the way they would bring their children with them, read the voting slips to them. There weren't many Asians but there were some. The second time Edwards was elected he died shortly afterwards and the next MP was a Tory, the son of one of the people who lived in the big houses. I remember watching a TV interview with Attlee who, when I was in the army, had inspected me once, and he recalled that in the 1930s Phillip Snowden, who was Chancellor, would refer to the MP of the constituency of Spenn Valley as a sewer.

I think most of my congregation would have voted for Sir John Simon, who was a National Liberal. I was more sympathetic to Labour. Hugh Gaitskell came and spoke at Cleckheaton, just down the hill, and I did go and listen to him. I was a bit disappointed; he made a cheap joke at the expense of Charles Hill, who had been the radio doctor during the war and had been a Conservative politician.

I suppose the outstanding event was the Suez Crisis that happened within weeks of my being ordained as a minister at the church. I had two lasting impressions. One was that I had spoken very cautiously to the congregation because I thought most would be Anthony Eden supporters. And the other was that I felt very isolated, as I had no natural circle of friends that I could talk to. I had just moved and I found that difficult. I was very unhappy about Suez. I was a *Manchester Guardian* reader even then! I felt that Harold Macmillan had a better grasp of things than Eden.

NEIL KINNOCK

Aneurin Bevan was our MP from 1929 onwards. He was elected after the local party organised the de-selection of the sitting MP, who was not very good. Bevan was a monumental character and was worshipped by my family, who knew him. My uncle used to say to me that one of the local pits was the biggest pit in the world. And I'd query that and he'd say well, it's so big because if it has all the people who say they worked with Nye when he was there then it must be the biggest as there's so many of them!

Tredegar was a Labour-only town. The first time I met Nye was in the 1950s. It was a Whit Monday Sunday school parade. All the Sunday schools would be tipped out on to the streets and they'd walk to the park in procession. Everyone wore their best clothes, which were always bought a size too big so that they could grow into them over the next year. So everyone had these new clothes on that were all too big for them. Hair would be brylcreem-ed as well and we'd all march behind the teachers and beneath the banners for every chapel; beautiful banners, blue backgrounds, wonderful maroon colours and green lettering. It was always the last Monday in May and, let me tell you, it was always sunny!

As I say, the march would always end in the park in Tredegar and on the steps traditionally would be the local MP, in this case Aneurin Bevan. He would then give a financial gift, something like £5, to each of the Sunday schools. Actually it was the council's money, not his. So, on this occasion I was chosen to go up and take the money. I shook hands with him, took the envelope and brought it back to our Sunday school teacher. And that was the first time I ever met him.

I had a couple of other encounters with him later on. One was in a pub in Trefil called the Quarryman's Arms. I was sixteen at the time and I was underage drinking with a couple of mates. So, there I was having a drink, you know, pints, smoking as well when, over on the far side of the pub, who should come in but Nye Bevan, his wife Jennie and his agent, Archie Lush. We looked up and such was our deference that as soon as we spotted them, we bolted for the door. But Archie Lush saw me and yelled, 'Kinnock, you bugger, I'll tell your mother!' I really thought he would and was terrified for days. Of course Nye and Archie were laughing their heads off.

My third meeting with Nye came just after his famous speech at the Labour Party conference in Scarborough about nuclear disarmament, when he stood up and urged delegates not to send him naked to the negotiating table. The Labour movement was split in two. I was a Young Socialist delegate and I was implacably against nuclear weapons. Any rate, come November we had the local general and trades council meeting in the constituency and Nye, as ever, attended. He got a right kicking and I have to say that in all my years as an MP, I was grateful that I never got a kicking like he got that night. But what I do remember is that Nye spoke to the meeting and he addressed them as if he was addressing the United Nations, such was the regard he had for them. The atmosphere was poisonous but he gave no quarter, and they gave none either. I never had an experience like that. He lacerated them. I came home and told my dad and he said, 'Well, Nye was right wasn't he.' And I said, 'No, he wasn't.' And my dad said, and I'll always remember this, he said, 'He's right. I'm afraid you can't dis-invent nuclear weapons, they're here now and they're for good, so it's just as well we've got someone like Nye to argue our cause.' I wish I'd remembered that line years later.

MARY JAMES

The big event I remember was the Hungarian uprising in 1956. I would be eleven at the time. My parents were very involved in accepting refugees from Hungary into the YMCA in Birkenhead. My job was to make up these toilet bags for the refugees. That has had a lasting impression on me. The youngest involved in the fighting were fourteen-year-old boys. They arrived in Birkenhead with not even a toothbrush. My job was to make up these bags – putting in a toothbrush, a facecloth, a bar of soap and so on. To me, the thought that people had had to leave home without even a toothbrush was just shocking. It was symbolic of the position they were in. My mother decided she had to learn Hungarian cooking so that we could cook appropriate food for them and they would not feel so isolated. Some of these refugees stayed in touch with my father until he died. Even though some of them went to America and beyond, they stayed in touch. They were a tremendous mix. One of them was a Count, which may not have been uncommon in Hungary. When I went to Oxford I met the son of one of the people who has started the revolution. He was a poet. So I learned later on a lot more about the Hungarian uprising. In the 1950s the big thing was these people coming and there were so many of them. It was just the men who came to us. I don't know what happened to the women.

BRIAN HULME

An event of great significance to me and my parents was the Hungarian uprising of 1956. I listened avidly to radio reports, and was deeply impressed by photos in the paper – the *Daily Mail* – of the Hungarian military leader, Pal Maliter, defying the Russian troops atop a tank in the streets of Budapest. It was heartbreaking to hear the Hungarian Prime Minister, Imre Nagy, making a radio appeal to the Western powers for military assistance – in vain, as it turned out.

The uprising's aftermath similarly left a deep impression – we learnt that Nagy and all the leaders who survived had been executed. My parents discussed quite seriously the idea of adopting an orphan refugee from the uprising – there was a camp set up at Ringway Airport (now known as Manchester International Airport) to house people who had fled. The idea of having a sister appealed to me greatly – we were just two boys – but I had misgivings about the suitability of our family, with parents who at best rarely communicated and who mostly avoided one another.

VERONICA PALMER

I really felt terrible about the Hungarian revolution because all those people were the same age as us. I was twenty-three and I felt for them trying to escape. I never at that time imagined I would ever meet any Hungarians. But

John had Hungarian friends. They had fled Hungary and came to work at his place and John brought them home to meet us. They came here with nothing, left their family and all their possessions behind. It must have been traumatic for them. They had no clothes and it was very cold. Years and years later, forty or fifty years later, we met up with them again. John met this young man at music classes and he got talking about these Hungarian friends from 1956 and strangely they knew them, so they arranged for us all to meet up again. It was lovely to see them. By then they were quite wealthy and owned restaurants. Obviously they can go back to Hungary now, but it was a long time before they were able to see their parents again. It wasn't until the wall came down in 1989 that everything began to change.

JOAN MATTHEWS

Korea was presented to us as standing up against communism. But of course there was till conscription. You had to serve two years in the forces. I worked in a school in Woking for a few weeks before I went to the LCC (London County Council). And a couple of the staff there had been in Korea and we saw pictures of troops in trenches with snow on the ground. And the language was all about hoards of Chinese coming at them. Not very nice really. It was such a long way away and of course when Vietnam happened we didn't get involved. Why were we so scared of the communists? God alone knows. You see my mother-in-law was a Russian. She was a grandee; she'd gone very downmarket when she married my father-in-law. She really did it to get out of Russia and get British nationality. She had only known him for three days. Whether money changed hands or not I don't know. Her brother went to the United States and became very wealthy. But she did tell me in a quiet moment that she thought the Russian aristocracy deserved everything they got.

I remember the Suez Crisis in 1956, and the Hungarian revolution. There was quite a few people who sympathised with the Russian viewpoint. You could read pros and cons in *The Times*, *Guardian*, and I did my best to be well-informed but didn't come down on either side. As for Suez, I was horrified; I thought it was a big mistake. I was very aware of the fact that the Americans had interfered and said stop. I can remember pictures of Anthony Eden and comments about his ill-health. Like many people I was also aware that the British Empire was falling apart and that we were not going to be able to continue having an Empire. We had to give way. One of the things I do remember about India is when I was working in Bethnal Green. The British army didn't leave India all at once. We had an incident where a ship arrived in London docks with troops from India on board and we had letters in the office asking if we could help with accommodation. I remember one of these letters said, 'I am a sergeant in the British army and I am arriving at India Docks at eleven o'clock on such and such a date. I am arriving with my wife and eleven children, please find me accommodation.' He had had British accommodation all the time he had been in the army in India, so he just expected it when he came here. He got it as we weren't going to have eleven children taken into care. That's what would have happened. That would have been in the mid-1950s.

Attlee was our Member of Parliament in Walthamstow. I remember him driving around in a car with a flashing light on top, which said 'Vote Attlee'. I never knew him but I did follow him. He was a clever man and a good man. And of course Aneurin Bevan was well thought of because of the National Health Service. Like many people, however, I was perplexed at the way Churchill was thrown out after the war. I remember being very bored and pushing Jo around in the pram in 1952 and propping a copy of Winston Churchill's *Gathering Storm* on the pram and reading it while trying to push the pram.

When I worked for the LCC I discovered that most politicians I dealt with were fine. I went into a little group called Members Inquires and all we dealt with were inquiries from Members of Parliament and local government. Anything that came in on headed notepaper to all departments was sent straight to our office. And I got to learn a lot about licensing and planning. A lot of MPs would ring us up and ask us things and putting anything down in writing meant you had to be a little bit careful. I found that everybody I dealt with, on all sides of the political spectrum, was really caring. Perhaps they are better at dealing with individual cases which are very meaningful to them. But I was very impressed with them and it makes me cross these days when people run down Members of Parliament because I think they do a good job on the whole.

MIKE PRIOR

I joined CND in the summer of 1958, when I was nearly sixteen. I had been a rather nominal member of the Young Communist League since I was thirteen, but I remember little of it. I was not in any sense political except for the fact of being surrounded by communists. I don't even remember being particularly taken with the idea of banning the bomb, though I do remember a beautiful girl from Southgate who was much taken with the notion. I joined, probably in part, because the Communist Party was not keen on CND, at least at its outset. There was already a body called the World Peace Council run by the party and they were suspicious of any rival who might turn out to be more popular. But by then my parents were regarded as politically unsound within the party and they encouraged me to take a rather different frame for my politics as well.

Ian Ralston

We used to get two newspapers on a Sunday, maybe the *News Chronicle*. But my dad would read the *Daily Express* – it was less offensive in those days. I think I started getting angrier with it in the late 1950s, early '60s. He would buy that at the station and then of course the *Liverpool Echo*, though we didn't get the *Liverpool Daily Post*. I recall my neighbour coming round one Saturday wanting to look at our *Echo* because they didn't get it. I said, 'Yes, what do you want it for?' He said, 'Well the group's just had its first record released.' I said, 'What's the name of the group?' and he said, 'The Beatles'. I said, 'I've never heard of them.' My brother had because he would go down the Cavern Club. This neighbour was a roadie but ended up as an executive for Apple.

Stephen Kelly

When the first Sputnik was launched this lad knocked on our door and said, 'Have you heard? There's a satellite in space, the Russians have sent it up and it's going bleep-bleep all the time.' From then on everyone was going around saying 'bleep-bleep'.

John Hectorball

I remember Yuri Gagarin – he came to Metro Vicks in an American-type limousine, but it was actually Russian. Billy Graham came to Metro Vicks as well. They used to talk and lecture in the car park. Billy Graham had everyone joining in singing and praying. He had a beautiful voice. He went to City's ground to talk. I was very impressed by him, but I wasn't religious. I never married, been single all my life. I did live in sin for eight years or so, but that was much later.

Mike Prior

Our campaigning in CND took on a slightly crazy aspect at times, like when we marched from Liverpool to Hull between Christmas and New Year. This all started out as a joke because we had no campaigning in our diaries, but in the end about 200 of us did it, starting in Liverpool on Christmas Day and ending in Hull on New Year's Eve – at one point going over the Snake Pass with snow falling and a police car at the front and one at the back shepherding us, it all seemed like a poor joke. Every evening we limped into a northern town or city to be met by the local adult CND. In Manchester we had beds but in smaller places they were school halls. Local Labour and Communist women came in with tureens of soup and pies, while volunteer doctors and nurses patched up our feet. And then in the morning local councillors, maybe even a mayor or two, marched out of the town with us. At every town the local newspaper had a photographer and there would be a story in the paper that evening. When we got to Hull, a long-time local Quaker centre, the local group arranged for each of us to have beds for the night. Along with two others I was called out and was then picked up by a Bentley and taken to a fair-sized mansion on the edge of the town. There was a large local company called Northern Dairies, which was owned by a Quaker family, and it was one of them who took us in. We had long, hot baths and afterwards they served us dinner around a large, polished, wood table. Then we were driven to a New Year's Eve party and picked up afterwards. And in the morning the Bentley took us to the station!

Chris Prior

When we moved down to Essex there were terrible floods, not the 1953 floods but some other. I must have been eleven or twelve. All the adults were saying, 'Don't come out, this floodwater's bringing up the sewage.' It was a filthy mess. They built flood barriers after that.

Veronica Palmer

We always voted Labour but we were never members of the Party. The first politician I can really remember was Harold Wilson, but that was in the 1960s. I'm not very political but I will always vote. My mother was Conservative and my father was Liberal. She always said, 'Don't vote Labour because they haven't got any money'. I voted Labour for years until Blair took us to war. I emailed him and told him, 'If you bomb innocent women and children – as happened in the Second World War – you won't get my vote.'

John Hectorball

I had two friends who were interested in the Young Communist League (YCL) and I used to help out by selling *Challenge*. They were unpopular; it wasn't a nice thing to belong to because of the Cold War, the Russians, and so on. We used to go on holiday, camping, there was quite a social life. We used to go to Delaware Forest. We had campfires, music and folk singing. There was always someone who could play the guitar – 'I am the man, the very fat man, who waters the workers' beer.' We used to sing all those socialist songs. I never joined the Communist Party; I was just in the YCL. I never took much notice of Eden and Macmillan. My socialist favourites? I went to see Harry Pollitt once at Belle Vue. [Harry Pollitt was General Secretary of the Communist Party of Great Britain.] He wasn't in good health; he'd been attacked at a meeting and it had left him poorly, but he was a wonderful speaker. There would be about 600 people at Belle Vue. Peggy Seeger came as well, and Pete Seeger. [Pete and Peggy Seeger were well-known American radical folk singers.]

MAX EASTERMAN

There was a lot of talk of politics in the house, and CND was a big issue. My father was very wary of CND and he believed that if you wanted a decent job it would be held against you, and I do think that if you wanted a job in the Civil Service you just would not get one.

JOAN WOOD

My husband was also involved in politics. We'd go on CND marches; we didn't go on the annual Aldermaston march, just the local ones. I liked Clem Attlee, I thought he was a very intelligent and well-educated man, but he wasn't as charismatic as old Churchill had been in the war. Although we didn't agree with Churchill's politics, we still admired him. I didn't particularly admire Eden or Macmillan. We picked up Michael Foot once from the Midland Hotel in the car; we were taking him to a meeting. He had a little dog, a little black bitch called Roxy. My husband was more involved than me. I sort of dropped out when I had a baby. My husband was a councillor in Manchester for about twenty years.

BRIAN KIDD

I remember the Munich disaster. It came over on the radio – there weren't many televisions then. I was kicking a ball about in Rome Street when I first heard – it must have been about four o'clock. I was just coming up to nine. When the news came through that they had actually crashed it was terrible. People were crying in the street – grown men – it was unbelievable. The school I went to, St Patrick's, was football mad; it was a real football area. The atmosphere in school the next day was shocking. I know when you are young you don't fully grasp the seriousness, but we could sense it then even though we were so young. People were mortified.

DAVID MEEK

I remember it all quite clearly. There was all this consternation over on the news side. Being a leader writer I was a little bit removed and in a separate office. The news went around the office like wildfire. It was about four o'clock and close to going home time when we became aware. At first you thought, oh, the plane has just had a bump, a technical hitch. But it quickly became apparent that this was not just one of those exaggerated reports. It was deadly serious and of course the entire office was then gathering around the tape machines.

BOB GREAVES

Everybody who was around at the time has their own memories of Munich. I was working on the *Daily Mail* but I was based in Leeds as a Yorkshire-based reporter. I got on the train in Leeds mid-morning, arrived in Manchester I think lunchtim'ish, stepped out of the station at Victoria and saw an evening newspaper placard – the *Evening Chronicle* or the *Evening News*, I don't know which. It said something very simple like 'United in Air Crash Drama'. And I thought, it'll be something small, never expecting it to be what it was. They'll have exaggerated it, I thought. So I got a paper and of course it was a very early edition and very little was known but it was obvious there had been a crash but there was little mention of deaths, just injuries. I got a taxi to the office and I think I, and many other reporters and journalists and production staff, probably walked out of that office the next time thirty-six hours later. I slept in the office certainly that night because as anybody can imagine all hell was let loose.

The *Mail*, like all other national newspapers, had their own personnel on the plane, some of whom were killed. Peter Howard, their chief photographer, and another photographer, whose name I can't remember, survived. Eric Thompson, that wonderful sportswriter, died. Because we had survivors from the *Daily Mail* who had access to telephones, they were able to tell us who was alive, who was injured and, more to the point, who hadn't survived. We in the *Manchester Daily Mail* office probably knew hours before the official news agencies, United, and the families.

A lot of those first two awful days was spent talking to members of the families back here, players and supporters and officials because, from our own man, and men on the scene, we knew an awful lot more. I was able to tell people in some cases that their loved ones were okay, seriously injured, slightly injured and, in two cases, breaking bad news to people.

I broke the news over the telephone to at least two families that their loved ones had died, and one of those families was the family of Willie Satinoff, who, from memory, was a textile merchant in Manchester and was one of the fans who was on the official plane. It was not an easy time and that's an understatement, but when there's a job to do – just like policemen and ambulance men and paramedics – you get on with the work, trying to do it as tastefully as you can but never forgetting, of course, that there's a product at the end of it, a newspaper. So it was half social worker, half journalist. Not an easy task but it helps you grow up, helps you grow up very quickly that.

The mood in the suburbs and the city, the mood everywhere, was just of quiet. I remember a lot of quiet. Nobody spoke for days and days in anything but hushed tones. I remember going to the ground at one stage, basically to pay my own little tribute, and everybody was either just standing and looking at the ground, the stands, the walls, or were walking around slowly in a semi-daze; hardly anybody spoke. I don't remember speaking to anybody and there were hundreds and hundreds of people coming and going, but a lot were just standing and offering their own prayers, paying their own tributes, but there was no conversation – the whole city was like that. As I say, whatever conversation there was, it was just very low, very quiet. It was like being at a funeral. I don't ever again wish to witness such mourning.

But of course the world goes on: a makeshift team, players you've never heard. In the oldest of clichés, life goes on. But those first few days were dreadful, dreadful. And my memory of the weather was that it was sombre and grey. Everywhere was sombre and very, very grey. People looked sombre and grey-faced. It was awful. I've rarely sat back and thought about it, but I don't want to see it again.

DAVID MEEK

The next day there was a strange, dramatic atmosphere in the office, but in order to be professional the editor insisted everybody carry on with their normal tasks rather than concentrate on this one story, because there was still the rest of the paper to produce. I wrote a leader on the tragedy and how all of Manchester was waiting with bated breath and anxiety to hear the full extent of the tragedy. It was that day that he asked me to cross over, as it became apparent that he needed a specialist to write about United, so he asked me to leave politics and join sport. News reporters had been dispatched to Munich to cover that end, but he needed somebody to find out what was going to happen at this end, to find out how the club was going to carry on as a football club. There were reporters dealing with the coming home of the survivors and arrangements that would have to be made for funerals. There was also a sporting story to be told about whether they would play the next game and there were stories to be written about the team that Jimmy Murphy would be trying to get out. And there was the postponed Cup Tie against Sheffield Wednesday that should have been on the Saturday, but was postponed for ten days or so.

It was my first game. I went by car from my home in Heaton Moor and I remember making my way there and wondering if I would ever reach Old Trafford because of the number of people on the road. There were as many coming away from Old Trafford as going because they had gone hoping to get in but had found it hopeless and had turned around and come away. It was a bizarre atmosphere at the ground. It wasn't so much a football match as a display of emotion. I remember Albert Quixall saying later, after he joined Manchester United, how difficult it was for Sheffield Wednesday to face this tidal wave of emotion, willing Manchester United to win, how difficult it was to get themselves in the right frame of mind to play a game of football. And I think other teams subsequently in that Cup run must have also found it difficult. It was as if the whole nation was willing them along and they were swept along on this tidal wave of emotion. But then of course a Cup final is so different from an ordinary football match. It was in the new surroundings of Wembley and because United's emotional adrenalin had faded a little the true strengths of the teams told and Bolton won easily really.

TERRY VENABLES

When I was growing up there was no televised football to speak of, and if you wanted to see a particular player or team, it meant going to one of their matches. It was February 1958 and United had just caused a stir by beating Bolton 7-2, and everyone was talking about Duncan Edwards. So I persuaded my dad to come with me to Highbury to see United play Arsenal. It was an unusual trip for two committed Spurs fans, and a day I will never forget.

United won a smashing match 5-4, but what happened afterwards gave the occasion a dreadful poignancy that still lingers. Just four days later the Busby Babes were decimated by the Munich air crash. Along with everyone else, I was devastated. So many died so young – my hero among them. It was a terrible tragedy, too awful to dwell on. I prefer to remember that lovely day out with my dad, standing behind the goal at the old Clock End at Highbury.

HUGH JONES

I was in Hong Kong when it happened. Of course communications weren't like they are today, you know. We found out on the camp. We got the information off another lad who was a very keen United supporter. He came from Manchester and was absolutely devastated, couldn't believe it. He thought it was just rumours going around. So I don't really remember much of the hype that went on in Manchester, only the papers that were sent out to me. I got the football *Pink*, my father used to send it every week. It would take four to five weeks to get there in those days, service mail. It was quite difficult to get information. I suppose there was radios. But you know on National Service, we didn't have radios in our barrack rooms, it wasn't a thing which was put in.

PAT McDONALD

The day of the crash I was in the Ferranti machine shop. I was walking down a passageway that ran between the lathes, parallel to the railway lines. Outside it was dark and misty and one of the charge hands stopped me. Had I heard about the plane crash? The United plane had crashed. The first thought that flashed through my mind was that this was part of their joking with me. I immediately rejected it; this would have been an untypically cruel joke. I can't remember how the rest of the afternoon went. I always used to cycle home then. I was thinking about it all the way home. I then remember my dad coming home and us both listening to all the news we could find. The other odd thing is how different it was then; there was no local radio, no Five Live, none of the news channels we have now. Certainly no Sky or CNN – how different it would be now. My dad and I just listened to all the scheduled news broadcasts – mainly on the radio.

LORD STAN ORME

I was working in a factory. It's a world apart. You didn't get information then. Everybody now has transistors on the machine or on the desk getting information minute by minute. But this rumour started in the factory that something had happened at Munich and it began slowly to seep through and people couldn't believe it. The whole factory went quiet. It still upsets me to talk about it. The shock continued through the whole of that week. On the Saturday I couldn't rest at home, I got on the bus and went to Old Trafford and ten thousand others were stood by my side. I've never forgotten it. We just stood there.

PETER HENNESSY

It was a very special decade in technological terms. If you read the *Eagle*, as I did, there was Peter Twist breaking the airspeed record, the first jet airliner, and you'd get a cut-out of the latest aircraft carrier for the Royal Navy – maybe the *Ark Royal* – all that stuff. We were on the rim of the most advanced technologies, including nuclear power and Calder Hall and all that. The Movietones at the cinema always made this a tremendous thing of British triumphs. There was a lot in it and I absorbed all that. One had a sense of being in a very advanced nation whilst having this ancient, monarchical background. It was a glorious time. With Suez I thought, Brits don't lose wars, and I was troubled by that. I didn't understand it but overall it was a burnishing of the traditional and the glow of the promise to come plus the new technologies. When you put all those together it's pretty illustrious and I knew that at the time.

I think there were certainly more advances in that era because things like antibiotics and the polio vaccine came through in a big way. Television became a mass consumer product and there was civil nuclear power, which was going to transform things. The biggest transforming event of the 1950s, although I didn't know about until many years later, occurred in 1958, when thirty-four-year-old Jack Kilby at Texas Instruments put together the first integrated circuits. There were rockets as well with Sputniks, and engineering, with boring but prosaic things like washing machines and long-playing records – the LP, the EP – and television screens, still minute but not bad picture quality. Also British entertainment began to do extremely well with *The Goon Show* and Tony Hancock, all that kind of thing. We all had a shared culture because, until 1955, there was only one television channel and from then there was only two throughout the rest of the 1950s. And we all listened in vast numbers on the radio – to the Light programme and Radio Luxemburg. The shared compost, as it were, of what we watched and what we listened to and what we read was really quite important and we were in many ways a rather narrow but glorious bunch of people. Looking back now we were very narrow but, compared to what we had been before, also very different. And also we began to get out of the Empire with a degree of dignity and that's why Suez was such a terrible shock to people a bit older than me. And the Queen was quite powerful and magical with a big following. You did feel, as a kid, that you belonged to a very definite success story nation.

Other titles published by The History Press

A 1950s Childhood: From Tin Baths to Bread and Dripping
PAUL FEENEY

Do you remember Pathé News? Taking the train to the seaside? Knitted bathing costumes? Then the chances are you were born in or around 1950. This delightful compendium of memories will appeal to all who grew up in this post-war decade, whether in town or country, wealth or poverty. With chapters on games and hobbies, holidays, music and fashion, the wonderful memories and delightful illustrations will bring back this decade of childhood, and jog memories about all aspects of life.

978 0 7524 5011 7

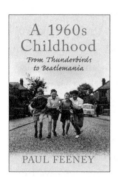

A 1960s Childhood: From Thunderbirds to Beatlemania
PAUL FEENEY

Do you remember Radio Caroline? Mods and Rockers? The very first mini-skirts? Then the chances are you were born in or around 1960. From James Bond to Sindy dolls and playing hopscotch in the street, life was very different to how it is now. With chapters on home and school life, games and hobbies, music and fashion, alongside a selection of charming illustrations, this delightful compendium of memories will appeal to all who grew up in this lively era.

978 0 7524 5012 4

A 1970s Childhood: From Glam Rock to Happy Days
DEREK TAIT

Do you remember cheesecloth shirts and chopper bikes? Who could forget the glam rock bands of that era, like Slade, Wizard, Mud and Sweet? What about those wonderful TV shows like *Starsky and Hutch*, *Kojak*, *Kung Fu* and *Happy Days*? Fashion included platform shoes, flared trousers, brightly patterned shirts with huge collars and colourful kipper ties. And everyone remembers that long, hot summer of 1976. So dust off your space hopper and join us on this fascinating journey through a childhood during the seventies.

978 0 7524 6344 5

Visit our website and discover thousands of other History Press books.

www.thehistorypress.co.uk